THE
COURT OF THE TUILERIES

VOL. II

*FROM
THE RESTORATION TO THE
FLIGHT OF LOUIS PHILIPPE. BY
CATHERINE CHARLOTTE,
LADY JACKSON*

*IN TWO VOLUMES
VOLUME II.*

WILDSIDE PRESS

Large Paper Edition

This edition is limited to one thousand copies, of which this is Number..............

CONTENTS OF VOL. II.

PAGE

CHAPTER I.

Grief and Despair. — *L'Homme du Duc d'Orléans.* — A Telling Phrase. — The Disgraced Minister. — Louis XVIII. and His Favourites. — The Pupil and His Royal Master. — Dissentient Views. — The Comtesse du Cayla. — An Ode to Peace. — Convincing the King of His Error. — Political Education. — Fooling Him to the Top of His Bent. — A Great King for France 1

CHAPTER II.

Political and Social Agitation. — Funeral of the Duc de Berry. — The "*Beau Roué*," Minus the *Beau*. — Hopes of the Bourbons Menaced. — Popular Conspirators. — The Theophilanthropists. — Execution of Louvel. — A Triple Abdication in Reserve. — A Betrothal. — Changing the Succession. — Vows Registered on High. — Disregard of Dignity. — Breach of Court Manners. — *Une Petite Comédie.* — Etiquette and *Esprit.* — An Amnesty . 13

CHAPTER III.

Mirabeau and the Marquis. — A Cradle for the Unborn Prince. — A Something Wanting. — Left to Their Own Devices. — Louis and the Fair Bordelaises. — "The Child of Miracle." — Rare Old Wine, and Garlic. — A Mystery Explained. — The Guarantee of Peace. — Was a Male Child Really Born ? — A Protest and a Violent Scene. — An Explosion in the Château. — The *Quid Pro Quo.* — The Pavillon Marsan in a Fright. — Preparing to Slide Backwards 27

CHAPTER IV.

Rather Theatrical. — A Well-got-up Scene. — Frightening the Saints. — The Royal Christening. — The Children and the Youthful Hero. — The Royal Sponsors. — The Civic Banquet and Ball. — Death of Napoleon I. — Grief of Général Comte Rapp. — " A Charming Phrase, *Ma Cousin.*" — A Partisan of the Right Divine. — A Mighty Conqueror Dies. — The Warrior's Return . . 40

CHAPTER V.

The Valiant Duc d'Angoulême. — The Congress of Verona. — Coquetry and Diplomacy. — Duc Mathieu de Montmorency. — A Sympathising Friend. — Imagination Taken Captive. — Madame Récamier's Letters. — A Great Enemy to Combat. — Author and Statesman. — Seeking in Vain. — Madame Récamier's System. — The Hero Is Off to the Wars. — Surprising the Garrison. — Impregnable Consciences. — The Hero's Return. — Hats and Gloves *à la Trocadéro* 51

CHAPTER VI.

Fêting the Hero. — Clinging to Life. — A Last Speech in the Chambers. — The Cause of Misfortune. — The Blessing of the *Rentiers.* — " Tell Him I Turn Him Out!" — The *Quid Pro Quo.* — " Atala of the *Salons.*" — Frequent and False Alarms. — A Wretched Condition. — " A King of France Must Not Be Ill." — The Strong Will Fails at Last. — A Conversion *in Extremis.* — The Death Chamber. — The Favourite's Portrait. — "The King, Gentlemen!" 65

CHAPTER VII.

A Feeble Ruler. — He Gave France the Charter. — Attending to Business of State. — The Dreaded Transition. — A *Ci-devant Jeune Homme.* — The Good Old Times. — Funereal Pomp. — The Lying in State. — The Funeral *Cortège.* — A Question of Precedence. — The Interior of St. Denis. — Charles X.'s Public Entry. — The Military Staff. — " No More Halberds." — *Les Enfants de France.* — The Royal Ladies. — The Funeral Oration. — The Royal Vaults Closed 79

CHAPTER VIII.

Resting on the Right Divine. — The Lapse of Fifty Years. — Napoleon's Mistake. — A Busy Time for the *Modistes*. — Regenerating French Society. — The New Converts. — "*Ad Majorem Dei Gloriam!*" — Lecturing in Vain. — Models of Kingly Perfection. — A Heaven Assigned Task. — Recriminatory Reproaches. — The Royalist Emigrants. — "*C'est un Polignac.*" — The Orléans Appanage. — The Heir of Philippe Égalité. — The Wealthiest Man in France. — Confidential Advisers. — Justified by Events 94

CHAPTER IX.

A Demigod for the People. — Sympathy with the Greeks. — Doubt and Disquietude. — A Most Gracious Reception. — A Flattering Distinction. — Congenial Sentiments. — Neither Part nor Lot in the Matter. — The Law of Sacrilege. — The "Fathers of the Faith." — An Odious Law. — The "*Déplorable*" Ministry. — Tearing Up the Charter. — A Touching Scene. — "The Worst of All Revolutions." — Piety and Etiquette. — Ah! Happy Woman. — The Legitimate Heir. — Youthful Courtiers. — A Military Toy. — A Wooden Army 109

CHAPTER X.

"Notre-Dame, Sire, or St. Denis." — Pious Horror. — *La Sainte Ampoule.* — A Comforting Miracle. — A Ponderous State Carriage. — The Grand Master's Opportunity. — Difficult to Decide. — "Working Double Tides." — "*Vive Charles Dix!*" — A Pleasing Novelty. — Ancient Customs. — An Offering of Fruits and Wine. — Just a Glimpse of Royalty. — Fashionable *Coiffeurs.* — Very Distressing. — A Brilliant *Tout Ensemble.* — A Mortifying Necessity. — "*Vivat Rex in Æternum!*" — The Merciless Rain. — Poems and *Chansons* 126

CHAPTER XI.

"Another *Grand Monarque.*" — An Empty Treasury. — Growing into Fashion. — "The Heart of Young France." — Funeral of Général Foy. — "*Les Enfants de la Patrie.*" — The Old Tactics Continued. — Sheathing the Sword for a While. — A Cure Effected. — "If You Think Thus, It Must Be So." — "The Grand Lama." — Mutual Satisfaction. — A Privileged Visitor. — No Lover Now, but Gambler. — The *Salon* of the Abbaye-aux-Bois. — Madame Vigée-Lebrun 143

CHAPTER XII.

Preparing for the Carnival. — The Jesuits and the Colporteurs. — The King a Jesuit Priest. — Talma's Last Part. — Primogeniture. — The "Three Hundred Spartans." — The Decree of the Cour Royale. — Reproving the Judges. — "Move On, Gentlemen." — Madame's New Year's Reception. — Death of the Duc de Montmorency. — A Change in Popular Opinion. — The Czar's Mental Depression. — A Reconciliation. — Death of Madame de Krüdener. — Her Last Words 157

CHAPTER XIII.

A *Procès* Gained. — Royal Ingratitude. — Loss of Court Favour — The Savonnerie. — An Ornament Lost to the Court. — The Sin of Light-mindedness. — The Governess and the Governor. — The Bourbon Temperament. — "*Contes à Ma Fille*." — M. Bouilly Presented to Madame. — Doubting the Pavillon Marsan. — Accepted on One Condition. — A Profession of Faith. — The Young Prince's Studies. — Principles Fraught with Danger. — A Flattering Leave-taking. — Madame's Methodical Habits 170

CHAPTER XIV.

A Crusade against the Jesuits. — Slaying the Hydra. — A Rigorous Law. — "They Shall Repent of It!" — Busy; Building and Improving. — Justice and Love. — The Faithful Three Hundred. — "The *Canaille* Must be Coerced." — A Mark of Royal Favour. — Not a *Vivat* Greets Him. — What Is the Reason? — False Hopes. — Two Great Events 185

CHAPTER XV.

An Eventful Day. — "Homage, Not Lessons!" — A Change of Mind. — "What Would Louis XIV. Have Done?"

— "An Act of Vigour." — Extinguished Forever. — Refusal to Pray for the King. — The Old Revolutionist. — "What if They Are *Canaille!*" — Grand *Fête* of the Jubilee. — Victory of Navarino. — A Sign from Heaven. — The End of the "Deplorables." — A Riot and a Massacre. — A Hint to the New President 196

CHAPTER XVI.

Disappointed Expectations. — Anything to Get Rid of Him. — An Exchange of Embassies. — To Rome He Went. — A Damaging Blow with a Fan. — A Visit of Condolence. — Royalty *en Voyage*. — The Château de Chambord. — Threatened with Demolition. — Bought by the Nation. — Ungraciously Accepted. — Some Sketches of Chambord. — Deceived and Undeceived. — A Long Deferred Journey. — Delighted with Chambord. — An Enthusiastic Welcome. — A Successful Expedition. — Saintly, Popular, and Powerful 209

CHAPTER XVII.

The Annual Visit to Dieppe. — Courtier and *Fiancé*. — A Concession to the People. — Astonishing the Chambers. — Madame's Costume Balls. — *La Mode* Suppressed. — "*La Muette de Portici.*" — Advancing without Walking. — Home Occupations. — Shopping in Paris. — Opposed on All Sides. — A Terrible Blow. — "*Le Mouton Enragé.*" — Radiant with Joy. — A Careful Guardian . . . 224

CHAPTER XVIII.

Seeking Repose. — Sinister Forebodings. — Political Tours. — A Sad Disappointment. — Patiently Biding His Time. — A Very Gay Season. — Incendiary Fires. — A Fearful Example. — Reliques of Saint Vincent de Paul. — Absolving the King. — Ministers in Council. — Torturing the Sealing-wax. — The Sentiment for Glory. — Mortified Exceedingly. — A Dreary State of Things. — Preparing for Royal Guests 237

CHAPTER XIX.

A High-handed Despot. — Royal Visit to the Opera. — An Exciting Opera. — The Tuileries Eclipsed. — An Unmindful Host. — Placed in a Dilemma. — A Lovely Night. — Seized with Sudden Frenzy. — Dancing on a Volcano. — " They Shall Suffer for It, the Rebels!" — Nothing New Intended. — Playing a Winning Game. — " God Preserve France and the King!" 251

CHAPTER XX.

A Thunderbolt. — The King Has Violated the Charter. — A Flag of Truce. — A Check to Court Gaiety. — " What News in Paris, Marshal?" — Strong in His Divine Right. — " Down with the Traitor!" — An Attempt to Buy Marmont. — Listeners in the Closet. — Whist and *Écarté* at St. Cloud. — Barricading in Paris. — Pleading Etiquette. — Unchanged and Unchangeable. — The Hôtel Laffitte. — War in Paris, Peace at St. Cloud. — The Battle Still Rages. — Cockade, Musket, and Uniform. — " *Drapeau Tricolore, Relève-toi.*" — Injudicious Play. — " She Is the Friend of the People." — Ready to Set Out for Dieppe. — " Yesterday It Was Possible." — France and the King 262

CHAPTER XXI.

Seen with a Shudder. — Sack of the Louvre and Tuileries. — "*Mort aux Voleurs!*" — Beginning to Grow Serious. — The Great Warrior in a Rage. — " Ah, Marmont, *Embrassons-nous!*" — " No Concession; Go on, Persist!" — Again, " Too Late, Too Late." — The Republic or Napoleon II.? — " Not a Bourbon, but a Valois." — " A Crown, or a Passport." — Saving the City from Anarchy. — Pleading in Vain. — Paris after Its Triumph. — Citizens Who Died for Liberty. — A Stifling Embrace. — A Treacherous Memory. — A Delightful Piece of News. — Tears and Tenderness. — The Civic Coronation. — Not a *Vivat* for La Fayette? 281

CHAPTER XXII.

Urging Charles Out of France. — The Cows of the Royal Dairy. — Madame in Male Attire. — An Embarrassing Position. — The Double Abdication. — Henri V. and Mademoiselle. — The Crown Jewels Demanded. — Unfavourably Received at Dijon. — Ready Cash for the King. — Sympathetic Sorrow. — Madame Soon Weary of Holyrood. — Migrating to Bohemia 299

CHAPTER XXIII.

Welcome News. — Taking His Walks Abroad. — Royal Hospitality. — A Mysterious Death. — Madame de Feuchères. — Flattering Proposals. — Flatteringly Received. — The Ruling Passion. — Not to Be Tempted. — Death of Benjamin Constant. — Quelling a Tumult. — M. Thiers's *Début* in the Chambers. — "*Chacun Chez Soi, Chacun Pour Soi.*" — Prince Talleyrand Dozing . . 310

CHAPTER XXIV.

Restoring the Tuileries. — The "Monarchy *à Bon Marché.*" — "We Are Subjects of the Law." — Caught in Their Own Trap. — A Sacrilegious Carnival. — Sack of the Archbishop's Palace. — Fast Waning Popularity. — Paganini's First Concerts. — The Opera and Opera Stars. — Madame la Comtesse Merlin. — Grand Musical *Réunions.* — *Petits Soupers Fins.* — The Literary *Salons.* — Private Concerts at Neuilly. — The Garden of the Great Lenôtre. — Cits and Citizenesses 322

CHAPTER XXV.

A Grand Carnival Ball. — King, Queen, and Family. — A Dreaded Enemy Advancing. — An Affray with the Ragpickers. — Ravages of the Cholera. — Disastrous Results of a Funeral. — An Ill-advised Adventure. — Madame and her Aides-de-Camp. — Death of Napoleon II. — The Prisoner of Blaye. — A Visit to Exiled Royalty. — Madame, Your Son Is My King. — The Sisters Elsler. — "*Le Roi s'Amuse.*" — Death of Général de La Fayette. 336

CHAPTER XXVI.

The Rule of Life in Paris. — Fieschi's Infernal Machine. — In Quest of a Wife. — "*Vive Napoléon III.!*" — The Marriage Bells Are Ringing. — Arrival of the Bride. — Wedding *Fêtes* and Presents. — A Great Theatrical Event. — *Les Débuts* of Mdlle. Rachael. — Success, Fortune, and Glory. — Rising with Her Circumstances. — Birth of the Comte de Paris. — Ste. Helena and Boulogne. — The Spanish Marriages. — Mr. Smith and His Passport. — M. Guizot "Disguizoted" — Death of M. de Châteaubriand. — Death of Madame Récamier . . 349

LIST OF ILLUSTRATIONS

VOLUME II.

	PAGE
MADAME CAMPAN	*Frontispiece*
COMTE RAPP	47
CHATEAUBRIAND	70
CHARLES X.	82
LOUIS PHILIPPE	106
METTERNICH	112
MADAME RÉCAMIER	150
CASIMIR PÉRIER	268

THE
COURT OF THE TUILERIES

CHAPTER I.

Grief and Despair. — *L'Homme du Duc d'Orléans.* — A Telling Phrase. — The Disgraced Minister. — Louis XVIII. and His Favourites. — The Pupil and His Royal Master. — Dissentient Views. — The Comtesse du Cayla. — An Ode to Peace. — Convincing the King of His Error. — Political Education. — Fooling Him to the Top of His Bent. — A Great King for France.

IT was with difficulty that the weeping Duchesse de Berry, who, reclining on the side of the couch, clasped in her arms the dead body of her husband, could be prevailed on to leave the sad scene of his death. Almost senseless, she was borne to her carriage and conveyed to her now desolate home in the palace of the Elysée Bourbon. Enthusiastically attached to her faithless husband, and always romantic in her sentiments, her first act, on reviving from the state of semi-unconsciousness in which for some hours she lay, was to cut off her beautiful hair. Those long, wavy, golden tresses, whose beauty had been the theme of many a sonnet, were the especial admiration of the late duke. To him, then, she sacrificed them; and, recommending her little daughter to the kind care of Madame de Gontaut, her lady in waiting, she declared that she, too, must die. She now cared not for life, and could not survive her husband.

These violent paroxysms of grief and despair at last gave way to a calmer state of feeling. Still she would not, she said, continue, after the funeral, to reside in France. This horrible crime had made it hateful to her, and she must entreat the king not to oppose her return to Sicily. She was reminded that it was her duty to remain in France; and the words of the late duke were repeated to her, — " Live, my Caroline, live for the sake of our unborn child," — faintly murmured as life was ebbing away, and while she, in the agony of her mind that she could not hold back the beloved one from the grasp of death, was protesting that she would die with him.

That her husband bade her live, and with his dying breath implored that she would not allow grief to overwhelm her, at once changed the current of her thoughts. And when the official journals announced that the Duchesse de Berry was *enceinte*, she was told that France also bade her live — live to disappoint those whose criminal hopes had led to the calamity that threatened extinction to the elder branch of the Bourbons, in order to elevate the Orléans family to that throne which, for two centuries past, they had coveted, and, from father to son, had been plotting and intriguing to sit on.

So strongly prejudiced was Louis XVIII. against the Duc d'Orléans, that he firmly believed the Duc de Berry to have owed his death to an intrigue in the Duc d'Orléans's favour, which, if he did not positively sanction, he also did not deprecate. The Comte d'Artois, the Duc and Duchesse d'Angoulême, with the priestly and ultra-royalist party, accused M. Decazes of complicity in the crime, the duchess especially stigmatising him as *l'homme du Duc d'Orléans*. His dismissal was required; also that of the ministry of which he was president, who, sharing his liberal opinions, were supposed to inspire the king with the idea of making concessions inconsistent with the monarchy by right divine.

"Had he been dismissed a twelvemonth ago," said the Comte d'Artois, "my son would still have been living." "His foot has slipped in blood (*Le pied lui a glissé dans le sang*)," wrote M. de Châteaubriand, for the sake of a telling phrase, with reference to the fall of the much maligned minister, though afterwards explained away as meaning nothing. But his fall — if fall or disgrace it could be called — led the king to exclaim, in his extreme annoyance at this cabal against his favourite: "I will raise him so high that his elevation shall excite the envy of aristocrats of highest rank." Forthwith the disgraced minister was created duke and peer of France, and thus was placed on an equality with the old nobility. Also he was appointed ambassador to the court of St. James's, and the king consulted him when naming his successor in the presidency of the Council. "As I have determined," he said, "to submit to the law of necessity, I will not separate from you, *mon enfant*, without having shown how keenly I feel what Syrus has so well expressed in the maxim, '*Amicum perdere est damnorum maximum.*'"

The king at the same time extended his hand towards M. le Duc Decazes, who, sinking on his knees, kissed it several times, and, unable longer to restrain their emotion, the monarch and his favourite mingled tears of regret at parting.

When the king and his brother again met, "You will not now complain," said the former. "You exacted of me the sacrifice of the man to whom I had given my fullest confidence. I have consented to it. M. Decazes retires."

"Would that he had done so long ago," sighed the count.

"You are unjust, my brother. Had the ministry been chosen by yourself, it could not have saved your unfortunate son. The crime is due to the revolutionary principles still rife among us," replied the king.

However, M. le Comte declared that he yet had reason to complain. The man who was concerned in the murder of his son, as he continually protested, had been rewarded by the king, instead of being made a striking example of the punishment awaiting conduct so criminal as his. But, besides titles and estates and responsible appointments, the brevet of minister of state and member of the Privy Council — which gave, for life, the right of *entrée* to the Council on all occasions — was also conferred on the new duke and peer of France, which raised him, as the king had said he should be, in social position to the very highest rank.

To Louis XVIII.'s many bodily infirmities was now added that of gradually decaying mental powers. He was conscious of this fact, and was then struggling to maintain his supremacy in the direction of affairs of state, and to resist the domination of the Jesuit-ruled Comte d'Artois and the still more evil influence of the narrow-minded bigotry of the Duchesse d'Angoulême. M. Decazes had for some time aided him in keeping the ultra and priestly party in check, and now and then thwarting their views. This, in their eyes, as the king was aware, was his minister's great crime, rather than any conviction of the truth of his asserted complicity in the assassination of the Duc de Berry, though it was put forward as a means of getting rid of him.

It has been doubted whether Louis XVIII., a man of so little feeling and so thoroughly egotistical, really had any sort of affectionate regard for any one of the several favourites who succeeded each other in his good graces. Was he not influenced, in this revival of the favouritism that was the rule of the ancient monarchy, by his profound veneration for the historical traditions of the old *régime* more than by any especial regard for the persons on whom his favours were lavished?

"If Louis XVIII. was not actually cruel," writes M. de Châteaubriand, "he certainly was not humane. But, though cold and unfeeling, he yet had a sort of passion for those favourites who administered to his pleasures and saved him trouble in the affairs of government." This is exactly what M. Decazes did. With much statesmanlike ability and moderately liberal opinions he possessed a pleasing manner, as well as the tact, when discussing affairs of state with the weary-minded king, to introduce apt quotations; to be reminded, by some remark, of a piquant *bon mot* or anecdote, and by these digressions to amuse his majesty and enliven the otherwise dreary business of government.

He flattered the king's vanity also by making it clearly appear that not only were his political opinions derived from him, — for Louis looked on his rather youthful minister as his pupil, when he was in fact his master, — but that the *bons mots* always so ready on his lips, and his facile and appropriate quotations from Louis's favourite Horace, were but sparks from those flashes of wit and wisdom that glittered so brightly in the king's discourse when he deigned to converse with him. Louis was in the habit of saying, with reference to measures suggested or advocated by M. Decazes, and invariably opposed by the ultra-royalist party, that his minister's system was his; the words he spoke represented his own will and wishes: "*Il exécute ma volonté, et voilà tout.*"

But in future the will of the Comte d'Artois, or, more correctly, that of his Jesuitical *entourage* — for will of his own he had none — was most frequently to prevail in the conduct of affairs of state. The decadence of Louis XVIII. from this time is remarkable. The dissentient views of his family isolated him in a great degree from the society of his near relatives, and with the Orléans branch he can scarcely be said to have held any friendly intercourse, so strongly was he prejudiced against the duke. Much pains were taken to keep far from him all persons of influence who would be likely to sympathise with his so-called liberalism. For Louis had begun to perceive — it being adroitly pointed out to him by M. Decazes — that concessions to the views of the constitutional party were more likely to give stability to his throne than persistence in the vain attempt to restore absolutism and priestly rule.

But it was to the minister's secret enemy, the fascinating Comtesse du Cayla, that much of the influence he had enjoyed was now to be transferred. Until then at the daily *tête-à-tête* politics had been by mutual consent eschewed; though she contrived sometimes with lively raillery to evade the prohibition. She still read poetry to the king, and wrote silly sonnets, which he corrected, believing that, her poetic powers being guided and fostered by his pure tastes, she would eventually astonish the world by producing a poem of striking merit. Doubtless she was herself amused at the king's idea of her possession of latent poetical powers. Talent of a much more matter-of-fact description developed itself — successfully, too, — at a later period; but at the time now referred to her most remarkably developed talent was for intrigue.

A specimen of her poetry — perhaps an early effort of her genius — is given by M. Capefigue, as having been presented to the king on the happy occasion of the signing of a general peace. It is as follows:

> " O paix! charmante paix!
> Secourable, immortelle,
> Par de nouveaux bienfaits
> Enrichis nos guérets des
> Présents de Cybèle.
> O sainte paix! viens régner
> À jamais!"

The king is said to have applauded the sentiment; but we are not informed what he thought or said of the verses. His own poetic efforts, the countess told him, reminded her of La Fontaine; though they grated a little on her ear sometimes from the absence in them of refinement.

But, notwithstanding these literary pastimes, a sort of void was created in the king's daily life by the loss of his favourite and *spirituel* minister; for, when the fair countess withdrew from the royal presence, the successor of M. Decazes, not having the same advantage of being both Minister of Police and President of the Council, did not bring with him the accustomed daily dish of highly seasoned scandal, wherewith, at times, the king was roused from a slight lethargy that of late had begun to creep over him, and his attention awakened for the discussion of more serious matters.

His interviews with his *amie de cœur* were, therefore, now often prolonged much beyond the stated two hours; or she repeated her visit in the course of the day, when it was not his evening for receiving ladies. Then, of course, she appeared, if only to see that her gouty gallant was not led astray by the wiles of some one or other of the courtly circle, as fascinating and intriguing, probably, as herself.

Louis, confessedly, was ill at ease with his new ministry, whose constitution he complained of as a sort of abdication of his political system. From this annoyance he sought distraction in the society of the countess. It was her business, however, — being in league for that purpose with the retrograde party of the Pavillon Marsan, — to convince him by flattery and cajolery that he was in error, and that the change which had taken place was calculated to impart steadiness to the throne — at this particular moment especially shaky.

She did not quite succeed. Yet, by degrees, "her exquisite tact," as the king termed it, her devoted personal attachment to him, — as he, prematurely in his dotage, imagined, — and, above all, the readiness and docility with which, like M. Decazes, she affected to gather and treasure up the words of wisdom that fell from his royal lips, obtained his fullest confidence.

Formerly he had expressed repugnance to feminine interference in affairs of state, and declared that the meddling of women in politics had greatly increased the troubles that beset him since his return to France. But although he did not now object to consult his *belle amie* on questions of government, and to hear her opinions thereon, it did not follow that he would adopt them. He was rather seeking — as indeed he acknowledged — to educate her politically, and would complain loudly of the tyranny of her persistence when she held to views that were opposed to his own. Often, forgetting the gallantry on which he piqued himself, his majesty would indulge in bursts of ill-humour.

Then he could, and sometimes did, swear terrible oaths.

The countess — when one of the *belles* of the imperial court — is said to have taken Joséphine for her model, and to have made a special study of the graces of manner that distinguished the empress. A certain graceful nonchalance, natural in her, was often assumed with considerable effect by Madame du Cayla. It fascinated Louis XVIII., even to calming him when he got into his tantrums. A quotation or two would complete the cure and, if she attempted Latin, would amuse him excessively. Casting politics to the winds, she would begin to talk of poetry, of plays, of actors, and authors; then, fooling him to the top of his bent, she would pray him to read to her, or allow her to read to him, some pages of the journal of his majesty's "*Voyage à Gand*," which she persuaded him she admired so immensely that she was never weary of hearing it.

She secretly contrived to obtain possession of the MS. of this journal, and had it very beautifully printed and elegantly bound. Then, by way of homage to her sovereign's great literary ability, she humbly presented it to him. Louis affected to be very angry, but in fact was greatly delighted to find in his fair friend so appreciative an admirer of his extraordinary talent and genius; while, to mark his satisfaction, riches with unsparing hand were lavished upon her.

Sometimes, however, he did wake up to consciousness that he was being played upon, and made some efforts to resist it. "Matters," he said to the Comte d'Artois on one occasion, "matters, my brother, are not yet so far advanced that I should for the present consent to annihilate myself completely." The saintly count professed himself deeply hurt by the reproach these words seemed to convey. Yet the ultra-royalists, the "immaculates of the Pavillon Marsan," were then plotting to place him on the throne, as more worthy to reign over them than his "liberal"— some even said "Jacobin"— brother.

"We want a real king," they said, "a great king, a Louis Quatorze, to tell revolutionary France, '*l' État, c'est moi.*'" This high-handed monarch they believed they had in Monsieur, the Comte d'Artois, if the old dotard so fond of posing as constitutional king would but vacate the throne, — would but die, but abdicate, — or if the *vrai chevalier* would allow his friends to compel his incompetent brother to yield his place to him.*

* Private Letters, 1816 to 1822.

CHAPTER II.

Political and Social Agitation. — Funeral of the Duc de Berry. — The "*Beau Roué*," Minus the *Beau*. — Hopes of the Bourbons Menaced. — Popular Conspirators. — The Theophilanthropists. — Execution of Louvel. — A Triple Abdication in Reserve. — A Betrothal. — Changing the Succession. — Vows Registered on High. — Disregard of Dignity. — Breach of Court Manners. — *Une Petite Comédie*. — Etiquette and *Esprit*. — An Amnesty.

FRANCE, both political and social, was strongly agitated concerning the succession to the throne during the seven months that elapsed between the death of the Duc de Berry and the birth of an heir. Eighteen hundred and twenty was indeed a year of trouble and trepidation; and not only in France, for the excitement that prevailed there influenced the population of other countries, stimulating Naples, Spain, and Portugal to attempt revolutionary action to free themselves from the oppression of despots.

The people, both men and women, assembled by thousands, and sometimes tens of thousands, in the streets of Paris. Joined by the students of the École Polytechnique, and those of the schools of law and medicine, they surrounded the Chambers and the Tuileries, crying "*Vive la charte!*" but without the accompanying "*Vive le roi!*" the object being to express disapprobation of certain measures of government — infractions of the Charter — relating to the elections and to a proposed check on the liberty of the press. In the conflicts between the military and the people, blood was shed, and several deaths ensued.

Meanwhile, the trial of Louvel, the assassin of the Duc de Berry, was proceeding with wearisome slowness before the Chamber of Peers. At the lying in state of the body at the Louvre, and at the funeral procession to St. Denis, all the obsolete usages of the ancient monarchy were revived, and both were marked by a degree of solemn splendour that France had certainly not witnessed for nearly two centuries, the pomp with which the so-called remains of Louis XVI. and his queen were conveyed to St. Denis being far surpassed.

It was, perhaps, intended to impress the minds of the people with a keener sense than was generally evinced of the greatness of the loss the nation had sustained, and to incite a deeper feeling of resentment towards his murderer. But the Duc de Berry was not popular. Besides his excessive arrogance he had many grave faults of character. The fascinations of his young wife had checked for a while his career of dissipation, but his vices, misnamed his gallantries, had caused discord and misery in several families, and vows of vengeance had been wreaked upon this modern Henri IV. by many an outraged husband and father.

The frequent menacing letters he received he tossed aside with a shrug of disdain. He was, in fact, in character the counterpart of his libertine father, the "*beau roué*" — minus the *beau*. At the instance of Madame du Cayla, the king had given orders for some time previously that the watchful eye of the police should be kept on his nephew, lest any mishap should befall him. Yet, when least expected, the fatal blow was given.

Much sympathy was naturally felt for the youthful widow; for whom, as soon as possible, apartments were prepared at the Tuileries, that she might be more under the eye of her severe sister-in-law than was possible at the Élysée. The excessive grief which at first overwhelmed the young Duchesse de Berry soon toned down, and her cheerfulness speedily returned, as is not infrequent with persons of lively temperament and elastic spirits. She displayed much courage, also, declaring that she was not at all alarmed, when a miscreant named Gravier — a discharged soldier, who had some grudge against the government — placed under her chamber window a sort of miniature infernal machine, charged with gunpowder, hoping that its explosion would terrify the duchess and prove fatal to the hopes of the

Bourbon dynasty. Gravier contrived to escape unobserved. But, finding that his first attempt was a failure, he ventured on a second, and was arrested as he was in the act of applying the match to the wick or cotton that was to ignite the gunpowder.

The man was tried and condemned to be guillotined. However, the duchess begged that the king would pardon him. Louis was not disposed to do so; but, on further entreaty, he spared his life, and sentenced him to a punishment far worse than death — the galleys to the end of his days.

Louvel's trial was not concluded until the beginning of June. On the 7th of that month he was guillotined on the Place de Grève. As many as twelve hundred persons had been interrogated, or had given evidence of some kind, concerning the assassin or his crime, so anxious was the government to make it appear that he was an agent of the *carbonari* or other of the secret societies then existing in France, that included several men of political influence and very popular with the people: Général de La Fayette, Benjamin Constant (lately returned to France), Général Foy, the banker Laffitte, and others, who, though they kept well behind the scenes, were known to be intimately connected with those societies, and with a deeply laid plot, then organising in Paris, which was to result in a change of rulers and a new form of government.

Active and secret measures were then being taken to thwart the objects of the conspiracy, without publicly impeaching the chief conspirators, which, indeed, the government feared to do, lest a rising of the people should lead to the desired revolution. But, in spite of every effort to find amongst those plotters and intriguers accomplices in Louvel's crime, nothing whatever was elicited to disprove the assassin's statement that abettors he had none. He was prompted solely by an impulse of his own to save his country, he said, from the rule of a race of tyrants. This patriotic wish — as this political fanatic believed it to be — he thought to accomplish by murdering, in succession, the king, his brother, and his two nephews.

He selected the Duc de Berry for his first victim, because, as he stated, it appeared likely that through him the line would be continued. He regretted that he had not been allowed to fully carry out his intention, which, according to his professed religious views, — those of the Theophilanthropists of the revolution,— was a praiseworthy one.* His love of mankind was shown in his desire to free them from oppression; and his love of God, or the Spirit of Goodness, in the attempt to carry that desire into effect. So reasoned this visionary — a man of obscure posi-

---

* The Theophilanthropists, while rejecting the teaching of Christianity, professed to learn from Reason the duty of loving God and man.

tion, a journeyman saddler, of about thirty to thirty-five years of age. He gloried in the crime, for which he deservedly suffered, and his false views enabled him to face death with the courage of a martyr.

The state of public feeling at this time towards the reigning family may be inferred from the fact that precautionary measures were taken to prevent an expected attempt to rescue the condemned criminal. Troops were marched into Paris during the night preceding the execution. A small number only was stationed on the Place to keep order; the rest were in barracks, ready to appear at a moment's notice if wanted. Happily they were not, though an immense crowd assembled on that fine summer evening to witness the horrible spectacle. The execution took place at seven o'clock. There were a few seditious cries which were speedily suppressed, "*Vive Louvel!*" grating painfully on the ear as the fatal axe fell and the criminal ceased to exist.†

The Opera-house, at the entrance of which the murderous blow was given, and where, in the *salon* adjoining his box, the Duc de Berry breathed his last, had not since that calamitous event opened its doors to the public. An order was given to raze it to the ground, and its demolition was at once proceeded with, the opera company giving their representations at the Théâtre Favart during

* Private Letters.

the eighteen months occupied in erecting a new building.

Anxiety as to the sex of the expected royal infant became very general as the *accouchement* of the Duchesse de Berry drew near. In the event of the birth of a female child, an intention to abdicate, and to prevail on his brother and nephew to renounce their claims to the succession, is attributed to Louis XVIII. It is asserted that he declared it to be his firm conviction that the sterile branches of the elder Bourbons could not maintain themselves on the throne in the presence of the new heir presumptive and his partisans. It would be better, then, he considered, both for the peace of France and their own safety, that "the three kings" should withdraw from a position fraught with so much peril.

It may, however, be doubted whether Louis XVIII. would, under any circumstances, have voluntarily surrendered his crown to the Duc d'Orléans, whom he believed to be at the bottom of every intrigue, and ever on the watch to displace him. But if the duke really was not displeased at being placed nearer the throne by the assassination of De Berry, he might have retorted that Louis XVIII. displayed neither grief nor dissatisfaction when the news of his brother's death on the scaffold reached Coblenz. The dancing and festivities at the emigrant headquarters were not even suspended that evening. That he should be joyous rather than grieved at the lamentable event was, indeed, quite consistent with the conduct he had invariably pursued towards Louis XVI. in his lifetime.

But lest the Duchesse de Berry should disappoint the hopes of "the three kings," an arrangement was entered into for the same object as that which gave Madame Royale in marriage to the Duc d'Angoulême. Mademoiselle, the daughter of the Duc de Berry, an infant six months old, was betrothed to the Duc de Chartres (the Duc d'Orléans's eldest son), then in his tenth year. The king afterwards expressed a wish that this engagement should be maintained, and the marriage take place in due time. The fates decreed otherwise.

The ultra-royalists, however, were for adopting another mode of securing the succession in the direct line. They petitioned the Chambers to abolish the Salic law, that Madame Royale might at once ascend the throne of her ancestors as the reigning sovereign of France. Louis's assumption of the *rôle* of constitutional king — not that he had any leaning towards it, but simply because he knew that without some such ruse he could scarcely hope to retain the throne till his death — displeased the immaculate partisans of the right divine.

In the hands of Madame Royale they felt assured that the sceptre would be more worthily wielded, and a real restoration follow. The Chambers, though essentially royalist, did not look favourably on the proposed change, and Madame herself by no means approved the step taken by her zealous *entourage*. She was far too much wedded to the rights and customs of the old monarchy; any departure from which she regarded as little less than sacrilege.

Yet another scheme was proposed, by M. de Vitrolles, with a view of keeping the Duc d'Orléans at a distance from the throne. He suggested that it would be well, in the state of uncertainty in which the elder branch was then placed, that the Comte d'Artois should marry the widow of the King of Etruria, daughter of Charles IV. of Spain, and that he should adopt her son, a Bourbon of the Spanish branch, to whom, should it become necessary, he might transmit the crown, and thus decisively set aside the pretensions of the Orléans branch. M. de Vitrolles was an ardent royalist, high in the favour of the Comte d'Artois. It was for this reason, probably, that his scheme received no other rebuke than silence, followed by a long-drawn sigh. That sigh, doubtless, was wafted heavenward, and reminded the too zealous M. de Vitrolles of the vows registered on high that bound the count to his *belle marquise*.

The Duc d'Orléans, whose spies were everywhere, just as everywhere his opponents had spies on him, had already written to the king to request that his rights might not at this anxious period be overlooked. Soon after, seeking an audience of his royal cousin, he appeared in person, always keenly alive to his private interests, to urge the same request.

"Your rights! Monsieur le Duc," replied the king, "and who desires to deprive you of them? Does not every one know that you are descended from a second son of Louis XIII., and that you take precedence of the Duc de Bourbon?" The rights of the Spanish Bourbons, who already, rather prematurely, had put forward their claims, were then brought on the *tapis* — the king opposing the duke's argument, that although nearer the throne than himself their formal renunciation of their claims was a bar to their succeeding to it. Louis became irritated at the duke's persistency in holding an opinion contrary to his, and especially on a theme so unwelcome as his pretensions to the throne.

Always inclined to take umbrage at the *bourgeois* habits and manners of Monsieur le Duc, *son cousin*, and to deprecate his revolutionary leanings, the king now reverted to a subject which he had already discussed with him, and with some asperity. This was the duke's disregard of the dignity of his station in sending his two eldest sons to the Henri Quatre College, which they attended on the same footing as the ordinary students. The young Duc de Chartres being affianced to Mademoiselle (the title conferred by the king on Miss Baby at her betrothal), his majesty considered that the course pursued by the Duc d'Orléans in the education of his sons was now even more derogatory to his high position than before.

Louis on the occasion in question was in an irritable, fractious mood, which was rather aggravated than soothed on perceiving that the duke, in defiance of court etiquette, wore gloves. It may be that this determined him to take advantage of the opportunity of giving the royal duke, who so loved to identify himself in all things with the *bourgeoisie* whose favour he sought, a lesson on his breach of court manners.

Under the old French *régime* gloves were not worn by men except when riding. Then, gloves *à la mousquetaire*, befringed, embroidered, and betasselled, were *de rigueur*. In the *salons* lace ruffles alone were recognised. To wear gloves there was an English innovation which pure royalists made a point of resisting. Louis XVIII. never wore gloves until the scrofula in his hands compelled him to cover them, and he then preferred green kid to all others. He was himself accused of an unpatriotic attachment to his blue coat and gilt buttons, an importation from England; but the Duc d'Orléans's habitual use of gloves he could not patiently tolerate.

As long, therefore, as the conference concerning the education of the young princes lasted, the king, while talking, kept continually twitching the fingers of the duke's gloves. At last he succeeded in pulling them off, and placed them on the table. The duke, with the same affected unconsciousness as the king had shown in what he had done, took up his gloves and put them on. Again by degrees the king removed them, and again the duke replaced them — neither appearing to be in the slightest degree distracted by it from the subject of their energetic conversation.

The gentlemen in attendance on the king that day, and who were of course mere lookers-on, were much amused by this little comedy, well understanding the motive impelling the king, while perceiving the duke's determination not to yield to it.

Louis XVIII. was, however, on all occasions extremely punctilious in such matters. He would never allow the slightest, even involuntary, breach of etiquette to pass unnoticed when engaged with his ministers in council. Yet business of state was always transacted by him in the most unsatisfactory manner. The reason of this was the extravagantly high opinion he had of his wisdom, learning, and wit; and of his requiring in consequence that all attention should be centred on himself. Instances have been given of ministers being unable even to introduce topics of the highest public importance, which they had met purposely to discuss, because of being compelled to listen to some interminably long story of the king's, garnished with innumerable quotations.

M. de Nettement gives an instance of the king's rigorous regard to etiquette when M. de Corbiére became minister. One day, while in the heat of argument, having his handkerchief and snuff-box in his hand, he placed them unconsciously on the king's table, beside which he was sitting. His sacred majesty seemed thunderstruck, and looked daggers at the offender, who, being but little accustomed, it appears, to the etiquette of courts, was not so readily awakened to a sense of his error as a more experienced courtier would have been.

From M. de Villèle's furtive glances and expressive gestures M. de Corbière at last comprehended the nature of his offence. Very quietly he then removed his handkerchief and box, remarking to the king as he did so, "Sire, it would be very much better if you always had ministers who empty their pockets instead of those who fill them." As his majesty to his other great qualities added the reputation of *un homme d'esprit*, his love of etiquette must of course give way to a *spirituel* reply. He smiled graciously on the witty Breton, who, with his snuff-box and handkerchief, was immediately amnestied.

The force of M. de Corbière's remark lay in the fact that M. de Villèle, the then head of the ministry, and a great adept in financial matters, had largely availed himself of the opportunities which elevation to power afforded him, to fill his pockets to overflowing. It was his ambition to possess a large fortune, and, having rapidly achieved his object, he was not unwilling to aid some among his official friends to do likewise. It was he who, a year or two later, proposed septennial parliaments, desiring, as asserted, to secure a longer ministerial existence, in order to introduce and bring into operation certain favourite financial schemes.

CHAPTER III.

Mirabeau and the Marquis. — A Cradle for the Unborn Prince. — A Something Wanting. — Left to Their Own Devices. — Louis and the Fair Bordelaises. — "The Child of Miracle." — Rare Old Wine, and Garlic. — A Mystery Explained. — The Guarantee of Peace. — Was a Male Child Really Born? — A Protest and a Violent Scene. — An Explosion in the Château. — The *Quid Pro Quo*. — The Pavillon Marsan in a Fright. — Preparing to Slide Backwards.

THE Marquis de Dreux-Brézé, who had held the appointment of Grand Master of the Ceremonies during the latter part of the reign of Louis XVI., was reinstated in that high office when he returned with Louis XVIII. to France in 1814. It was he who, in the name of the king, commanded the deputies of the *Tiers État*, assembled at Versailles in 1789, to withdraw from the hall where, in spite of an order to the contrary, they continued to hold their sittings. "Go, tell your master," replied Mirabeau, in a voice of thunder, to the marquis's message, "that we are here by the will of the people, and will remain here, unless thrust out at the point of the bayonet." Very often he spoke of this scene, and piqued himself greatly on the air of superlative disdain with which he had received the "plebeian count's" insolent reply.

M. le Marquis was a perfect grand master — a very incarnation of the etiquette and ceremonial prevailing under the old *régime*. With a shudder at the *décadence* in manners that had since fallen on courtly France, his thoughts probably reverted to those early tumultuous scenes of the revolution, when on the 19th of September, 1820, all his arrangements, thoughtfully made for introducing a deputation of the *dames de la halle* of Bordeaux in due form to the king, were cast to the winds by *les dames*, in their unseemly, obstreperous haste to rush into the presence of royalty.

But although these women of the people showed so little respect to the marquis's programme of the ceremonial with which they were to be marshalled in and presented to his majesty, they were actuated by feelings and intentions profoundly loyal. They came to offer, in the name of the sisterhood of *la halle* generally, a very handsome cradle for their *prince;* any doubt as to the sex of the child whose advent was now daily expected they would not listen to. The king had promised, in the event of an heir to the throne being born, to reward the loyalty of the Bordelais to the Bourbons by conferring on him the title of Duc de Bordeaux.

It appears they had intended to prepare a suitable speech, to be spoken on presenting the cradle;

but, after much cogitation, nothing worthy of meeting the ears of royalty suggested itself even to the most loquacious of the party. They knew what they wished to say; but all agreed that, expressed as they expressed it, there was wanting a certain ring, a *je ne sais quoi*, which they felt, but were unable to define. In this dilemma they applied to a local poet, who advised an application to M. de Châteaubriand. M. de Châteaubriand, being fond of popularity, at once consented to relieve *les dames* from their embarrassment by preparing a short address for them.

The prettiest of their number, he thought, should be charged to deliver it. But, with much good taste, they were unwilling to make so invidious a distinction, the deputation being composed of picked specimens of Bordelaise *halle* beauty. The most venerable of the party — the matron of the *halle* — was therefore chosen as their spokeswoman, M. de Châteaubriand proposing to introduce them. However, some one unfriendly to him whispered in their ear that he was so much in disfavour with the king, that they would do better to ask M. de Sèze * to accompany them to the Château.

M. de Sèze having communicated this request to M. de Châteaubriand, the latter was so much offended that he would have nothing further to do

---

* The *avocat* who, in 1792, undertook the defence of Louis XVI. on his trial.

with *les dames*. The spokeswoman had got the speech by heart; that they were welcome to. For the rest, he left them to their own devices, or to the direction of M. de Sèze, if he chose to take charge of them. This he declined to do. Hence the unceremonious manner in which the *dames de la halle* of Bordeaux presented themselves, and the consequent shock to the Marquis de Brézé's nerves and rigid sense of etiquette.

The king was suffering less that day, therefore in a mood to be amused by the *naïveté* of the fair Bordelaises, and to admire the elegance of their offering. He was pleased, too, with their speech, and still more with their own earnest, untutored expression of royalism, which he pronounced to be true royalism, flowing from the heart, such as he would like more frequently to hear. He endeavoured to converse with them also in their own *patois*, of which his memory still retained a few sentences. Their delight was of course immense. They seized both his hands and kissed them with enthusiasm; and, to the horror of M. le Marquis, seemed about to fall on his sacred majesty's neck and embrace him, a liberty which, he declared, as the ladies were so young and so pretty, he should have felt no difficulty in pardoning.

They were a little disappointed at not being able to pay their homage to the Duchesse de Berry, and to lay their offering at her feet. But, on taking leave of the king, they prayed him to send their princess to them, and their little prince also, as soon as both were strong enough. This Louis promised them he would do.

Ten days after this interview, the 29th of September, a hundred and one guns announced to the Parisians, as they had done nine years before, the birth of an heir to the throne. On both occasions an heir was anxiously expected — on the former, as promising the continuance of a new dynasty; on the latter, as averting the threatened extinction of an ancient one. Yet both these children, whose birth was hailed with so much rejoicing, were destined neither to wear a crown nor to leave posterity to inherit one. Short, indeed, is human foresight; but who will pretend to foresee, or to provide against, what may or may not happen in France, where, as Rochefoucauld says, everything happens. It did indeed seem possible on more than one occasion that Henri V. might yet ascend the throne of his ancestors, and the white banner wave once more on the Vendôme column. These royalist hopes are now ended.

It was considered of happy augury that the "child of miracle," — the "dynastic shoot of legitimacy," — as the royalists foolishly named the new-born babe, was born on the *fête* of Saint Michael the Archangel. Saint Michael is regarded as one of the protecting saints of France, and, as the ejecting of rebel angels from heaven had chiefly been assigned to him, no other patron saint, the pious relatives thought, would be so likely to sympathise with and aid the little prince in the arduous part he might eventually, as king, be called upon to play.

But the royal infant came into the world, as the king expressed it, almost *incognito*, none of the high officials and other personages whose presence is deemed necessary at royal births being in attendance. The king, the Comte d'Artois, the Duc and Duchesse d'Angoulême were summoned in haste between 2 and 3 A. M., but arrived only some time after the prince. The attesting witnesses were, therefore, Maréchal Suchet, Duc d'Albuféra, and the officers and two or three men of the national guard on duty that night at the Château, they being then the only persons immediately within call.

That Henri IV. might live again in Henri V., the child's lips, by the king's order, were, as the Béarnais's had been, rubbed with garlic, and a few drops of the rare old wine of Jurançon poured down his throat. He seems, like his prototype, to have uttered no objection to it. It was, therefore, predicted that he would be brave and gallant as Henri IV. had been — a hero in love and war.

A gossiping letter from Paris of that date says: "The royal *aubade*, or morning serenade, which under the old *régime* it was customary at break of day to play beneath the king's bedchamber window, was revived for the occasion of this child's birth. At the first peep of daylight, then, the stillness that prevailed within and around the Château was suddenly broken by the animated strain ' *Vive Henri Quatre !* ' sounding more joyous than ever, from the absence of noise and that uproarious chorus which usually accompanies it. It was remarked, however, as an ominous fact, that Henri was separated from his Gabrielle. By and by it was ascertained that Madame Royale had divorced them."

The king, it appears, who always heard these strains with pleasure — though he had never cared to be roused from his slumbers by an *aubade* — noticed the absence of the "*Charmante Gabrielle.*" Later in the day this mystery was explained to him by Madame du Cayla. Madame Royale had thought that a more appropriate song of welcome to this "child of miracle," or miraculous child, would have been the triumphant one with which the angels greeted the birth of the Saviour. She was not aware that a serenade was commanded; it was, therefore, both a surprise and a shock when "*Henri Quatre*" so jovially broke the peace of Saint Michael's morn. Too late to put a stop to that scandal, she, however, succeeded in suppressing what would have inevitably followed it.

"And will inevitably follow," rejoined the king. "' *Henri Quatre*' *seul* will suffice for the present; '*Gabrielle*' will arrive in due course." Louis was greatly elated. "We have now nothing to fear for the future," he cried. "The people will feel that, too. The birth of the Duc de Bordeaux is a great event — the crowning blessing of the Restoration."

Congratulations flowed in from all quarters. The *corps diplomatique*, at a special audience, offered their felicitations on this happy event — this blessing vouchsafed by Providence to gladden the paternal heart of the king, and to console the bereaved parent and widow. The Nuncio, in the name of his colleagues, spoke of the royal infant as the "child of Europe — the presage and the guarantee of the peace that was to follow a long period of agitation." The royalists were very demonstrative in proclaiming their joy; and, in their enthusiasm, believed that the future of "the monarchy of Saint Louis and Henri IV." — the term then generally in use — was contained in the cradle of the new-born babe.

Victor Hugo did homage to this hope of the Bourbons in a birthday ode, and a public subscription purchased the grand old château and domain of Chambord as a nation's offering to him. The public christening was deferred until the following spring; but a preliminary private ceremony took place. The child was named Henri Dieudonné, and the king conferred the promised reward on the loyal Bordelais by giving them a Duc de Bordeaux.

None was more profuse of congratulatory

speeches and exuberant felicitations than the prince who was placed by the birth of this child at a greater distance from the throne. The king accepted them, as he said, for what they were worth, and thanked him accordingly. But the minute pains that were taken in every particular to put the Duchesse de Berry's *accouchement* and the sex of the child to which she had given birth beyond a doubt, served only to increase the number of those who were incredulous on both points.

"Tell me," said the Duc d'Orléans to Maréchal Suchet, "tell me, M. le Maréchal, for, knowing your honourable character and loyal sentiments, I can fully rely on your word, did the Duchesse de Berry, whose *accouchement* you *almost* saw, really give birth to a male child?"

"On my word of honour, I affirm that she did," replied the marshal.

"Enough, M. le Maréchal. As you affirm it, I no longer entertain any doubt on the subject," said the duke.

Yet immediately afterwards a protest was published in the London newspapers in the name of the Duc d'Orléans against the rights of a prince believed to be a supposititious child. He at once disavowed it. None the less it was attributed to him, and a violent scene took place at the Tuileries between the duke and the king — violent, indeed, only on the part of the king, who gave way to passionate anger and indulged in language by no means courtly; the duke remaining perfectly calm, and denying all knowledge of the protest attributed to him or of the real author of it.

But another name, dear to the people, that stirred their emotions and raised their hopes as the unfamiliar one of Duc de Bordeaux was powerless to do, was now often brought forward by those who were hostile to the government or were concerned in plots to overthrow it. It was the magic name of Napoleon — not the once mighty conqueror, the new Prometheus then slowly dying of physical and moral suffering on a rock in the midst of a wide waste of waters, but his son, Napoleon II., the poor prisoner of Schönbrunn.

To the supposed partisans of this unfortunate youth was attributed the placing of a small barrel of gunpowder in the Tuileries on the staircase leading to the apartment in which the business of state was transacted. Fortunately, in exploding, it did comparatively little damage. Differently placed it might have destroyed a large part of the palace. Some windows were blown out and a door or two shattered. No one was injured, but the noise of the report caused great alarm to many. It was at first believed to be an attempt of the Bonapartists to blow up the Tuileries. The royalists attributed it to an Orleanist design on the king's life. But Louis himself dismayed his brother and the Duc and Duchesse d'Angoulême by charging the *ultras* of the Pavillon Marsan with being the perpetrators of the deed.

Their intention, he said, was not so much to do mischief as to make a great noise, in order to frighten him into sanctioning extreme measures, political and religious, which they desired should pass into laws. Whether these measures were or were not wholly repugnant to his own views, Louis was still sufficiently sagacious to perceive that the nation would resist them. His infirmities were great, and he had no wish, as he informed his brother, to end his days in exile. "Keep a stricter watch," he added, "on the proceedings of your friends. Open your eyes to their extravagant pretensions, for they compromise you."

The count was offended; Madame Royale nearly fainted. The *belle amie* preserved a strict silence; she had probably said all she wished to say *en tête-à-tête*. Henceforth, however, if her influence increased with the king, though already it was as great as it well could be, it positively declined with the Pavillon Marsan. That she ceased to play so well into their hands from this time was evident by her refraining to dissuade the king from giving the priestly and *ultra* party the *quid pro quo*, as he termed the fright he, with malicious enjoyment, put them in by sending off leave of absence to M. Decazes.

The "dear child" delayed not a moment in obeying his sovereign's summons. Doubtless he expected a command to form a new ministry; while the saints and *ultras*, in terrible alarm, saw in the favourite's return his majesty's speedy relapse into Jacobinism. Long interviews *en tête-à-tête* ensued, and many marks of the king's favour were conferred on him. Every day his appointment to the presidency of the Council was expected, the royalist ministers being ready to offer their resignation whenever that calamity should descend on them.

The attitude of fear and trembling into which the Comte d'Artois and his party were thrown, though threatening the most determined opposition to a ministry under M. Decazes, assured the king that the reins of power were still in his hands, if but loosely held; and this much gratified as well as amused him. Nevertheless, he was but too conscious of his incapability of offering any sustained resistance to their views; and when, after having kept them on the *qui vive* so long as seemed good to him, he counselled the ambassador to return to his post, "*Mon enfant*," he said, "I must submit to my destiny. And," he added, quoting Voltaire, "'*Semiramis n'est que l'ombre d'elle-même.*'"

He seemed to foresee the result of the Comte d'Artois's accession to the throne, and to strive, by such feeble opposition as he was able to offer to the exaggerated views of the count's party, to ward off the evil day, at least till he had vacated the throne.

Yet, strangely enough, during the past year the king had greatly increased his household, and surrounded himself with the pomps and vanities of royalty and courtly etiquette to a much greater extent than he had done during the first six years of the Restoration. It was as if he were preparing for the revival which Madame Royale and the future Charles X. dreamed of — a real restoration, as the ultra-Royalists termed it; and perhaps it was so, as he would often say he desired that the transition from his own system to that of Monsieur and the party who governed him should not, for his brother's sake, be too abrupt. He cared little indeed for the people; but he thought the stability of the throne might be endangered by a too sudden change from that "enlightened constitutionalism" which he believed to be embodied in his Charter, to the uncompromising absolutism of the old monarchy, priestly domination, and the effete forms of the old *régime.*

CHAPTER IV.

Rather Theatrical. — A Well-got-up Scene. — Frightening the Saints. — The Royal Christening. — The Children and the Youthful Hero. — The Royal Sponsors. — The Civic Banquet and Ball. — Death of Napoleon I. — Grief of Général Comte Rapp. — "A Charming Phrase, *Mon Cousin*." — A Partisan of the Right Divine. — A Mighty Conqueror Dies. — The Warrior's Return.

THE legislative session of 1821 was opened by Louis XVIII. in a manner that gave the ceremony the air of a theatrical spectacle. Instead of repairing to the Chamber of Deputies, as he had hitherto done, to read his opening speech, the deputies and peers were ordered to assemble at the Louvre, to meet their sovereign in the Salle des Gardes de Henri IV. The king's state of health was made the pretext for this change, the real motive being that he had long regarded this annual visit to the legislative chamber as derogatory to the dignity of the crown.

The representatives of the people should wait on their king. What place, then, so suitable for receiving their homage, and acquainting them with his will and pleasure, as the ancient palace of the Louvre — that grand old edifice, so closely associated with the greatness and majesty of the old French monarchy and the triumphs of kingly power. The moment was favourable, too, he conceived, for abolishing a practice so entirely contrary to courtly *convenances*, and, at the same time, doing a service to his successor, having in view the proximate revival of the old forms and ceremonies, and the high-handed manners that were to restore the lost prestige of royalty.

Accordingly the king was wheeled in his chair along the picture gallery to the Salle Henri IV., where, at the end he entered, was placed the throne. When he was comfortably seated upon it, his brother and his nephew in chairs of state on either side, and a numerous and brilliant retinue composed of the great officers of his civil and military household grouped around him, the magnificent red velvet and gold-fringed curtain that hung in folds across the hall parted in the middle, and was rapidly drawn to the sides, forming an effective drapery to the well-got-up scene it disclosed to view.

This grand *coup de théâtre* was vehemently applauded. The artful old king then, in whining, piteous tones, informed his peers and deputies that the term of his days was approaching, and that, in *some sort*, he proposed to deliver up the guidance of the helm of state to his brother. He, however, afterwards made known to those partisans of Monsieur who, putting faith in his declaration, thought to presume upon it, that in *no sort* did he intend to transfer the direction of affairs to other hands beyond what bodily infirmity compelled him.

Further to amuse himself, by giving another fright to Monsieur and his party, he spoke of a desire to consult with, and to seek the advice of, M. de Talleyrand. This brought Madame Royale, in great alarm, to the king's *cabinet de travail*, to remonstrate with him, or to entreat — according to the mood she found him in — that he would not carry out so terrible an idea. He did not intend it; his grand chamberlain was by no means so high in his favour; but it diverted him to frighten the saints, and to laugh and jest on the subject with the lively Comtesse du Cayla.

His increasing incapacity for attending to public affairs was evident to all; but those who wished for his end had to wait longer for it than, from his state of bodily suffering, seemed possible. Sometimes he sank into a perfect torpor, and from hour to hour his death was looked for, when, gradually, he would rally in the most remarkable manner, and become quite cheerful — so much so that some of the people about him fancied that, at times, much of that helpless languor was assumed. The following day he would probably be out in his *calèche*, accompanied by two or three of his courtiers, and, although driven at a rapid rate, complain loudly of its slowness.

However, at about this time a cessation of gout

and a general mitigation of suffering brought with them a renewal of mental vigour, and enabled him to attend the christening of the Duc de Bordeaux at Notre-Dame on the 1st of May, 1821. The ceremonial generally — arranged according to the programme prepared, with scrupulous attention to the minutest details, by that able official the Marquis de Dreux-Brézé — was of imposing grandeur. New state carriages of unusual splendour were prepared expressly for this great national event. Both the civil and military household attended. Being augmented to nearly double their former number, and having an additional quantity of gold lace on their uniforms, they composed, of themselves, a very glittering pageant.

Draperies, and in some few instances, old tapestry, with garlands and festoons of flowers, decorated the fronts of the houses and were suspended across the streets along which the royal *cortège* was to pass. White flags, inscribed with loyal sentiments and complimentary couplets, fluttered from many a window along the route of the procession. The balconies were filled with ladies and children, dressed in white and wearing bouquets and wreaths of white and blue flowers. The little ones, being especially interested in the youthful hero of this May-day *fête*, clapped their hands and waved their handkerchiefs with an energy most amusing to behold. The royal ladies were resplendent, and the fineness of the day contributed not a little to bring out the flash and sparkle of the glittering gems of which they wore a profusion.

"The Duchesse de Berry was radiant, all smiles and graciousness; Madame Royale gravely placid, and wearing a stately plume; *le gros goutteux* looked better than could be expected, but fussy and important, as though *l'enfant du miracle* had been a miracle expressly vouchsafed to himself; Angoulême sleepy and heavy, and very much bored; *le vrai chevalier* still the *ci-devant jeune homme*, you know; the Orléans party, duke, duchess, and Princess Adélaïde, meekly resigned, duke rather pleased than otherwise; Monseigneur le Duc de Bordeaux, a fine plump babe, and, when held up to gratify the faithful lieges, apparently much astonished at the noisy hubbub, the fuss and folly, the glitter and glare, and the stuff and nonsense going on around him."[*]

All the treasures of the venerable old church of Notre-Dame were brought out to worthily decorate the interior, and grand and solemn music was composed for the occasion. The King of Naples and the hereditary Princess of the Two Sicilies, represented by Monsieur and Madame Royale, were the sponsors, Cardinal de Talleyrand-Périgord officiating. Great rejoicings, public and private festivities, illuminations, grand balls, and theatrical entertainments followed.

On the 2d of May, being the anniversary of

[*] Private Letters.

Louis XVIII.'s first entry into Paris, the king felt well enough to drive through all the principal streets and along the boulevards in a carriage-and-six, attended by the Ducs de Ragusa, d'Aumont, and d'Havré, and a brilliant escort. He was anxious even to be present at a grand banquet and ball given to the royal family at the Hôtel de Ville by the municipality of Paris. But his physicians, MM. Portal and Alibert, absolutely forbade it; the consequences, they feared, might prove fatal. Louis therefore unwillingly obeyed.

He was, however, partly consoled for this enforced absence from a festive scene which, though of frequent occurrence before the Restoration, was now a novelty, by the certainty of learning every detail connected with it from his *belle comtesse*, who had a talent for narrating with liveliness and *esprit*. The municipality were not less hospitable or less inclined to dance and dress than of old; but politics, and the struggles and intrigues of opposing parties to further their own views and thwart their opponents', had led to an almost total cessation of civic festivities. But now, to *fête* the youthful heir and hope of the Bourbons, all former festive triumphs were to be surpassed in the extent and splendour of the arrangements for this grand banquet and ball.

To attend on Madame Royale and the Duchesse de Berry, the latter, since the birth of the heir, being regarded by the royal family with more consideration than before, the king had appointed twelve ladies of the highest distinction, and had placed Madame du Cayla at the head of the list; thereby occasioning much jealous feeling and giving rise to murmuring and dissatisfaction.

After the rather prolonged festivities in celebration of the royal christening were ended, the king was again falling into the semi-lethargic state that now so frequently oppressed him, when an event which had occurred on the 5th of May, but was not positively known in France until the 5th of July, roused him from his stupor and once more infused new life into him. It was the death of the Emperor Napoleon, officially announced that morning at the council of ministers. A grand reception was immediately arranged to take place in the evening at the Tuileries, and Louis, who had been purposely brought from St. Cloud, was wheeled into the Salle des Maréchaux to receive the felicitations of the court. The *corps diplomatique* also assembled to offer their congratulations on the auspicious event, and a ball was given, as though the king had gained some great victory.

Several of Napoleon's generals and marshals were present when the event was first announced. But only one among those on service at the Château that day was affected by the sad details of his former " great captain's " last hours. So overwhelmed was he with emotion that he was compelled to withdraw, that he might in private give

Comte Rapp.
Photo-etching after the painting by Gros.

way to his grief. This officer was Général Comte Rapp.

"I owe everything to Napoleon," he said, by way of apologising to the king for his inability to restrain his feelings in his presence. Louis had noticed his grief, and is said to have replied: "Comte Rapp, your affliction does honour to your heart; I esteem you the more for it."

Yes, the exile of Ste. Helena being no longer either a menace or a terror to the coalesced kings of the Holy Alliance, Louis XVIII. could affect to speak of him as one capable of appreciating the many great qualities of that remarkably gifted man whose death so greatly rejoiced him.

"It was not only martial glory that he achieved," said the king, "but every kind of glory." This was malice on his part, and he was glad to perceive that on some who were present it had its effect.

But the Duc d'Orléans replied: "Sire, the greatest glory of all — that of restoring the crown to its legitimate owner — he failed to achieve."

"A charming phrase, *mon cousin;* I am glad to hear it from your lips," rejoined the king.

In 1818 the Emperor Alexander suggested the transfer of Europe's prisoner to a climate less fatal to him; but Austria harshly refused to join in this request to England. "The Iron Duke," as asserted, logically replied to it, in the name of his government, that "Sir Hudson Lowe did not complain of the climate!" The estimable governor, it appears, had recently reported that the health of the prisoner was not at all seriously affected.

However, "the modern giant was dead," as Louis XVIII. informed the countess, and, though there had been a commotion of the elements at Ste. Helena, his death had not shaken the world. "Heaven grant," he added, "if glory remains with his ashes, that it may not be reflected on any belonging to him in a manner dangerous to the rulers of Europe. His death has freed them from much disquietude, and has also given stability to my throne."

As for his son, he knew there was nothing to fear from him. Austria had taken care of that. Never was there a more bigoted partisan of the right divine. The young Duc de Reichstadt almost despised himself for being the son of a man who had set it at naught and usurped the place of France's saintly descended and ancient line of kings. What wonder, then, that the longing for an honourable career, and the promptings of ambition, with which in boyhood he is said to have been animated, thus constantly repressed by the sentiments so diligently instilled into him, should at length prey on his mind! A sense of utter isolation and a settled melancholy took possession of him, and led to that languor and mental inanity, that weariness of life when but on its threshold, that terminated in an early grave.

But, gratifying as the death of Napoleon I. may have been to the Bourbons, it spread consternation throughout France when it became generally known there. Deeply the patriots of the empire mourned for their emperor, and old soldiers wept for their general, openly accusing the kings of the Holy Alliance of sacrificing him to their vengeance and their fears. Many there were who refused to believe that the prisoner of Ste. Helena *could* die without having again seen France, and for a long time continued to cherish a hope of his return.

Chiefly, however, among the rural population a sort of superstitious awe was excited — which tended greatly to deify the memory of Napoleon — when they heard, with fear and trembling, that a tempest, sublimely grand in its terrific fury, swept over the island, and was at its height when the spirit of their hero departed. The four winds of heaven seemed to have united their forces to shake the rock to its base. The lightning flashed and the thunder rolled with startling *fracas* over the great man's humble dwelling. Thunder is rarely or never heard at Ste. Helena, so that many of the inhabitants were much alarmed at the awful sound accompanying the explosion of heaven's artillery. It imparted something of the supernatural to the weird grandeur of the sudden unchaining of the elements at the moment of the fallen hero's death, and, as it were, harmonising with the meteor-like suddenness with which he first burst on Europe as a mighty conqueror.

Notwithstanding, some of his old soldiers would still exclaim, "He *could* not die!" and the persistency with which restored royalty turned its back on Fontainebleau, which formerly had been the scene of so many of the stately revels of the old French court, confirmed their idea that *he* was there — a prisoner, no doubt, but *there* — and some day would reappear, or, as they said, return. Return, indeed, he did; but they who hoped to see him return alive were — with a rare exception or two — themselves no longer living when, in 1840, "home was brought their warrior, dead!"

CHAPTER V.

The Valiant Duc d'Angoulême. — The Congress of Verona. — Coquetry and Diplomacy. — Duc Mathieu de Montmorency. — A Sympathising Friend. — Imagination Taken Captive. — Madame Récamier's Letters. — A Great Enemy to Combat. — Author and Statesman. — Seeking in Vain. — Madame Récamier's System. — The Hero Is Off to the Wars. — Surprising the Garrison. — Impregnable Consciences. — The Hero's Return. — Hats and Gloves à *la Trocadéro.*

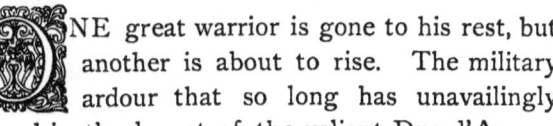NE great warrior is gone to his rest, but another is about to rise. The military ardour that so long has unavailingly burned in the breast of the valiant Duc d'Angoulême will shortly blaze forth in a flame so bright that its rays shall dazzle all Europe. It belongs, of course, to grave historians and military writers to relate in detail the particulars of the Spanish war, whose object was to restore to the despot Ferdinand VII. the sceptre he had so unworthily borne, and of which the Spanish people had temporarily deprived him. Very briefly only its origin and results can, or need, be noticed here.

In the autumn of 1822 there were assembled at Verona, that city of palaces, so rich in the architectural *chefs-d'œuvre* of Palladio and his school, the Emperors of Russia and Austria, the Kings of Prussia, Naples, and Sardinia, with many other sovereign princes, dukes, grand dukes, and archdukes, and the several ministers and ambassadors representing the potentates of the Holy (or Unholy) Alliance. As at Vienna, imperial and royal ladies accompanied these great personages. Among them was Maria Louisa, ex-Empress of France, attended by her husband, Count Neipperg; the wives and daughters of the plenipotentiaries completing the courtly throng.

A continual round of amusements — grand breakfasts and dinners, *fêtes champêtres* in shady glens, or at night in illuminated Italian gardens, with concerts, balls, and theatres, and other gay doings — enlivened the dull business of diplomacy. The Congress was to begin its discussions on the 9th of September; but an adjournment took place, in consequence of the startling communication of Lord Castlereagh's suicide, until the Duke of Wellington's arrival in October. England was not of the Holy ones, but her own interests and those of her allies made it necessary that her representative should also attend.

At Vienna the chief question to be solved was how best to apportion the spoils of war, and with that the gaieties of the Congress did not seem so inconsistent. At Verona it was the graver one, how most speedily to suppress insurrection and restore unpopular monarchs to their thrones; yet they danced and flirted and coquetted as unceasingly as before, for

> " The ladies' eyes were bright,
> And their spirits light,
> And their bosoms without a thorn; "

and this apparently helped on the more serious business wonderfully.

It must have done so ; for in the preceding year a Congress had been held at Laybach for the same political objects. But it was a poor, dull place; the ladies vouchsafed not the charm of their presence ; and the assembly soon broke up, promising to meet at a more convenient place and season, but announcing to rebellious populations that the sovereigns of Europe were determined to suppress Jacobinism and anarchy. Nevertheless, Greece, Naples, Sardinia, Spain, and Portugal had revolted, and raised the standard of freedom. Another Congress is arranged, and palatial Verona is selected for this *réunion* of royalty.

Louis XVIII., necessarily absent from the Congress, was diplomatically represented by Duc Mathieu de Montmorency (once a Jacobin, now a saint*), and, after some difficulty with the king,

---

* The duke was one of that enthusiastic band of young nobles who accompanied the then youthful Marquis de La Fayette to America to offer their services in the cause of independence. It was on a motion of his, then a deputy to the States General, that the constituent assembly on the 4th of August, 1789, decreed the abolition of the privileges of the nobility — the family of the

M. de Châteaubriand was recalled from his embassy in London to join him,— M. de Villèle believing that the viscount's political views were more in accordance with his own. But, all royalist though he was, the king and his brother could scarcely tolerate the poet-statesman, the "Atala of the *salons*," the idol of a flattering circle of fine ladies.

Towards the end of December, Duc Mathieu returned from Verona, when M. de Villèle induced the king to refuse to ratify the arrangement the duke had entered into with the Congress, — namely, to recall the French ambassador from Spain, and to send troops to the frontier. The Minister of Finance was not willing to incur the expense of war; the treasury was too empty, he urged, perhaps because he had appropriated so much that should have gone into it. He preferred to send remonstrances and menaces to insurrectionary Spain; more than that he considered premature.

Montmorencys being one of the most ancient and distinguished of its members. He was then one of the disciples of Madame de Staël, and emigrated with her in 1792, when Pétion, shutting his eyes to the fact that the duke and two other friends were with her disguised as servants, conducted them safely out of Paris. The duke's brother, the Abbé de Laval, was soon after guillotined. His grief and remorse were so great that it was feared his reason would be affected. A great change in his sentiments was, however, the result of his brother's death, and from a revolutionist he became a fervent royalist and an austere Christian — austere towards himself, but full of benevolence and kindly feeling towards others.

The duke declared that his honour was compromised by the refusal to fulfil the promises made by him to the Congress, and at once resigned his office of Minister of Foreign Affairs.

His wrongs were poured forth to the sympathising Madame Récamier, of whom for many years he had been one of the most devoted of devotees, and perhaps one of her sincerest friends. So devout himself, he was constantly in dread lest the admiration and flattery of the world should turn the thoughts of that "dear and lovely friend" from those higher things towards which he would lead her mind to dwell more frequently upon. Especially at this time he was much grieved that she, who hitherto had been the sun round which so many planets revolved, in the depth of her admiration for genius, seemed to have allowed her imagination to be taken captive by the vain, fretful, and capricious M. de Châteaubriand, and to have given him that place in her heart which so many had wished, but sought in vain, to occupy.

A very few days after M. de Montmorency had resigned his post, M. de Châteaubriand returned to Paris, bringing with him copies of the diplomatic notes already despatched by the several Powers recalling their ambassadors from Spain. Louis XVIII., being one of the kings of the Alliance, was expected forthwith to do the same, and without delay to send aid to his brother Ferdinand to put down the insurrection. M. de Châteaubriand had not opposed armed interference in the affairs of that country; he approved of the war, as he informed Madame Récamier, who was also the *confidante* of his hopes and fears, as she was of M. de Montmorency's and so many others'.

Scarcely can one inquire into the particulars of any event, social, political, literary, or artistic, occurring in the capital of France during a period of almost fifty years, from the time of the Directory to far into the reign of Louis Philippe, without meeting with the name of Madame Récamier, directly or indirectly, connected with it.

Such a woman, though often spoken of by her own sex as a mere vain, inanimate beauty, or an artful coquette with little beauty to boast of, must have had attractions beyond those of a lovely face and perfect form which jealous woman closed her eyes to. Her letters display much kindly feeling, elevated sentiments, and that quality of the mind so highly valued in France, and which throws mere beauty into the shade — *esprit*.

That she was no *intrigante* appears from her conduct towards the great viscount, on the occasion in question. His overweening vanity led him to desire, ministerially, to conduct the Spanish war — to covet, in fact, the *portefeuille* which his rival in love and diplomacy, from a delicate sense of honour, had resigned. He obtained it, too, at the instance of the Duchesse de Duras, one of those ladies whose ardent worship and flattering attentions ministered to the melancholy viscount's vanity. She was an extreme royalist, and of rather a stormy temperament. Her *salon* was the resort of many literary celebrities, and she was herself the author of two novelettes, "Ourika" and "Édouard," which had great success in the fashionable world, and, like her noble friend's "Atala," their titles had given names and perhaps vogue to some of the ugly hats, dresses, fichus, etc., then much in favour.

Her influence at court was great; for, although among the first to avail themselves of Napoleon's permission to the emigrants to return to France, she and her husband had stood aloof from the court of the "usurper" in an attitude of proud disdain. The king's sagacity told him that M. de Châteaubriand, once in the ministry, from sheer restlessness of character and insatiable love of popularity, would oppose his colleagues, and that, if not intriguing to enter the Cabinet, he would infallibly cabal to get out of it with *éclat*. "He had a great enemy to combat," he said.

"An enemy, Sire," exclaimed the duchess; "some envious —"

"No, madame," interrupted the king; "his great enemy is himself."

But the enthusiastic duchess was of opinion that to place M. de Châteaubriand in the ministry was to ensure that the greatness and the honour of France would be unflinchingly upheld.

With a compliment to him as an author, and a slightly disparaging remark on his qualifications as a statesman, Louis promised the desired *portefeuille*, and M. de Châteaubriand was summoned to the royal presence. Of course he affected unwillingness to accept the weighty responsibility of that great mark of royal favour his sovereign was disposed to confer on him. Modestly he shrank from undertaking its arduous duties; yet finally, as in duty bound, he yielded to the royal command. Immediately, he writes and despatches a note to Madame Récamier:

"The king sent for me at four, to offer me the *portefeuille* of Foreign Affairs. He kept me an hour and a half in his cabinet preaching to me, I resisting. At length he ordered me to obey. I obeyed; so that I do not return to London. I remain with you. But this ministry will kill me."

He survived, however; though, as minister, not very long. He expected to dominate in this ministry, and to make his tenure of office in it the culminating point of his political career.

Numerous were the congratulations, interwoven with delicate flattery, received by "Atala" from his circle of admiring lady friends; but he sought in vain amongst these scented epistles for one addressed in the "charming little handwriting of Madame Récamier." She is much grieved; she is deeply offended; and thinks that the melancholy poet has acted towards his friend and hers very ungenerously, if not dishonourably — his first act as minister being to persuade M. de Villèle to carry out the measures to which the Duc de Montmorency had pledged himself, and which, rejected, had led to his resignation. He must interpret her silence as he pleases. For a moment he was amazed at it; but ambition seems to have blunted his usual susceptibility, and the great things he dreamed of achieving, since his accession to power, to have put all minor matters out of mind. But as his appetite for praise was now more than ever voracious, he sought it from Madame Récamier by giving her full details of his speeches in the Cabinet councils; what he said at sittings of the Chamber; the measures he proposed and opposed. Not receiving his due meed of admiration, he spoke querulously to her, and displayed much ill-temper.

It was a part of what was ironically called "Madame Récamier's system" never to allow disputes or reproaches to ruffle the serenity of her friendships. She feared, however, that M. de Châteaubriand would some day lead her into breaking this rule. To his consternation, then, he learned that "the soft light that guided his path" was about to be withdrawn. She announced that she was going to take her adopted daughter (a niece of M. Récamier) to Italy for her health and change of scene. Her old faithful friend, M. Ballanche, who thought life worth living only in the light of her eyes, escorted them, accompanied by a young friend of his, M. Ampère, whom he had lately introduced at the Abbaye-aux-Bois, and who, though but twenty-two, was soon as ardent a worshipper of the enchantress as others who came within the circle of her influence. Madame Récamier was absent from France upwards of a year and a half, and during that time scarcely a line, after the first week or two, when the captious poet-minister reproaches her with indifference to his woes, seems to have passed between them.

Madame Récamier has kept the generalissimo a long time waiting. He had donned his helmet and buckled on his trusty sword. His impatient steed has been pawing the ground, and he, with his foot in the stirrup, ready to mount and away to the wars. But at last he is fairly off. His army, it appears, has really for some time been waiting for him on the frontier, ostensibly as a *cordon sanitaire*, the plague or yellow fever being reported at Bayonne, but actually with a view of deceiving the people and the troops themselves. For the war is not popular. They are not going forth, as of old, to conquer new kingdoms or to subdue an enemy, but to chastise a people driven by a tyrant's oppressive sway into rising against him and demanding constitutional freedom.

Ferdinand, if not exactly a prisoner, was under so much restraint and strict surveillance that probably he would have granted what the Spaniards required of him if the French had not interfered. By restoring him to his throne and the country to the monks and the executioner, they occasioned those fearful reprisals, those horrid massacres and revolting cruelties, carried out with such savage vengeance, with which the narrow-minded *rey absoluto* — a bigot and a libertine — signalised, under the protecting shadow of the white flag, his restoration to power. The great feat of the war was the taking of the Trocadéro. It gave the final blow to the revolution by opening the way to the capitulation of Cadiz.

The duke being desirous of witnessing this brilliant feat of arms, Général Guilleminet, who commanded, placed his generalissimo in a safe position, where he could see what took place, yet be out of the reach of any random shot. It is asserted [*] that all the garrison of this strong fort, which commanded the entrance of the Isle of St. Léon, was asleep when it fell into the hands of the French commander. When the *vivas* of the attacking party roused the sleeping sentinels, it was too late to give the alarm to their drowsy comrades, for the French were already in the entrenchments.

The generalissimo doubted not that the victory — such as it was — was due to him. At

[*] P. Lacroix, "*Histoire de France.*"

once he wrote off to the Comte d'Artois: "My father, I am fully satisfied with myself. I alone decided on an enterprise which none of our generals dared take upon himself to recommend to me! God has blessed it, and I have just returned thanks to Him at the foot of the Altar!"

The *avocat* Martignac followed the expedition in the character of civil commissioner. He carried with him some magic means — narcotics, perhaps — of "bringing over impregnable consciences," which is said greatly to have aided the military in taking impregnable fortresses.

But to the French nation the most galling incident of this inglorious and unjust war, which cost France 400,000,000 *francs* (16,000,000 pounds sterling), and 15,000 men, was the taking from the Hospital of the Invalides forty-eight banners and the keys of the city of Valencia, trophies of the preceding wars of Napoleon in Spain. This same M. Martignac was charged by the valiant generalissimo, who was anxious to get back to Paris, where an ovation was in preparation for him, to place these trophies in the royal palace of Madrid, and, in his name, to announce their restoration to King Ferdinand. The remembrance of the first Spanish war, it appears, importuned the minds of the French Bourbons more than it troubled the Spaniards themselves, and it was desired to efface it by the glorious souvenirs of the second.*

A grand *Te Deum* was sung at Notre-Dame in celebration of the duke's great victories. On the 2d of December the rolling drums and the merry fifes proclaimed the return of the conquering hero. The municipal authorities, and a brigade of the household troops, drawn up at the *barrière de l'Étoile*, attended to greet him, the bands striking up, as he with his brilliant staff and invincible battalions approached, " *Vive Henri Quatre !* " followed by " *Charmante Gabrielle !* " — a compliment to Madame Royale, as "the girl he left behind him."

The roar of the cannon of the Invalides mingles with shouts of " *Vive le héros du Trocadéro !* " as that doughty and very lusty personage passes under Napoleon's triumphal arch. Now he enters the garden of the Tuileries; he alights — neither lightly nor gracefully, it is to be feared — in front of the Pavillon du Château. The royal family are in the balcony, all drowned, as the exaggerated phrase is, in a flood of tears.

He enters the palace; he passes, with heavy tread, into the Salle des Maréchaux. The king is there; the hero falls on his knees, and needs a friendly hand to help him up again. The monarch's face is bathed in crocodile's tears; he opens his arms and essays to embrace his nephew's

* P. Lacroix, "*Histoire de France.*"

ample form. "My son," he exclaims, "you have gladdened my heart. I am satisfied with you." The rest of the family press around him, and mutual embracings follow.

The next day Trocadéro hats were all the rage, with a sort of *mousquetaire* glove, named for this special occasion " *Gants à la héros du Trocadéro.*"

CHAPTER VI.

Fêting the Hero. — Clinging to Life. — A Last Speech in the Chambers. — The Cause of Misfortune. — The Blessing of the *Rentiers*. — "Tell Him I Turn Him Out!" — The *Quid Pro Quo*. — "Atala of the *Salons*." — Frequent and False Alarms. — A Wretched Condition. — "A King of France Must Not Be Ill." — The Strong Will Fails at Last. — A Conversion *in Extremis*. — The Death Chamber. — The Favourite's Portrait. — "The King, Gentlemen!"

LOUIS XVIII. survived the return of the Duc d'Angoulême from Spain nearly ten months; yet the hand of death may be said to have been upon him some time before that event. In spite of it, however, he insisted — pitiable spectacle though he was — on being present at most of the religious ceremonies and courtly entertainments with which the hero of the crowning incident of the Spanish war was as extravagantly fêted as if he had achieved a second Marengo or Austerlitz. The king's remarkable force of will alone bore him up under his acute bodily sufferings, and supported him, time after time, in, as it were, his struggle with death, enabling him from week to week, day to day, and hour to hour, to evade the clutch of the grim enemy.

Contemporary writers do not willingly credit Louis XVIII. with fortitude, or ascribe to resignation his uncomplaining endurance of the anguishing pain he must often have writhed under. He clung desperately to life, because he too plainly foresaw the downfall of the throne under Charles and his advisers, and — more agonising still — the very probable elevation of the Duc d'Orléans to kingly power. To avert this catastrophe, he strove sternly to hold out and to prolong the miserable remnant of his days, if a determined will and the principle of life that was so strong within him could accomplish it. By opposing some of the fatal measures of the priestly and ultra-royalist party to which the Comte d'Artois had abandoned himself, he is said to have believed that the nation might glide more gradually from what he considered to be his own liberal system of government to a despotic one, therefore with less risk to the stability of the throne.

If this was his object he did not succeed in it; for Charles X. and the priests of the congregation who guided him began virtually to reign before Louis XVIII. was actually dead. The state of the king's health, however, was as much as possible concealed from the public. Indeed, as he still looked florid, ate enormously, took long drives at a rapid pace, and had never been seen from the time of his first entry into France out of his chair or his carriage, the few who felt any interest in the matter saw no cause for alarm. So wonderfully, too, did he rally that he opened the Legislative Chambers at the Louvre on the 23d of March, seated on his throne in the Salle Henri IV., as when, three years before, he had announced his abdication of power and approaching end.

His speech was a long one, urging on the Chambers the advisability of holding septennial elections rather than annual ones, as decreed by the Charter; also the conversion of the five per cent. *rentes* to three per cent., a measure that gave M. de Châteaubriand — in whom M. de Villèle had found a colleague less in agreement with his views than he had expected — the opportunity of caballing, as the king said, to go out of the ministry with *éclat*. It appears, too, that while secretly seeking to thwart his colleague's measure, his speech in the Chambers seemed to approve it.

This attempt to reduce the rate of interest on the public funds occasioned quite a commotion in France, small *rentiers* being the most numerous of the state's creditors. To them, of course, the reduced rate of interest meant a large reduction of income, while the state was to realise by it 600,000,000 *francs*, the greater part of this sum being already promised, to pay the yet unsatisfied demands of the emigrants. M. de Villèle was an able financier, and it does not appear that there was any injustice in his scheme, as the interest paid by the state had become out of all proportion to the ordinary rate of money, while the *rentiers* who objected to the change were offered the alternative of receiving back their capital in full.

Those who availed themselves of the opportunity of opposing the minister by opposing his measure, condemned it as a most flagrant and scandalous denial of justice. The peers vigorously pronounced against it. The Archbishop of Paris, Monseigneur Quélen, also favoured the "cause of misfortune," and pleaded on behalf of the *rentiers*. Ignorant of finance, he qualified as iniquitous a scheme that, to ease the burden of the state, reduced the income of the man who depended solely on his *rentes*, and condemned him and his family to straitened means. Not in vain did he lift up his voice — his eloquent pleading securing victory to the cause of *malheur* by 128 votes against 94. He was lauded to the skies, and the fervent blessing of the *rentiers* descended upon him.

M. de Villèle had not foreseen this defeat, the proposed reduction having been assented to on the 5th of May by the Chamber of Deputies. It irritated him greatly; and greater still was his irritation when he discovered that he owed it mainly to M. de Châteaubriand. He had spoken of the scheme, if not very warmly, yet favourably, in the Chamber of Peers; yet it was he who was said to have organised there the opposition to it.

The archbishop's fluent discourse was also attributed to him, and it was remarked that he had absented himself when the measure was put to the vote.

But of the charges brought against him, that which probably M. de Villèle could least pardon was the hint M. de Châteaubriand was said to have dropped of the approaching formation of a new ministry. Every one knew this meant that he was to be the head of it, and that he firmly believed he was the only minister, the supreme political arbiter, who could save France. The aggrieved financier lost no time in laying the matter fully before the king. Roused to anger by this check to a measure of which he vehemently declared his approval, he gave way to one of the Bourbon explosions of brutal ill-temper, and, raving at the top of his voice, "Tell him I turn him out! (*Dites-lui que je le chasse!*)" sank back exhausted in his chair.

M. Alibert was instantly summoned, and by the aid of restoratives and the soothing voice of the countess — the "modern Madame de Maintenon," as she was now often called — his majesty was restored to consciousness and calmness. This occurred on the 6th of June, at about midday. An hour or two after, M. de Châteaubriand entered the Tuileries in full court dress as minister, as was usual, to pay his respects to the king and royal family, and to assist at the council. When about to enter the king's apartment, he was informed by a gentleman-in-waiting that an important communication awaited him at his hôtel. He returns immediately, opens his letter, and reads, to his great consternation:

"MONSIEUR LE VICOMTE: — By his majesty's orders, I transmit to you the enclosed decree.
"JOSEPH DE VILLÈLE."

The decree ran as follows:

"The Comte de Villèle, President of our Council of Ministers, is charged *ad interim* with the *portefeuille* of Foreign Affairs, replacing the Vicomte de Châteaubriand."

In less than an hour the viscount replied to M. de Villèle in a style as laconic as his own:

"MONSIEUR LE COMTE: — I have left the hôtel of Foreign Affairs. The department is at your orders.
"CHÂTEAUBRIAND."

The manner of his dismissal was, in one sense, a terrible blow to his *amour-propre;* in another, his vanity was immensely flattered by the great outburst of popularity he obtained by it. On the 7th of June he announced in the *Journal des Débats* that he had broken with the government; and, whether in the Chamber of Peers, in his various pamphlets, or numerous articles in the *Débats*, he kept up a vigorous onslaught against his former friends who had abandoned him. Former opponents, however, whose chief strength lay in the press, now gathered around and supported him.

Châteaubriand.
Photo-etching after the engraving by Hopwood.

Not a word of all this does he vouchsafe to Madame Récamier. Since he became the "champion of the cause of misfortune," his circle of female worshippers is also enlarged, and he now needs not her sympathy; though, as he afterwards confessed, he missed it greatly. She, on her side, seeks no information from her capricious friend, and offers him no word of consolation. But she is informed of every circumstance of his defeat and his duplicity by her friend, Duc Mathieu de Montmorency.

He now has hope that the "even tenor of her life may not be ruffled by the contact of one so capricious, so fitful, so uncertain of temper as 'Atala of the *salons*,' who is always overshadowed by a causeless melancholy, and to whom the greatest success has failed to give contentment." Once more the duke flatters himself that the "sweet privilege" of holding the first place in her heart, and of guiding her safely through the snares of this wicked world to the pathway leading to a better, will again be his. Meanwhile, he advises her to "seek help from Him who alone can both fortify and recompense."

The dismissal of M. de Châteaubriand and the injunction to M. de Villèle to retain his post of President of the Council, in order to take his revenge in spite of present defeat, appears to have been the last public act in which Louis XVIII. took any real part. That even a month or two later, when in a state bordering on somnolence, his nearly palsied hand was guided to give the sanction of his name to measures which he would have rejected had he comprehended their import, is of course well known. But he was then utterly incapable of repressing the furious zeal of the Congregationists — otherwise the Jesuits — who, with the Comte d'Artois as their nominal chief, but actual slave, were busily preparing "to rule with vigour."

They, however, deemed it expedient that, until their plans were fully laid, as little as possible should transpire outside the Château of the king's actual condition. There had been many false alarms during the last three or four years, one day he was said to be dying, the next he was out driving or engaged with his ministers, so that these fluctuations were little heeded. Until the *gros goutteux* was actually dead, none would believe that he was dying. He was never reported ill enough to keep his bed. Nothing would induce him to do so. "A King of France must die," he said, "but must never be ill."

His last monthly reception of the ladies of the court took place at St. Cloud on the first Monday in August. A sad ceremony it must have been, his head drooping on his breast and falling sometimes to his knees; attendants at his side carefully raising it, he being powerless to do so. When, a second time, the gentleman-in-waiting mentioned the name of Madame du Cayla, "Ah!" he said, his attention momentarily aroused, "I saw a pretty foot, and should have recognised its owner." It was on her that his thoughts now seemed chiefly to dwell. His anxiety was no longer about France and his throne, but the Comtesse Zoé, who was more to him than either.

His physicians considered it advisable that he should be removed to the Tuileries, to which he consented. But on the eve of the *fête* of Saint Louis he was actually out for a long drive in an open *calèche*, his helpless appearance exciting much commiseration. Yet on the morrow he received, as was usual on that day, the municipal authorities, the *corps diplomatique*, and the court. By a sort of supreme effort of the mind to triumph over bodily infirmity and to be himself again while the reception lasted, he succeeded in keeping an erect position, and, in a voice scarcely less loud and deep than it had been for years past, to say something complimentary to most of his visitors.

He fancied that he could do the same with impunity on the following day; and, in fact, did so, refusing to listen to the advice of his physicians to adjourn the audience. He was always ready with, "A King of France must not be ill," as a reply to advice that he cared not to follow. On the 28th he went to Choisy, this time, which was the last of his drives, in a close carriage, but as fast as six horses could carry him — he continually exclaiming that his coachman drove them at the pace of a *voiture de place*. In this rapid movement he hoped to find some abatement of the pains that racked him; but this last drive seems to have had a contrary effect.

His strong desire to live and, one may almost say, persistence in living, and that in bodily torture that would to most persons make death a welcome visitor, are very remarkable. His swollen legs and feet are described as shapeless masses of rankling sores, yet he uttered no cry of pain. Brief intervals of comparative freedom from it sometimes occurred, and with them a revival of mental powers. Then, the countess was summoned to a confidential interview, or his brother was called to listen to his warnings and his advice. At last, by his order, bulletins were issued, revised by himself, by no means alarming ones, until the 10th of September, when M. Portal was of opinion that the imminence of his danger should no longer be concealed from the public. Still he absolutely refused to be kept in bed; not only must a King of France never be ill, but "he must die standing or sitting."

But strength of will at last failed him. On the evening of the 14th the agonising pain of his wounds triumphed over the unnatural strain on his powers of endurance. He fainted. Availing themselves of his inability to resist, his physicians ordered him to be placed in his bed. To die in peacefulness was not, however, permitted to Louis XVIII. He was supposed to hold the philosophical doctrines of Voltaire and his school, and to be a deist, if not, as many suspected, an atheist. Therefore the zealous devotees who surrounded his bed urged on him the necessity of a renunciation of these principles before the last sacraments could be administered.

The Duchesse d'Angoulême and Monsieur persistently importuned him to edify the world by a striking conversion *in extremis*. But his mind was wandering, and he seemed scarcely to comprehend what was required of him. It was in consequence reluctantly determined to summon Madame du Cayla to the aid of the Congregational priests. She already had secretly served them so well by using her favour with the king for the furtherance of their views — probably to maintain her position at court after his death — that her all-powerful intervention was now sought to overcome the deist monarch's repugnance to confess and be shrived.

She is said to have succeeded, which it may be permitted to doubt. Perhaps she was less ardent than when, but a few days before, she obtained the tracing of his signature to the papers that put her in possession of the Château of St. Ouen and its dependencies. His edifying devotion, and the

Christianlike obedience with which he had submitted to the practices of the faith and received extreme unction, were, however, duly announced to an astonished and incredulous public. At the same time an *"ordre supérieur"* required the fair countess to withdraw from the court. Louis XVIII. had made a will in which she was particularly interested, and of which it was feared she might obtain possession and thus rescue it from the destruction awaiting it.

The king had now fallen into a sort of trance. Surely the supreme moment must at last have arrived. Many present feel that it is near at hand for them, unless speedily released from the pestiferous chamber. The physicians approach his bed and anxiously feel the dying man's pulse. All eyes are upon them. They resume their seats, and despairing countenances seem to say, "Will it never cease to beat?" Yet hastily, and for the second time, the Duc d'Orléans, with his wife and sister, is summoned to see the end of the man who so thoroughly detests him.

As he enters that crowded apartment — from which from time to time some one is led or borne out fainting — there are signs, in that almost senseless corpse, of returning animation, and glimmerings of reviving intellect in the reopening eyes. The discoloured, blackened countenance assumes a severe expression. What is he so earnestly gazing at? Black-robed priests stand at his bedside, and all that could bring back earthly souvenirs has been removed — even to the portrait of his favourite, the Duc Decazes, which has so long hung opposite the foot of his bed. It is that his eyes so earnestly seek. Convinced that it is not there, the indignity thus offered to king and minister affects him so strongly that the departing spirit about to wing its way to the unseen world is momentarily arrested in its flight.

With startling energy — though death is closing with him, and the final struggle with his defiant spirit can be but briefly delayed — he commands in reproachful terms that the picture be replaced. He is obeyed. He then asks for the Duc de Bordeaux. The child is brought, and the king's helpless hand is placed on his head. A blessing is murmured; the once strong voice sinking almost to a whisper as he utters, "Let Charles X. be careful of this child's crown." His eyes then revert to the portrait, and remain fixed upon it until closed in death.

The dial in the king's bedchamber was striking four on the morning of the 16th of September when M. Portal announced to the Comte d'Artois that the king was dead. The door leading to the Gallery of Diana was then thrown open; the Comte de Damas advanced. "The king, gentlemen!" he said, addressing the crowd of courtiers assembled there. Charles X. then entered. All kissed his hand, and many knelt; while he, much affected, and followed by the princes and princesses, left the Tuileries immediately for St. Cloud.

CHAPTER VII.

A Feeble Ruler. — He Gave France the Charter. — Attending to Business of State. — The Dreaded Transition. — A *Ci-devant Jeune Homme.* — The Good Old Times. — Funereal Pomp. — The Lying in State. — The Funeral *Cortège.* — A Question of Precedence. — The Interior of St. Denis. — Charles X.'s Public Entry. — The Military Staff. — " No More Halberds." — *Les Enfants de France.* — The Royal Ladies. — The Funeral Oration. — The Royal Vaults Closed.

DURING the century that elapsed between the death of Louis XV. in 1774 and that of Napoleon III. in 1873, two emperors and four kings reigned over France, of whom Louis XVIII. alone died peacefully in his bed in the palace of the Tuileries, and was buried at St. Denis with his ancestors. "The affairs of the world," wrote Prince Metternich, recording the king's death in his diary, " go on better now, so that kings may die in peace. But the old king was a feeble ruler."

Dead, however, he excited more interest than when living; and though liked no better, yet, in view of what was expected to follow, he was almost regretted. If the government of the kingdom had been to him, on the whole, a mere congenial amusement, and the two or three hours he daily passed in council with his ministers but a whiling away of time which, in his infirm and afflicted condition, would have hung very drearily on his hands, at all events, willingly or not, he had given France the Charter. As far as he was able, too, he had made royalty bend to its yoke. True, it pleased him to retouch and modify as well as sometimes to evade it — "to pass his measures by finessing with the Chambers, and to conduct affairs of state generally after the fashion of a party of piquet." *

Sometimes it was difficult to secure his attention to public business, however important; an instance of which occurred during the Spanish war, and is mentioned by M. de Châteaubriand. An army of 40,000 men was invading Spain, when a despatch relating to its operations was received, the substance of which it was necessary to communicate immediately to the king. MM. de Châteaubriand, Villèle, and other ministers at once sought an interview, and found him surrounded by papers, written and printed, one of which he was reading. Instead of allowing them to enter on the subject of the despatch, he began reciting to them the Cantata of Circé. Having finished that, he took up another paper, and read several couplets from the "*Sabot perdu*" — a composition of very doubtful delicacy. It, however, amused him exceedingly, and interested him

* Arnault.

so much that he could not be brought to attend to the object of his ministers' visit, notwithstanding its gravity. The despatch in question was therefore laid beside him, with a hope that it might attract his attention, the ministers then taking leave of the literary monarch.

"If you would reign with peace and tranquillity," he said to his brother, when approaching his end, "follow my example. Take a middle course, and (using a nautical phrase) steer the vessel of the state through troublous water and opposing currents by judicious tacking, as Henri IV. did, and as I have even more successfully done; for I die in my palace, while the hand of an assassin laid him low in the streets." But Charles X., as King of France, is expected to discharge, and without delay, the engagements of the Comte d'Artois towards his party; and already the "immaculates" are kissing the feet of the modern Louis Quatorze, who, booted and spurred, and whip in hand, is about to dash into the midst of the articles of the Constitutional Charter.

This dreaded transition, however, from the rule of the temporising deist king to that of the uncompromising bigot, takes place quite peaceably; and Charles X., whose advent to power the majority of the nation so dreaded, begins his reign with a certain degree of popularity; resting chiefly on his immense advantage over his predecessor in personal appearance and distinction of manners.

Louis XVIII. at his death wanted but two months of completing his sixty-ninth year, and Charles X. is but a twelvemonth younger, so that his personal graces have for a long time been on the wane. Yet the "*beau roué*" bears up pretty well, and carries jauntily the weight of sixty-eight frosty winters. As with Louis XVIII., a brief renewal of youth, or rather a subduing to a certain extent of the traces of anxiety and advancing years by satisfaction with his changed position, was shed upon him soon after his return to France, like the bright glow of autumn sunshine, beautifying the fading and falling glories of summer. A little sleet has fallen on his once abundant black hair, of which, if less luxuriant than in days of yore, he still has an ample quantity. It is carefully arranged, and appears to be slightly powdered, but by no means does it look, to one who is not too near him, like the frosty poll of an elderly gentleman.

He still condescends to earthly vanities in fondness for embroideries and diamonds, and in the splendour of his uniforms. So that when, with a flowing plume, and seated erect as a young man on a highly trained and high-bred, curveting, prancing steed, displaying his equestrian skill to admiring groups of ladies, to whom with infinite grace he raises his hat and bends almost to his

Charles X.
Photo-etching after the painting by Charles.

saddle-bow, he yet looks wonderfully well, and seems to claim the old epithet of *le vrai chevalier français*.

Of course, it was not merely the delight of the dowagers of the Faubourg St. Germain with the graces of a *ci-devant jeune homme*, albeit now a king, which induced the calm that had spread, not only over Paris, but throughout France. Like the Duc d'Orléans, the nation was watching and waiting. No measures of severity were attempted; therefore, perhaps, none were needed. No seditious cries were heard, and no popular movement indicated the existence of an insurrectional plot. The *carbonari* and the republicans seemed to have disappeared entirely, which Charles and his advisers attributed to the terror inspired by the promptitude and thoroughness with which the great Angoulême had put down the Spanish insurgents.

The new reign was to be inaugurated with great pomp. The funeral of the deceased king and the coronation of his successor afforded excellent opportunities for reviving the ancient splendour and etiquette of the old monarchy, and for reintroducing at the Tuileries, until Versailles was restored and refurnished, the usages and customs of the ancient court of France. This sufficed to excite public curiosity and to amuse the Parisian mind for a time by its novelty. It diverted attention, too, from other measures by which the return of the good old times was silently, gradually, and effectually to be accomplished.

For the moment, then, politics did not greatly absorb the thoughts of the Parisians. All parties seemed agreed to put them aside for a season. Charles, who had made so hasty an exit from the Tuileries, was at St. Cloud in strict seclusion, praying, some said fasting (a terrible penance for a Bourbon), and at spare moments arranging with the Marquis de Dreux-Brézé the ceremonial to be observed at the late king's funeral. Most patient research was needed for the due formation of this imposing spectacle; for at the funerals of the "*Grand Monarque*" and the "Well-beloved" as little ceremony as possible was observed in conveying the body from Versailles to St. Denis. In both cases the removal took place in the night, to avoid the insults of the people, who followed with gibes and jeers wherever on the route the scanty *cortège* was recognised.

For the lying in state of the late king his bedchamber was fitted up as a *chapelle ardente*. The walls were hung with black velvet, relieved by draperies of crimson and gold. Several girandoles containing numerous wax lights were placed along the sides of the apartment; the glass shades being veiled with crape, to subdue the glare to a dim religious twilight.

On the state bed, curtained with crimson velvet heavily fringed with gold, and surmounted by the royal arms, lay the fast-decomposing corpse of Louis XVIII. A superb mantle of state was thrown over it, on which lay the insignia of the Order of the Saint Esprit. The crown was placed on a cushion at the head of the bed. Since the lying in state of Louis XIV. at Versailles, in 1715, no such spectacle had been witnessed in France. Louis XV. having died of the most malignant type of smallpox, no lying in state was possible. All Paris, therefore, desired to obtain a glimpse of the splendours of the royal chamber of death.

A glimpse was indeed the utmost that could be obtained, because of the pestiferous atmosphere; those who were admitted being urged to pass as quickly as possible through the chamber without regard to the solemnity of the scene. Ample particulars were, however, supplied by the newspapers. The censorship of the press had been reëstablished when the late king's dangerous state became known, in order to provide against any untimely or disquieting publicity being given of the secret arrangements for the approaching accession of his brother. It was now withdrawn, or partly so, any comments on the government of the past, or a reference in any sense to that of the future, being strictly prohibited.

On the 23d of September the remains of deceased royalty were transferred from the Tuileries to St. Denis. The newspapers were not only permitted, but expected, to give the fullest details of these sumptuous obsequies, that the minds of the absent, as well as of those who were privileged to gaze on them, might be impressed with wonder and awe. The pompous *cortège* was arranged in strict conformity with all accounts written and traditional of the usages of the ancient monarchy on the lamentable, or otherwise, occasion of the departure of its sovereigns for another and perhaps a better world. A faithful representation was thus produced both of the customs and costumes of a period of which, of course, no trace existed in the memory of the people. They gazed on it with mingled feelings of curiosity and displeasure, but with little, if any, reverence. All the great officers of the crown attended, surrounding the new king, who, as chief mourner, was on horseback, besides heralds-at-arms, standard-bearers and others, all wearing the historical costume of the sixteenth century. The crown, with the rest of the insignia of royalty, was placed on a magnificently embroidered cushion, and borne under a canopied car, drawn by six richly caparisoned horses, each led by a *palefrenier* in antique costume.

Yet, as a spectacle, this grand show lost much in completeness and effect by the absence of the two great dignitaries of the Church — the Archbishop of Paris and Monseigneur Frayssinous, the king's grand almoner. That they and their respective train of priests were not in attendance was doubtless a grief to the king, whose voice was powerless to command in such a matter. To the people it was inexplicable, except as a reflection on the supposed Voltairean principles of the late monarch.

Perhaps it was injudicious on the part of those distinguished ecclesiastics, as the Church was looking forward to reign supreme, to allow a paltry question of precedency to influence them on so solemn a public occasion, and thus to give rise to much unfavourable speculation. The very little respect in which the priesthood generally were held was not increased when the public became aware that a dispute of this nature had run high between the archbishop and the grand almoner. Priestly pride forbade either to yield an inch of his pretensions. The funeral *cortège* was therefore deprived of a conspicuous part of its solemnity, and, as a pageant, was shorn of some effects of contrast by the absence of the violet and crimson robes of the high ecclesiastics, and those more sombre ones of the various grades of their attendant clergy.

The deep tones of the great bell of Notre-Dame and the hoarser ones of the cannon of the Invalides mingled with the chant of a band of white-robed choristers as the procession slowly wended its way from the Tuileries to St. Denis. Arrived at its destination, the coffin was placed under a splendid catafalque in the nave, there to remain until the final interment in the royal vault. The grand old abbey was draped throughout with black velvet embroidered in gold with *fleurs-de-lys*. Massive silver lamps were suspended along the nave, and groups of wax tapers dimly lighted the more remote parts, forming, with the ancient sculpture of the interior of the edifice thus brought into relief, and with the rays of coloured light gleaming from the painted windows, a highly impressive and solemn scene.

Three weeks have elapsed, and again the air vibrates with the booming of the cannon of the Invalides. But now it announces a *fête;* and instead of the lugubrious tolling of Notre-Dame's great bell resounding through Paris, the merry church chimes are ringing. The period officially appointed for general mourning and sorrow is to be relieved of a portion of its gloom by Charles X.'s public entry into his capital, with as much royal state and as many old-world ways as attended his predecessor out of it.

Not a vestige of mourning is now visible at the Tuileries. The black velvet draperies have all disappeared, yielding place to royal purple, crimson, and gold — richness and brilliancy reigning throughout. Lavender and pastils have been unstintingly burned, and every apartment, small and large, is redolent of perfume, from the bottom to the top of the Château, which now is ready to receive its new master.

Every house along the streets through which the pageant is to pass is gaily decked with tapestry, or what does duty for it; while every flower the lateness of the floral season affords is there, waving in loops, wreathing in the balconies, or formed into devices of welcome to the king, with "*Vive notre roi!*" "*Vive Charles X!*" A stranger would have said, "Surely this monarch lives in the hearts of his people." Perhaps he did, as long as the pageant was passing and the streets were thronged, the weather fine, and all around gaiety and animation.

From St. Cloud to Notre-Dame (where a *Te Deum* and a mass are to be sung), regiments of infantry stationed at short intervals line the road; the gaps, or intervening spaces, being occupied by squadrons of cavalry. The household troops form part, and a very showy part, of the procession. The king's military staff is composed of marshals of France. They are really superb, so elaborately ornamented are their uniforms, so dazzling their numerous grand cordons and crosses, and so spotlessly pure their waving plumes.

Those rare gems, the Regent and the Sancy, which have shed lustre on so many of the illustrious personages of France, and played a brilliant part in many a state ceremony, are already transferred, it is remarked, from the hat and sword of the late king to those of Charles X. He comes, as usual, caracoling along. His horse, trained to this by Franconi, tosses his head, paws the ground, prances a little, showing off all his circus tricks to show off himself and his rider. By the side of this *ci-devant* juvenile king rides one who, at a very short distance, looks like his good fat elderly father, but who is in fact the elderly dauphin, the son of that smiling, bowing, elegant horseman, who, with the hopeful heir-apparent, is surrounded by a quaintly dressed company of men-at-arms with their halberds.

Vivas for the king are loud, long, and hearty; and, as this pleases Charles, he bows his acknowledgments very graciously. But enthusiasm is increased and hopes rise high when, with condescending smiles, he waves his hand towards his antique guard, who had seemed disposed to use their weapons to disperse the *canaille* so eagerly seeking to approach the sacred person of their monarch. His gesture appears to deprecate violence, and the people thus interpreting it, exclaim, "No halberds!" while some among them, giving it a wider significance, add, "No more (*plus*) *de halberds!*"

The king smiles, as if assenting; and, in their joyousness and momentary warmth of feeling, the people accept a wave of the hand and a smile as the happy presage of an intention to usher in the new reign by a liberal policy.

The Duc d'Orléans, who, but for his gold-embroidered uniform, stars, and crosses, might, from his want of dignity, be supposed to have no place here, rides on the left of his royal cousin. The old Duc de Bourbon-Condé, too, is present, but in his carriage. The grand state carriage prepared for the royal christening also figures in the procession; probably time was wanting to construct another of more antique fashion. It is occupied by the Duchesse d'Angoulême, now Madame la Dauphine, and three of her ladies. Following, in a splendid equipage, which some of the spectators declare they recognise as an imperial one (probably Maria Louisa's) with a change of emblazonments, is the Duchesse de Berry.

By the general shifting of position consequent on the king's death, the duchess has become Madame. The Comtesse de Gontaut, who is governess to the royal children, accompanies her with little Mademoiselle and the Duc de Bordeaux. They are pretty children of four and five years of age, apparently much interested in all that is taking place in the animated scene around them.

Madame is almost the only member of the royal family who has any real popularity. She still looks almost as girlish as when she tripped unattended into the tent at Fontainebleau. Her bright fair hair has grown again in all its former luxuriance, and she has lost none of her liveliness and love of gaiety, though she has devoted much time to study, and to acquiring proficiency in artistic pursuits, for which she has shown much talent. Her love of the arts and her patronage of them give her a place in the history of the Restoration which neither the Duchesse d'Angoulême, Louis XVIII., nor Charles X. can lay claim to.

The Duchesse d'Orléans and Madame Adélaïde, with attendant ladies, have also their place in this grand procession. The clerical element, too, is not wanting. The archbishop is present, also the grand almoner. How they have settled the question of precedency is not recorded. But there they are — the archbishop and his *coadjuteur*, the grand almoner and his deputy. Squadrons of cavalry bring up the rear, as much for protection as military parade; for who can tell what trivial unforeseen circumstance may, like a spark on tinder, rouse into flame the fire that smoulders in the breasts of the populace, and change this grand show into a scene of riot, and even of bloodshed?

Madame la Dauphine had urged the king to give strict orders for the prompt and rigorous suppression of any seditious cries. None, however, were heard, fortunately perhaps for her, as well as for others. "À *bas les Jésuites!*" is said to have been here and there uttered; but, if so, a deaf ear was judiciously turned to it. The entry of Charles X. into his capital may therefore be pronounced a success.

In the evening the Tuileries, the Palais Royal, and all official residences were brilliantly illuminated, and generally the windows of private houses were lighted up with lamps or candles. The theatres were open gratis to the public; but, as it was a period of deep mourning, Charles and his family, in the dusky October twilight, returned to St. Cloud.

On the 31st the ceremony of removing the coffin of Louis XVIII. from the catafalque to the royal vault took place, with a vast deal of ecclesiastical pomp. The funeral oration, delivered by the king's grand almoner, excited considerable attention, as the errors of the late king's political system were alluded to, and a hint given of the counteracting of their evil results by that of his successor, on whom the blessing of Heaven was invoked to aid him in his arduous task. "The King of France," he said, "ought not to allow the revolutionary spirit to subsist in his kingdom;" concluding his discourse with the announcement that "the new reign would be that of a Christian who would put into his government the religion that lived in his soul."

The coffins of the king and the Duc de Berry were placed side by side — the last of their line to repose in the Abbey of St. Denis.

CHAPTER VIII.

Resting on the Right Divine. — The Lapse of Fifty Years. — Napoleon's Mistake. — A Busy Time for the *Modistes*. — Regenerating French Society. — The New Converts. — " *Ad Majorem Dei Gloriam !* " — Lecturing in Vain. — Models of Kingly Perfection. — A Heaven Assigned Task. — Recriminatory Reproaches. — The Royalist Emigrants. — " *C'est un Polignac.*" — The Orléans Appanage. — The Heir of Philippe Égalité. — The Wealthiest Man in France. — Confidential Advisers. — Justified by Events.

NO date is yet fixed for that grand, solemn act, the king's coronation, which Louis XVIII. preferred to forego, and rest solely on his right divine, rather than acknowledge the fact that during nineteen years of exile, which he chose to call absence, he had not been reigning monarch of France. Pius VII., equally firm in maintaining a contrary opinion and in upholding the authority of the Church, died in August, 1823. But although Louis lingered on for another twelve months, he was in a too critical state of health to reopen the question, even had it been certain that the new Pope would be less firm or less scrupulous than his predecessor. This was an advantage to Charles, for the French like novelty in their pleasures.

Fifty years have elapsed since Louis XVI. was

crowned at Rheims and Marie Antoinette declined to be crowned. Charles, whose turn is now come, late in the evening of life, to wear the crown himself, assisted at that ceremony as a youth of eighteen. It was thought as gorgeous and imposing a spectacle as France had ever witnessed; but "it is to be far surpassed," say *les on-dit.* Few, probably, who were eye-witnesses of it will be present on the later occasion to draw a comparison between them. But many survive who but twenty years since were spectators of a similar scene in the Abbey of Notre-Dame, and who will doubtless be carried back to it in thought when they witness the coronation of Charles X. in the ancient Abbey of Rheims.*

But it will surely be the men who played the principal part in the scene, and present so strong a contrast in character, with whom thought will be more busy than with the pomp of their surroundings. "Had Charles more firmness of character," said Prince Metternich, "he would be distinguished among ordinary sovereigns, for ordinary sovereigns there are." A great concession this. Of course good, easy Francis II. was not one of them,

* M. de Talleyrand, who had been present at the three coronations of Louis XVI., Napoleon I., and Charles X., and at so many other displays of imperial and royal pomp in France and elsewhere, being asked, when Louis Philippe was reigning, which was the grandest spectacle he had ever seen, replied, — as we learn from "Leaves from the Diary of Henry Greville," — "The coronation of Napoleon."

Heaven having vouchsafed him such a *rara avis* among ministers as a Metternich to take the helm of the state. Of Napoleon, he thought that more firmness than he possessed was not possible in human nature. His great mistake, he considered, was want of confidence in Prince Metternich. Together, they could have ruled Europe. The emperor might then have reigned to the end of his life, and some rays of glory have been reflected on the prince.

Fate, alas! did not favour this arrangement; and France, instead of still living flourishing and happy under a Napoleon I. or II., counselled by a Metternich, is now making believe to mourn the loss of her legitimate sovereign. Her garments are gloomy; the *salons* of the *beau monde* are closed, almost ere they had reopened, and there is a suspension of court revels, which also could scarcely be said to have begun. It is fitting that a decent period should be devoted by the nation to sorrow; especially as the winter is neither convenient nor pleasant for the due display of the trappings of royalty, splendid *toilettes*, and all the accompaniments of a grand religious and state ceremony.

Great preparations, however, are needed to begin the new reign with *éclat*, and will afford active employment to all concerned during the months of mourning. The *modistes* are timidly venturing to invent new fashions, chiefly for the

English ladies. But for the *grandes dames* of the French court, they, and other *artistes* of *la mode*, are searching the public libraries for correct information concerning the forms, fashions, and fabrics connected with their several employments or manufactures that were in vogue in the court of the sixteenth century. For hair-dressers, *lingères*, glovers and fan-makers, shoe-makers and stay-makers, the weavers of rich silks, velvets, and gold brocades of Lyons, as well as lace-makers, jewellers, and coach-builders, with every trade and profession, in short, that administers to the needs of high rank and wealth, the pencils of able artists are also engaged in delineating antique costumes, etc., for guidance in their reproduction.

Meanwhile, the devout monarch and his son, and especially Madame la Dauphine,— Monsieur le Dauphin, notwithstanding the martial ardour that burns in his broad manly breast, being a mere nullity under the orders of his wife,— are praying and alternately fasting and refreshing themselves the livelong day in their oratories. They ask to be Heaven's favoured instruments in achieving the great work of regenerating French society in both its upper and lower strata. There must be more reverence for the sacred person of the king, more humble trustfulness in the priesthood.

They would bring back those happy, glorious days when men sank prostrate in the dust if but the shadow of that highly estimable, moral, and pious monarch, the fourteenth Louis, perchance fell on them when condescending to take his constitutional walks abroad. Ah! those were the palmy times of Church and state. The faithful were then a more docile flock, more attentive to the authoritative voice of the shepherd — the wily tongue of some eloquent Jesuit priest. But the denunciations of the Church and the "*Moi, le roi*" and "*Mon bon plaisir*" of the king are not now such potent spells as of old.

Such, however, is the servility of a considerable portion of mankind that the same thing occurred at the beginning of Charles X.'s reign as during the latter part of Louis XIV.'s, when the monarch, after a long career of depravity, having taken to piety, the court and society, in order to retain favour, also put on the garb of hypocrisy.

Many conversions were now made by the priests of the Congregation, the sincerity of which was more than doubtful. But the propaganda had the disposal of the most lucrative and important posts in the government, and since Charles's accession numerous dismissals had taken place; thus offices more or less desirable in an influential or pecuniary point of view were vacant. These were inducements held out to those whose principles, religious and political, sat loosely on them, to make the sign of the cross, cry "God and the king," and daily, with bowed head and on bended knees, mutter long prayers in the churches. Some distinguished military men are said not to have been proof against such seductions.*

A hundred or more of the deputies had become acolytes, and a large supply of pardons and indulgences was always at hand in Madame la Dauphine's oratory to obliterate past or present offences. When M. de Portalis went to Rome to conclude with the Pope the terms of the Concordat, he brought back with him a sackful of those valuable documents. These safe-conducts to heaven were a present from the Pope to Madame Royale, to be distributed at her discretion to those who were worthy. The extravagant joy of Madame, and the Pavillon Marsan generally, on receiving so great a treasure, much diverted the sceptical Louis XVIII. "*Ad majorem Dei gloriam!*" he exclaimed, quoting the device of the Jesuits, when jesting on the subject with his *amie intime*. Perhaps she had as little faith in the efficacy of such pardons as the king himself; but being for ulterior purposes a secret agent of the priests of the Congregation, she was compelled, gently and smilingly, to reprove her royal lover's profanity, and whisper the reproachful word, "Jacobin."

Another enemy in the Congregational camp, and a terrible thorn in the side to Madame la Dauphine, was Madame la Duchesse de Berry.

* E. Malpertuy, "*Histoire de la société française au 18me et au 19me siècle.*"

The long devotional exercises in which her austere sister-in-law indulged, and would have had her take part, were to her simply weariness of mind and body. Yet she was a true Bourbon in her belief in the supremacy of her race and the divine right of its kings. Doubtless, too, she was a sincere Roman Catholic.

But she possessed an irrepressible gaiety of temper and an amiable disposition little in harmony with the gloomy formalities and solemn nonsense in favour at the Tuileries. She held aloof entirely from politics, and would not be bound by the chains of the Congregation. Madame la Dauphine lectured in vain; the lively young duchess could not be broken in; the old stiff etiquette of the court and its newly revived grave ceremonial surpassed her powers of endurance. On more than one occasion she is said to have shown so much disregard of, and utter indifference to, them as greatly to disconcert some of their most obsequiously severe observers, while affording much secret amusement to others. To the Orléans family she was much attached, and at that time they apparently were to her. If Louis's antipathy to the Duc d'Orléans could have been overcome, her "dear uncle" would have had his much-coveted title of royal highness long before Charles came to the throne.

Within a week after the king's public entry into Paris he seemed to confirm the favourable interpretation the people put on his deprecating gesture to the men-at-arms when about to attack the crowd with their halberds; he abolished the remaining restrictions on the liberty of the press. All shades of opinion united in a chorus of praise, in acknowledgment of the boon. Popularity was said to be his object, and at once he seemed to have obtained it. All the great qualities of the pious Saint Louis and the gallant Henri IV. were attributed to him, combined with the personal graces and artistic tastes of François I. — the happy union of the distinguishing characteristics of these three French models of kingly perfection forming a Charles X., the *vrai chevalier français*.

It was hoped that this general concert of insincere praise and flattery, which credited him with intentions and motives very different from those that really influenced him, might show him the wisdom of adopting and acting upon them. But Charles did not care to see more than his blind guides told him. He therefore made the fatal mistake of believing the nation to be willing slaves, ready to bow the neck to his yoke, and to wear the chains with which the Church was to bind them. It was a satisfactory smoothing of the way to the accomplishment of his heaven-assigned task — as he imagined it to be — of restoring the throne and the altar on the foundation from which they had been hurled in 1789.

He had feared the changed spirit of the age

without comprehending it. But, as faction and turbulence seemed to have died out with the reign of his temporising predecessor, he was now prepared to do as his priests and his *ultras* bade him — " act with vigour." That the *Carbonari* and other secret associations were organising their forces to " oppose with vigour " was, of course, not made known to him. He seems, indeed, never to have sought, or desired, to know the feeling of the people respecting any of the oppressive measures sanctioned by him and brought forward by his ministers. By divine right, it was his to command ; his people's to kiss the rod and obey.

With these enlightened views he took his seat on the throne of France ; and when, by reason of his acting upon them, he was ignominiously expelled from it, there is every reason for believing that these views were in no respect changed.

Charles X.'s first address to the Chambers, on the 22d of December, was received with much dissatisfaction. He spoke of satisfying the remaining unpaid emigrants' claims for indemnity as "closing the yet open wounds of the revolution," the balm needed for that purpose being the sum of forty millions sterling. Perhaps it was the magnitude of the sum, considering what large amounts had already been expended in satisfaction of those claims, that raised such a storm against it.

The discussion of this question revived all the sad souvenirs of the past, and with increased bitterness. In the heat of passion recriminatory reproaches passed between those who had fled the country, or whose relatives had done so, at the breaking out of the revolution, and those who had remained to share in the perils and distress consequent on the general overthrow of the social system during that period of terror and bloodshed. The latter were strong opponents of this project of indemnity, regarding the emigrants as cowardly and unpatriotic, and deserving no recompense for the loss of property they had wilfully abandoned in abandoning their country.

The emigrants were, however, the most zealous of the royalists, whatever they had been before they became emigrants. For not all who fled were actuated by love for the royal family; some among them were actuated rather by a desire to keep their heads on their shoulders, leaving royalty to take care of its own. But it was singular that those most in favour with the Bourbons were those who first took alarm and decamped in haste. The Comte d'Artois was one of them; he and his wife and sons, and the Polignacs, who had so large a share in bringing misery on the country, and influencing for evil the unfortunate Marie Antoinette, fled on the evening of that very day that saw the destruction of the Bastille.

Jules de Polignac — the son of the Duchesse de Polignac, the bosom friend of the frivolous queen — was Charles's friend. He was a man of mediocre capacity, whom Louis XVIII. persistently rejected as minister. When urged by Charles to appoint him a member of his council, "He is the very man to overthrow the throne," he invariably replied; and overthrow it he did, for in his advice Charles had more confidence than in that of any other, and that confidence cost him his throne.

So generally was his incapacity known, even amongst the people, that his name was used to express the worthlessness of any article, the stupidity of a person, or the inferiority of an animal, such as a horse, a mule, etc. The drivers of hackney carriages, when a horse was slow in his movements, was obstinate, or had any other bad quality, were accustomed to say, "*C'est un Polignac.*"

Yet Jules de Polignac was, to some extent, trained to be the avenger of Louis XVI. When he was a boy, with his relatives in exile, it was customary to awake him once or twice in the night, and to ask the sleepy youth, "What are you thinking of, Jules? (*À quoi penses-tu, Jules?*)" Sometimes he would reply rather surlily, "*À ven-g-e-r,*" and be asleep again before the full answer was given. But again he was shaken and the question repeated. More thoroughly roused, he would then get through his lesson, if not with much ardour, "Of avenging my king (*À venger mon roi*)."

If doing all the harm to France that his very

limited opportunity and capacity permitted during his short tenure of power be accepted for avenging his king, he did it. But he brought down the throne of the elder Bourbons, which might have been called avenging France for the wrongs she had suffered at their hands, but for the calamity which followed.

But we have wandered away from the Indemnity, which, in spite of the opposition it encountered, passed the Chambers; M. de Villèle — who was still the head of the ministry, and contrived, from the date of his first appointment to the presidency of the Council, to retain his post eight years — spending millions of *francs* to secure votes for his measures.

Greater still was the disapprobation expressed of the proposal for adding considerably to the revenues of the princes, and especially the replacing of the Orléans branch in hereditary possession of the ancient appanage assigned by Louis XIII. to his brother Gaston. In 1814 Louis XVIII. restored it to the Duc d'Orléans simply by royal ordinance, but would not reëstablish the hereditary privilege in his favour. So determinedly was it opposed that M. de Villèle was compelled to inform the Chambers, very distinctly, that it was the will and good pleasure of the king that it should be assented to (*le roi le voulait*), together with the rest of the *projet de loi* he had ordered to be laid before them.

Various motives, apparently, influenced both deputies and peers in this matter. Twenty-five only against 278 had the courage of their opinions, and voted against it, notwithstanding the orders from headquarters. Many of the liberal party, who, though opposed to the measure, regarded the Duc d'Orléans as their chief, abstained from voting; amongst the latter was that fervent patriot, Général Foy, who risked his great reputation by thus silently supporting the Duc d'Orléans's material interests.

But Charles X. was not content with making his cousin the most considerable landed proprietor in France; he promised him also a share in the largesses of the Indemnity, to the extent of a million and a half sterling. Nor did he stop here. He ordered that restitution should be made to him of all portions of land, estates, *rentes*, and shares in financial transactions, that the heir of Philippe Égalité could claim within the domain of the state. His claims appear to have greatly exceeded his father's belongings, though by his marriage with Mademoiselle de Penthièvre he came into possession of vast estates assigned by Louis XIV. to his illegitimate son, the Comte de Toulouse. Not an acre was anywhere overlooked or escaped the grasp of Louis Philippe d'Orléans to which, on any pretence, he could furbish up a claim.

By these concessions, which violated certain articles of the Charter, the duke became from this

Louis Philippe.
Engraved from painting by Philippoteaux.

time the wealthiest man in the kingdom. But lest, perchance, the canker-worm that long had preyed on the heart of his serene highness of Orléans might mar the full enjoyment of this overflow of fortune's gifts, Charles stayed not his lavish hand until he had signed the decree that made his serenity royal. Thus, by removing the feeble barrier which Louis XVIII. was so anxious to keep closed, Charles seemed to reopen to his cousin the road to the throne.

The prodigality with which the new king heaped favours on the Duc d'Orléans was, however, by no means for the purpose of making him any sort of amends for the suspicion with which his predecessor had regarded him, and for his having compelled him to live wholly apart from the court; for Louis scarcely tolerated the duke's residence in France, much less his presence at the Château. Charles, though he did not quite share his brother's prejudices, was to a certain extent influenced by them. But, instead of making it so evident to the duke that he suspected, mistrusted, and was on his guard against him, he would have heaped coals of fire on his head by seeming to repose confidence in him, and bestowing on him every mark of favour.

When Charles came to the throne, his confidential advisers — the Duc de Polignac, and the equally sagacious and competent statesman, the Duc de Rivière — recommended this course. On the onerous terms above named, the price and the pledge of reconciliation and peace between the crown and the Duc d'Orléans, they flattered themselves they had bought him. First, the king believed that he was sure of his gratitude, as a prince of the blood, for concessions that released him from slights put upon him by Louis XVIII. Secondly, he made sure, too sure, that at least his neutrality, as virtual head of the liberal party, was secured; his secret influence as such being regarded by the government as dangerous, in view of the changes and innovations they proposed to introduce.

Charles X. was more confiding, but less discerning, than Louis XVIII., who, with some traits of character resembling those of the cousin he so cordially detested, judged him and his probable course of conduct, as events proved, with far greater accuracy than his brother.

CHAPTER IX.

A Demigod for the People. — Sympathy with the Greeks. — Doubt and Disquietude. — A Most Gracious Reception. — A Flattering Distinction. — Congenial Sentiments. — Neither Part nor Lot in the Matter. — The Law of Sacrilege. — The "Fathers of the Faith." — An Odious Law. — The "*Déplorable*" Ministry. — Tearing Up the Charter. — A Touching Scene. — "The Worst of All Revolutions." — Piety and Etiquette. — Ah! Happy Woman. — The Legitimate Heir. — Youthful Courtiers. — A Military Toy. — A Wooden Army.

THE fleeting popularity of Charles X. seemed destined scarcely to endure until the grand affair of the coronation should have taken place. The attendant round of festivities in which the nation would then be immersed was arranged with a view of elevating the monarch on a pedestal, to be worshipped by the people as a demigod. Another object was to divert public attention from disturbing events then threatening not only the despots of Europe, but menacing also some tyrannical governments of the American continent.

Mexico and Peru had declared their independence, and the Spanish-American colonies were in a state of revolt; while — most annoying and embarrassing to the "right divine" views of the king — the United States had decreed a grand triumphal *fête* in honour of Général de La Fayette. The general himself, being then at Washington, was receiving the honourable reward of a life devoted to the cause of liberty. The paternal government, very painfully anxious to prevent any further perversion of the minds of France's revolutionary children, determined to lay such restrictions on the press that not an echo of these naughty doings should penetrate the serene French atmosphere, and disquiet king and people. The latter were, however, permitted to expend their enthusiasm for liberty in the cause of Greek independence, and to get up subscriptions, make collections, and solicit contributions to aid the Greeks, in rebellion against Turkish despotism.

These demonstrations of sympathy with the oppressed were allowed by the government, ostensibly because the struggle of the Greeks was not with their legitimate masters, but with an alien race; the real motive being that Russia and Austria desired the humiliation of Turkey, and that France, as a party to the Holy Alliance, was bound to assist in realising their views.

This shortly after brought to Paris that most egotistical of statesmen and diplomatists, Prince Metternich. He had hitherto been wavering whether he would or would not condescend to take the journey, being then at Milan. "It is true," he writes, "that I am one of the most active diplomatists of whom history makes mention. But I think it would be an excess of activity to make a journey to Paris to felicitate Charles X. on his accession. However, I do not say that I will not stretch a point to visit France when the coronation takes place."

It then seemed greatly to depend on the good behaviour of the king and his ministers. He feared that Charles was making concessions to the liberal party only to gain popularity. If he had shown marked affability to individuals of perverse opinions merely for the purpose of opening to them a way of repentance, he, of course, could but applaud conduct so moderate. "But the consequences of a flattering reception," he wrote, "awarded to the *coryphées* of liberalism, could not be contemplated without disquietude by persons of a reflective mind."*

His wife, either the second or third, was then in Paris, very ill. Summoned hastily to her bedside, he arrived on the 14th of March, and the princess died on the 19th. But he soon consoled himself with a third — if the deceased lady was his second, or a fourth if she was his third; for the prince followed the good example of his emperor, and in the course of his career took four ladies to wife. This death does not seem to have necessitated his leaving Paris,— his duties to the

* *Metternich Mémoires*, 1824–25.

living probably were paramount to those to the dead,— for he stayed on, and had reason to be satisfied that he did so.

Of course he thoroughly impressed on the king the gravity of the responsibilities he had succeeded to as a member of the Holy Alliance. Charles, he says, received him in the most gracious manner and with his most winning smile. He evinced towards him a perfect unreserve, a real *abandon moral*, and also openly expressed his great confidence in him, confirming it, which was better still, by substantial distinctions. With his own royal hands he gave him the Order of the Saint Esprit, saying that he had intended it should be presented to him at his coronation; but, as a mark of his *gratitude* and *affection*, he gladly availed himself of the opportunity of personally investing him with it.

Further, the king invited him to dinner *en petit comité*. This was a distinction which had never but twice before been accorded to any but royal personages since the existence of the monarchy. Those exceptions were the Duke of Wellington, after the battle of Waterloo, and Lord Moira, who was an intimate personal friend of Louis XVIII. during his exile.

Only the king, the dauphin and dauphine, and Madame — the Duchesse de Berry — were present. It is to be hoped that the greatness of the honour did not spoil the famous diplomatist's appetite, for

Metternich.
Photo-etching after the painting by F. de Fournier.

Charles from his youth was renowned for his dinners and suppers, and to the end of his career employed quite an army of cooks. He was also a first-rate connoisseur of champagne; and probably now enjoyed the good things of life more than ever — piety driving him to occasional fasting, and fasting stimulating his relish for them.

This visit of Prince Metternich appears to have been productive of much evil, but no sort of good, to France. He records with great satisfaction the delight with which the ultra-royalists regarded the intimacy to which the royal family admitted him, and the alarm of the liberal party, who saw in it an end to the liberty of the press. Madame la Dauphine seems to have found in the prince's political sentiments the echo of her own, and to have discoursed long and effusively of her high esteem and affection for the Emperor of Austria, both she and the king being thoroughly convinced, she said, that, "supported by his powerful minister, the emperor was the living guarantee of the salvation of Europe and its rulers."

Monsieur le Dauphin meekly listened — as was his wont — to his wife's positively expressed opinions, without venturing to speak of his own. M. Metternich ascribed this to his mind having been perverted by the liberalism of the men he came in contact with in Spain. Although considering him a man of very mediocre abilities, he yet "dreaded," he said, "the influence of his liberalism on the mind of the king." With very little reason, one would suppose, as neither father nor son dared to have an opinion of his own, being alike dominated by narrow-minded bigots and Jesuit priests, as well as by the iron sceptre of Madame la Dauphine.

What was thought of the law of indemnity, which had so greatly increased the vast possessions of the son of Philippe Égalité, and put such a good round sum into his purse, by this self-applauding minister who kept Austria and her titular ruler in such good order — for it was Clement I. who governed, though Francis II. reigned — he does not say. What remained, however, of the forty millions sterling was then being distributed literally on the principle of "Whosoever hath, to him shall be given; and whosoever hath not, from him shall be taken even that which he seemeth to have." For when Général Foy pleaded for the restitution to old officers, reduced to poverty, of the poor pittance of pension attached to their crosses — given, in many instances, on the battle-field — or for some compensation for its withdrawal, the general's *protégés* were told that they had neither part nor lot in the matter.

They had fought and bled, they might urge, for their country. Possibly. But not under the white banner and lilies of Saint Louis. They had taken no part in the late glorious war for upholding the throne and the altar of Spain. They had not shared in the glory of that ever memorable achievement of the French arms, the surprise of the Trocadéro, when the garrison was caught napping, which added so brilliant a page to military history.

The complement of this "just and beneficent" law of indemnity was the law of sacrilege — a law so monstrous that it cannot be passed over even in these pages without a brief remark. It had its origin in a happy thought of the Keeper of the Seals, M. Peyronnet, whose sumptuously decorated dining-room (paid for by the nation) proved so fertile a theme, as a minor grievance, for murmur and complaint, as well as jest and song.

What did the great diplomatist think of this law? He is not explicit on the subject. His opinions and views, if of less value and importance than he was disposed to attach to them, nevertheless received much consideration in Europe at that time. As he was in Paris, too, professedly in a strictly private capacity, and at a particularly dull moment in the social life of the court, though a very agitated one among opposing political parties and the people, he doubtless availed himself of his leisure for closely observing what was passing around him.

From his account of the state of demoralisation into which all classes had fallen, and the general tenor of his remarks, one may infer that he approved the measures of the government in adopting the "system of missions" as a possibly effective remedy for so degraded a state of things. "These missions," he says, "are like those which labour for the conversion of savage tribes — that is, the Jesuits, calling themselves 'Fathers of the faith,' preach to the people terrifying things of the wrath of a jealous and vengeful God, and of eternal torments. The consequence is," he continues, "that the system is morally decried and materially thwarted by the liberal faction."

The law of sacrilege, however, came to the aid of the priests. It was a revival of the temporal power of the Church in the state, and was intended to gratify and console the clergy for their disappointment in not receiving pecuniary indemnity for the Church lands which the revolution had confiscated and incorporated in the national domain. If Charles, by a royal ordinance, could have reëstablished the Inquisition, he was sufficiently fanatical to have done so. He therefore warmly approved a law that seemed to be the reopening of a door to all the frenzied jurisprudence of the ancient ecclesiastical tribunals.

Death was the punishment which some forms of sacrilege, metaphysical and otherwise, involved, and Scripture was quoted in proof of its expediency. The bishops suggested for the minor forms of punishment, public penance, barefooted, with taper in hand, cord round the neck, winding sheets, red veils, etc., and by and by, probably, there would have been the weekly spectacle of an *auto-da-fé* on the Place de Grève.

This odious law was first presented to the Chamber of Peers. M. Peyronnet, while describing it as urgent, yet vaunted its extreme moderation. He, however, expressed a hope, though it seemed to be but a faint one, that it might prove sufficiently stringent to check the spread of *atheism;* thus were the philosophical ideas of the eighteenth century alluded to. As he read and explained his law, astonishment became general. Those who most vehemently opposed it contested alike its urgency and its necessity. MM. de Châteaubriand, de Broglie, Pasquier, and others spoke long and eloquently against it — M. Molé concluding his speech by stigmatising it as a law "insulting both to heaven and earth, to religion and to the age."

But infamous as it was, it obtained the support of 127 votes, against 92 in its condemnation. The only change made was the substitution of the galleys for the punishment of death, which met with general and strenuous opposition.

M. Chifflot, the *rapporteur* of the second Chamber, introduced the law of sacrilege to the deputies with the remark that "it was a blessing that France had long looked for." A storm of indignation responded. Benjamin Constant, Général Foy, Royer-Collard, and all the eloquent orators of the liberal party, vehemently denounced it. In spite of this, the majority of votes was again in its favour.

The public mind was excessively agitated in consequence. The law of indemnity, notwithstanding the increased taxation it entailed, sank into insignificance compared with it. The ministry, already unpopular, were declared to be individually and collectively dishonoured by such a measure, and henceforth were stigmatised by the *sobriquet* of *le ministère déplorable.* The king was not excepted from the contempt which this epithet was intended to convey. On the contrary, a full share was dealt out to him.

It was clear that he had no regard for the feelings or wishes of the nation, but was determined to brave it, and to restore the despotism of a forgotten period, whose slavish ideas were wholly out of harmony with the times he lived in. The obnoxious measures so hastily introduced, the forerunners of others in reserve, had been long prepared for the expected event of his accession — so often deferred by Louis XVIII.'s frequent repulses to the approaches of death and his persistence in living.

Notwithstanding this expression of public opinion, very openly declared, M. de Villèle, replying to the question pointedly put to him by Prince Metternich, "Will you remain, or will you consent to be overthrown?" said, "I have decided to remain; and it is not easy to put aside a resolute man." He might have added, especially when he is favoured by a weak king, has the control of the treasury, and, by pecuniary grants, pensions, and places, can buy the support of the two Chambers. So the *déplorables* kept on their way, rejoicing at the success of their inroads on the liberties of the people, and the gradual tearing up of the Charter, which, with the memory of its author, was now cherished as neither had been before.

The pious king meanwhile had edified the court by humbly washing the feet of twelve so-called beggars in the chapel of the Tuileries on Good Friday. "The beggars" were chosen from among his servants; and they displayed their feet with some pride. Beautifully prepared for the occasion with powder and perfumes, they made quite a pretty show.

The ladies were admitted by tickets, for the chapel would not contain all who desired to witness the performance, and many heartburnings resulted from ineffectual efforts to obtain the *entrée*. The more successful applicants were of course much touched by the graceful humility with which the *vrai chevalier* went through his part, gazing on him with admiration, subdued by tearful emotion.

But the great event of the coronation is drawing nigh, and, in anticipation thereof and the round of *fêtes* to follow, the Parisians are struggling to bear up for a while under their political grievances, trusting to pass safely through the festive period without becoming metaphysically or otherwise amenable to the law of sacrilege.

Six months have elapsed since Louis XVIII. was gathered to his fathers, and here and there, with the expiration of the term devoted to mourning, a *salon* is reopened. But a *société intime* only is received. For the present no grand receptions take place. M. de Talleyrand entertains his old colleague, and aims many a shaft at the ruling powers, with whom he is by no means in favour. He does not scruple to ask his brother diplomatist what he thinks of the Paris and society of the day compared with what they were, and as he knew them twelve years or so back. He replied that "restorations are usually but a change for the worse — 'the worst in fact of all revolutions,' as a great statesman (Mr. Fox) once remarked; and that, from all he sees and hears, he does not find the Restoration referred to an exception."

The Palais Royal is also open, and all shades of opinion are still courteously received there. The Duchesse d'Orléans is graceful and dignified, her courtly air and manners being a set-off to those of the *bon homme* her husband. Great changes are intended, great improvements meditated at the Palais Royal, for increasing the value of the property and rendering the gardens and galleries more reputable places of resort. The duke, *en atten-*

dant the commencement of his building speculations, is spending a portion of his million and a half in adding to his already large collection of modern pictures. He is much pleased to show them to his friends, and to be the cicerone of connoisseurs in his own picture-gallery; to name the painters; to hear their several excellences descanted upon; to have the prices guessed at, and to congratulate himself on his astuteness when he finds he has made some excellent bargains.

Madame, since the reconciliation between the Duc d'Orléans and the Tuileries, is a more frequent visitor at the Palais Royal, where, in the cheerful society of her aunts and young cousins, she seeks relief from the oppressive dreariness of the piety and etiquette of the gloomy court of Madame la Dauphine. There dullness reigns supreme. But Madame's own bright and happy temperament diffuses a halo of sunshine around her; and very shortly its rays will light up the dismal Pavillon Marsan.

The duchess, with her elevation to the dignity of Madame, will hold there her separate court — its heretofore solemn inhabitants, for the most part, migrating to that part of the Château inhabited by the late king. She will reassume the sceptre of *la mode*, which she swayed for a brief period at the Élysée, as undisputed queen of the revels. Already she has drawn up a wonderful programme of what is to take place; and it is to be hoped that she may be permitted to carry it out, as it is by no means all frivolity.

In her and her children — whom she desires to educate on an approved plan of her own — much interest is taken; and those who have the privilege of visiting Marie Caroline like to hear her talk of these things. There is a charm in it, she is so earnest, though so easy, fluent, and gay. It is a prattle — light, bright, brisk, and refreshing, Prince Metternich says, as a glass of sparkling hock. The disconsolate widower declares that it both soothes and cheers his melancholy spirit to pay his homage to her. She will never be old, he prophesies. Ah! happy woman!

One would almost accuse him of a wish to lay his heart at her feet as once he laid it at the feet of another Caroline. But she, though a queen, was a Bonaparte; this one is a Bourbon, and mother of a king expectant, which makes a slight difference. He, however, has not yet laid aside his old *rôle* of *beau garçon*, and, as the king has brought jaunty old *beaux* into fashion, the prince, though a trifle too young, being but fifty-two, doubtless still shines with *éclat* in the *salons*. Madame, he acknowledges, receives him with much cordiality. She is usually profuse in praise of the great merits and virtues of the Austrian imperial family. She has learned their estimable qualities chiefly from the report of the

Duchesse d'Angoulême, whose high opinion of the Austrian ruler and his minister is founded on her thorough approval of the system of education (a gradual reducing to idiocy) which the great diplomatist recommended, and the meek Emperor Francis adopted, for the son of Napoleon.

But Madame was anxious that the Austrian minister should carry back to Vienna a glowing account of the legitimate heir. With his sister he was, therefore, always brought into the apartment to receive the homage of the great man, also the meed of warm admiration which the infantine beauty the fond mother saw in her son led her to expect, and naturally to believe, to be fairly his due. Flattered to her heart's content both children no doubt were, though Metternich afterwards said of them, rather slightingly, that "they were small and weakly."

The little Duc de Bordeaux was then four and a half years of age, and it was not unusual for the officers of the household and persons of distinction who frequented the court to seek permission to present their sons to him — children of the same age or a few years his seniors. He had thus at this early period of life acquired the habit of extending his hand, with a sort of childlike grace and dignity, to be kissed by his youthful courtiers. The object of these presentations was to secure for the sons of these men who already basked in the sunshine of royal favour the patronage and protection of the heir to the monarchy, when both the heir and the juvenile aspirants for his smiles should have attained to years of discretion.

M. de Beaumont-Vassy, in his "*Mémoires secrets du XIXme siècle,*" mentions having at about this time been presented by his father * to the little Duc de Bordeaux. "Carefully dressed," he says, "as on a *fête* day, I ascended the staircase of the Pavillon Marsan, my father holding me by the hand. We were shown into a spacious *salon*, where my attention was immediately and particularly attracted by a large circular mechanical table, around which were displayed groups of wooden soldiers, representing detachments of the various corps of the *garde royale* — infantry, cavalry, artillery.

"I was wholly absorbed," he continues, "in the contemplation of this attractive table, when Madame de Gontaut (governess to the royal children) entered, leading in the little prince — a fair child, of a lively expression of countenance, and with short light hair. He looked very earnestly at me. 'Kiss Monseigneur's hand,' said my father. I advanced a few steps, and Monseigneur, with great gravity, held out his little fat hand, on which, as directed by my father, I reverently imprinted a kiss."

Suddenly, however, the child's eyes rested on

* The governor of the Military College in Paris.

the above-named table. Eagerly he ran towards it, his lesson in courtly etiquette being at once forgotten. "The ice was broken," as M. de Beaumont says, and, by gestures more natural than in the little farce at playing at royalty, he beckoned to his delighted young visitor to follow. "A spring concealed beneath the table being touched, the bands of the wooden regiments immediately raised their instruments, and a military march was played — all the troops then forming in line and defiling before the prince."

As he was a colonel of the royal guards, these wooden soldiers probably formed the division he was supposed to command — the ingenious toy being constructed to render military evolutions thus early familiar to him, and the passing in review of an army he was destined never to possess, except in these wooden toy-soldiers.

CHAPTER X.

"Notre-Dame, Sire, or St. Denis." — Pious Horror. — *La Sainte Ampoule.* — A Comforting Miracle. — A Ponderous State Carriage. — The Grand Master's Opportunity. — Difficult to Decide. — " Working Double Tides." — " *Vive Charles Dix !* " — A Pleasing Novelty. — Ancient Customs. — An Offering of Fruits and Wine. — Just a Glimpse of Royalty. — Fashionable *Coiffeurs.* — Very Distressing. — A Brilliant *Tout Ensemble.* — A Mortifying Necessity. — " *Vivat Rex in Æternum !* " — The Merciless Rain. — Poems and *Chansons.*

WHEN Louis XVI. was about to be crowned at Rheims in 1775, the reforming Minister of Finance, M. Turgot, strongly urged on the king the advisability of saving the impoverished treasury the expenditure of two millions of *francs*. Expensive preparations would not be needed, he said, if the ceremony took place at Notre-Dame. The king stood aghast. "Or," said M. Turgot,— for the king's exclamation and look of horror had prevented his minister from saying all he had intended,— "Or St. Denis." His majesty was still silent; the feeling that overcame him temporarily deprived him of the power of intelligible utterance. A subdued shriek, as if he had been suddenly stabbed or attacked by acute pain, was his sole reply.

It was not indignation at the idea of saving two millions which thus moved the king; for, as all the world knows, he was inclined to be economical, and would really have been so had he known how, or would have allowed others to know and to be so for him. His horror at M. Turgot's proposal was pious horror. Since the foundation of the monarchy in the fifth century, when Clovis I., the first Christian king of France, was baptized at Rheims by Saint Rémy, and afterwards crowned there, having been anointed with the holy oil brought down in a phial by angels from heaven and placed in the saint's hands for that purpose, all succeeding Kings of France had been anointed and crowned in that city.

One exception there was; but that was the heretic king, the ever popular and gallant Henri IV., who, however, thought and said that if Paris would on no other terms open her gates to him, "*la belle ville* was worth a mass." Of course Louis could not foresee that France's next ruler would select Notre-Dame for his coronation, and for the reason which M. Turgot, secondly, urged on the king — that the capital was a more suitable place for the crowning of the monarch than a second or third rate city of his kingdom. But, could he have foreseen, it would have been no sufficient reason for *him*, but one decidedly against it.

Louis lamented the empty condition of the

state's coffers; but, whether the nation became bankrupt or not, crowned at Rheims he would be. "Crowned elsewhere," he said, "he should not consider himself King of France." This settled the question; but neither with two millions nor four could M. Turgot settle the bill for the coronation.

Early in May, 1825, the *Moniteur* announced the glad tidings that the *Sainte Ampoule* was still intact. Without it the ceremony would probably have been deprived of much of its sacred character. With it Charles must have felt fully conscious that he, no less than Clovis, was especially distinguished as Heaven's anointed, For it may be mentioned, though perhaps scarcely necessary, that the *Sainte Ampoule*, or phial of holy oil, brought from heaven to Saint Rémy for the *sacre*, or anointing, of Clovis, was destroyed at the revolution. Rhul, one of the deputies of Rheims, took it from the recess in which it was kept, near the altar, and, rushing from the cathedral to the public square, dashed it on the stones. Of course it was broken into many pieces, which, with the contents of the phial, were scattered in all directions.

From the temper of the times (1793), one must be well assured that the excited populace who looked on at this silly act approved it. Or should there, perchance, have been one among them to whom it caused grief and pain, certain it is that he dared not show it — except at the risk of his life — in the vain attempt to gather up the scattered atoms of glass, and the oil or other liquid the phial contained.

Yet, says the veracious *Moniteur*, aided by a miracle of skill and foresight, they were collected and preserved — and, *O mirabile dictu!* not in fragments. During the intervening years they have *become miraculously* united, and have assumed their former shape; while, greater wonder still, the sacred phial now contains as ample a supply of holy oil as when the angels first presented it to Saint Rémy, with a promise that it should never be perceptibly diminished. With the announcement of this miracle to cheer and edify Charles and the faithful, the coronation is fixed for the 29th of May.

The mouldering, time-worn cathedral of Rheims was fast falling to ruin when Louis XVI. was crowned. But no steps were taken to arrest its decay until the Emperor Napoleon I. ordered its reparation. The interior of the ancient edifice now preparing for Charles's coronation wears more of a festive than solemn aspect, being draped throughout with rich velvet hangings alternately of white and blue, the latter embroidered with *fleurs-de-lys* in gold, the white with the arms of France on an azure field.

To the emperor also is Charles indebted for the good roads over which he will pass so easily from his capital to the cathedral city, in the very magnificent, if somewhat bulky, carriage prepared for the state procession. When he, with his brother, last travelled in that direction, the forced labour of the *corvée* was called into requisition to make the highways passable for the ponderous royal carriage, eighteen feet in height — to suit the lofty tower, with a waving plume surmounting it, which the queen carried on her head. It was found necessary, too, to remove the venerable old gate of the town of Soissons, before the gigantic vehicle could proceed on its journey.

The programme of the royal pageant, issued by M. de Dreux-Brézé, differs scarcely at all from that of the coronation of Louis XVI., which was arranged in strict conformity with that of his predecessor, the boy-king Louis XV., fifty years before. This again was conducted in close accordance with the usages established at that of Louis XIV. — an interval of upwards of sixty years having occurred between the two events. So that during the lapse of two centuries but three kings had been crowned in France.

The only innovation, or perhaps it should be called revival, — as it does not seem to have occurred to the marquis's predecessor, — is the attempt to bring the costumes of the ladies of the court circle into harmony with those that prevailed at the period when a coronation, apart from the solemn significancy of the religious ceremonial, became also a grand court pageant. What an opportunity this affords the grand master to show how deeply he is versed in that branch of antique lore intimately connected with the duties of his important office. Madame is greatly interested in the matter, her studies and researches on this occasion leading to the development of a taste for artistic archæology, which eventually had favourable results scarcely to be expected from one so gay and apparently so giddy.

To turn back many pages of historical court costume was to find it too generally stiff and unbecoming. The flowing court robes of Marie de' Medici, — one of the few crowned queens of France, — and the similarly fashioned dresses of her ladies, seem to have met with favour. However, some old gossiping letters from Paris of 1824 and 1825, from one who was interested in the important question, and which passed into the hands of the writer of these pages, state:

"After all this tumbling and turning over of old volumes and piles of engravings, the making up of specimen models, and the sketching and colouring of some rather ugly as well as rather pretty — shall I say? — figures of fun, I fancy it is now very generally decided to adopt none of them, that is to say, *in toto.*

"Our *couturières, modistes, coiffeurs,* and the rest of them, will take a hint here, adopt a suggestion there, and utilise them to show off a beauty in one and conceal a defect in another. Thus shall we be either an amalgamation of periods, or of no period at all. Do you think, *chez vous.*

that we are all boiling over here with delightful expectations of what the royal 29th is to bring forth? *C'est autre chose*, believe me. I dare not say more on such weighty matters than that the sky is overcast and the horizon murky.

"The king spends more time than ever in his oratory, knowing nothing, and, *on dit*, caring for nothing. Another *on dit* is that, in preparation for the 29th, he is working double tides. (N.B.—for 'working' read 'praying.') While yet a third—floated by the better informed, or the more malicious—says, whisperingly, that his majesty's wrinkles have deepened of late.

"His confidential and able *valet* and *parfumeur*, whose duty it is to ward off the touch of time from his royal master and attend to his youth and beauty,—which means to dye his hair with judgment, keep his hands and complexion smooth, his backboard straight, lest it should get awry and out of its place when he bows very low, touch up his eyes and eyebrows, with other minor but no less necessary duties of his office (no sinecure, I tell you),—this man—I perceive that the thread of my story is slipping through my fingers—this man, then, I repeat, has discovered a new cosmetic, an infallible balm for the effacement of those lines and furrows which time, without respect of persons, traces on the human countenance, even though it be that of a king. Retirement is said to be necessary for completing the operation, which the royal sufferer is patiently undergoing. Hence—so say malicious tongues—his majesty's increased devotion!"

In the afternoon of the 28th of May salvos of artillery, and the sudden pealing forth of the bells of the cathedrals and other churches, announced the king's near approach to Rheims. The streets were crowded. The picturesque old city had been decked out gaily to welcome once more a Bourbon king. It was the season of flowers, and fully had the inhabitants availed themselves of the abundance with which in that district they grow and flourish, to vary the monotony of the inevitable and too often dingy draperies.

One prolonged deafening shout of "*Vive le roi!*" "*Vive Charles X.!*" greeted the king as his carriage passed through the gates and took the road leading to the cathedral. An escort of *gardes du corps*, followed by men-at-arms with their halberds, rode on either side. Next came Monseigneur le Dauphin and Madame la Dauphine in a splendid state carriage and attended by a numerous escort. The hearty applause bestowed on them, unmingled with cries of "*À bas les Jésuites!*" or "*À bas les plumes!*" was a novelty to Madame la Dauphine, and a pleasing one, no doubt. Madame, Mademoiselle, and the youthful heir, all smiles and bows and kissing of hands, always excited much interest, and more especially so on the present occasion. For the good citizens of Rheims had no doubt whatever that the little fair-haired boy who so gravely kissed his hand in acknowledgment of *vivas* for the Duc de Bordeaux would, and at no distant day probably, come among them to be crowned.

The Orléans family; the grand officers of the king's household and of the establishments of the rest of the royal party; the marshals of France and the general officers ; the heads of the various departments of the state, with delegates from the principal cities of the kingdom ; a detachment of the *garde royale*, and a squadron of cavalry, made up the king's *cortége*, following as far as the grand gate of the cathedral. There, under a dais, stood Cardinal de Latil, Archbishop of Rheims, in full pontificals, waiting to receive the king.

It had on former occasions been customary for the archbishop to address from this dais a long allocution to the king on his arrival, evoking the ancient supremacy of the Church over the Crown. The monarch, in acknowledgment of this supremacy, then entered the church, and brought from the altar a bowl or vase, placed there for the purpose, and presented it to the archbishop. Louis XVI. took with him to Rheims some offering of the kind and placed it on the altar, in token of submission to the Church's authority. This ceremony appears to have been omitted at the coronation of Charles X. But it was noticed as equally remarkable, considering the pretensions put forth by the Church at that time, that the cardinal archbishop should have refrained from asserting the supremacy of the Papacy over the crowns of kings.

His address, which was rather political than religious in sentiment, was apparently intended for the enlightenment of those who accompanied the monarch rather than for his especial edification.

"Do not suppose," said the cardinal, "that our kings come hither to receive the holy sanction in order to acquire or to confirm their right to the throne. No — their rights are far more ancient. They hold them from the order of their birth, and from that immutable law which has associated religion with the throne of France, and to which religion attaches a duty of conscience."

The address ended, the municipal authorities of Rheims, headed by the mayor, wearing his civic robes and chain of office, and carrying the keys of the city on a salver, approach the king. The keys are presented to him. The mayor recites a loyal speech, which doubtless has caused him much time and trouble to get by heart. The king responds, briefly but graciously, and restores the keys into the trusty hands of the worthy mayor. Four men bearing an elegantly decorated hamper or basket then come forward. It is the customary offering of the fruits and wine for which Rheims was famous. The mayor again steps forward. "Sire," he says, "we, citizens of the loyal city of Rheims, humbly offer you, in the name of our city, of the best we possess — our wine, our pears, our hearts."

This address may have grated a little on the royal ear, and sent a spasm through Charles's heart; for the form used to be, "We, your sacred majesty's faithful subjects, humbly," etc. But, as one of the deputies exclaimed in the Chamber when on Louis XVIII.'s return to France he promised his *subjects* a constitution, "there are no longer any subjects in France, but citizens only."

After the interlude of the keys and the wine and fruits, the preliminary ceremony of the 28th terminated with a sermon, delivered by Cardinal La Fare. It is described as being a long series of imprecations on the revolution and the men who figured most prominently in it. On the king leaving the cathedral, the *cortége* re-formed and passed at a rather brisk pace through the principal streets and square of Rheims, in order to excite the enthusiasm of the people, and to prepare them, by just a glimpse of royalty and its surroundings, for the morrow's festivity.

So general, so all-absorbing, were the preparations for that morrow, and so urgently needful was it that all, whether of high or low degree, should be early on foot, that not many thought it worth while to seek repose that night. A night's rest might well be sacrificed to an event that occurred scarce once in half a century. The court *coiffeurs*, and those of their professional brethren most in repute in Paris, had followed in the rear of the royal *cortége*. To them, almost more than all the rest of the *artistes* of the *toilette*, the coronation was a source of profit. Small fortunes were made by them, their charges being enormous.

The *coiffure* of the day was not becoming.

The hair was drawn up to the top of the head and elevated in puffs or bows on wires, not so exaggerated then as this fashion afterwards became. A bunch of stiffly rolled curls adorned each side of the head, and the back of the neck was left uncomfortably bare. By the skill and taste of the artistic *coiffeur,* this stiff and packed-up head-dress was brought into harmony with the features and dress of the lady on whose head he operated. But it was not this kind of *coiffure* that suited those costumes which, by some slight modification of the reigning mode, or adaptation to one of earlier date, were called historic, or of the Marie de' Medici period.

The skilful *coiffeur* had his drawings and models with him, and, having already thoroughly studied them, the modern head-dress was soon transformed into one of earlier date or historic character. These men were the *élite* of their profession, worthy successors of the great Léonard, who could manipulate a tablecloth becomingly into a lady's hair, or mingle with it fifteen yards of gauze besides innumerable ornaments — feathers, flowers, jewels, etc. If their fee was a large one, the perfection of their work merited it.

All through the evening of the 28th, all through the night, and until long after sunrise on the 29th, they worked steadily on. Yet many ladies could not obtain their services, and, sad to say, were compelled to seek the aid of the local professors, and even — as they also were fully employed — in the last extremity, to summon their own *femmes de chambre* and despairingly to put their heads into their hands. One of the ladies who sulkily did so, expecting, as she said, that her maid would turn her out a great fright, was saluted by another lady issuing triumphant from the hands of the court *coiffeur* with "Ah! madame, how charmingly your hair is arranged, — elegant, artistic, most becoming!" This was consolation indeed. It dispelled her sulks, and brightened up her face with smiles for the day.

The morning of the 29th beamed brightly, and the bells rang it in with a merry peal. Though so early, a brilliant crowd was already filling the old basilica, the ladies being anxious to get to the places assigned them. A double row of seats was arranged for their accommodation in the tribunes and galleries of the nave. All wore full court dress. If there was any variation in style it was too slight to be perceptible. Of pearls and diamonds, rubies, emeralds, and other precious stones, there was a very dazzling display, forming with the richness of the dresses, — superb velvets and laces, heavy silver and gold embroideries, — together with the beauty of many who wore them, a brilliant and harmonious whole.

As described at the coronation of Louis XVI., between six and seven hundred seats, in rows one above another, filled the choir. They were occupied by the peers and deputies, lieutenant-generals, *préfets*, mayors, etc. A separate tribune was reserved for the *corps diplomatique*, the nuncio being placed at their head.

When all had taken their seats, and the archbishop, bishops, and attendant clergy, wearing the vestments customary at high festivals, were also in their places, at or near the altar, the ceremony of fetching the king took place. He entered, attended by cardinals and bishops, and was conducted to the seat prepared for him. Around him stood all the officers and domestics of the royal household, ranged according to their relative rank, and each with the insignia of his office.

The king wore a sort of tunic of white satin, and a velvet *toque* with white feathers and a diamond *aigrette*. He is said to have looked remarkably well, his brow smooth, with scarce a trace of a wrinkle. After the *Veni, Creator*, the king, still seated and covered, — the new crown and royal mantle lying before him on the altar, — repeated the coronation oath, his hand placed on the Gospel and on a cross said to contain a piece of the true cross. He had the mortification of not daring to dispense with the oath which bound him to govern in conformity with the laws and Louis XVIII.'s Charter.

The white satin tunic was then exchanged for a velvet one, and he was assisted by the chief huntsman and the dauphin to put on a pair of velvet boots and gold spurs. The archbishop girded him with the sword of Charlemagne, and Charles, thus equipped, knelt, and was anointed with the seven unctions of the *sacre*. A deacon's robe, of velvet embroidered with *fleurs-de-lys*, was then put over his tunic. On one shoulder was placed the royal mantle of state; a ring, blessed by the archbishop, was put on the forefinger of his right hand. The sceptre and hand of justice were presented to him, and the crown was put on his head. He was then led to the throne, and the royal family assembled round him to receive his embrace.

In a loud voice the archbishop then cried, "*Vivat rex in æternum.*" All present arose and responded in a joyous shout, "*Vive le roi!*" The doors were thrown open, the people rushed in, also crying "*Vive le roi!*" A flourish of trumpets then proclaimed that the king was crowned. The cannon roared, the church bells clanged, and the band struck up a military march. Thousands of birds, as at the coronation of Louis XVI., were freed from their cages, representing the *vieilles franchises* of France. "*Noël et largesse!*" cried the heralds-at-arms as they scattered coronation medals among the people.

It must have been an attractive and animated spectacle — scarcely, however, differing at all from that which took place at Rheims fifty years before, the actors only being changed. The coronation had been preceded by an amnesty that included political offenders of the late reign. Crosses of Saint Michael and Saint Louis were now distributed, and the touching for the king's evil was not omitted. It was remarked that the king, while performing this ceremony, seemed to have more faith in the efficacy of his touch than the poor sufferers who were brought to be healed by it.

Charles returned to Paris on the 6th of June. A grand pageant had been arranged for his entry into the capital; but the weather had changed, and the rain descended mercilessly on all the finery. He was, however, harangued at the gates by the authorities of the city, and he assisted at the *Te Deum* chanted in his honour at Notre-Dame. But his popularity was already on the wane, and the people received him coldly. His courtiers made up for this chilling reception by overwhelming him with congratulatory addresses, laudatory verses, and discourses.

The festivities began on the 10th, and continued a fortnight. This — aided perhaps by the return of fine weather — put the people into better humour, and a sort of political truce ensued. A large batch of dukes, marquises, and counts was created, and numerous grand crosses distributed, amongst the faithful of course — Victor Hugo, for his loyal birthday poem, participating in these honours.

Lamartine offered his congratulations to the

king in a coronation ode. Ancelot contributed the first act of the opera of "Pharamond," produced for the celebration of this event; while Rossini, for the occasion, shook off the *dolce far niente* which for two years past had taken possession of him, and composed for these *fêtes* "*Il viaggio a Reims.*" As appears to be the rule at coronations and royal marriages in France, the *fêtes* terminated with a deplorable accident in connection with a grand display of fireworks. Several people were killed and many much injured.

The success of the coronation and the brilliant *fêtes* that followed it fell far short of the triumph expected. Royalty was neither stronger nor more venerated than before — "one of Béranger's *chansons* being sufficient to strike it to the heart under its mantle of state, and fully to prove to many of its partisans that all this obsolete pomp could achieve nothing unaided by the enthusiasm of the people." *

* P. Lacroix.

CHAPTER XI.

"Another *Grand Monarque*." — An Empty Treasury. — Growing into Fashion. — "The Heart of Young France." — Funeral of Général Foy. — "*Les Enfants de la Patrie.*" — The Old Tactics Continued. — Sheathing the Sword for a While. — A Cure Effected. — "If You Think Thus, It Must Be So." — "The Grand Lama." — Mutual Satisfaction. — A Privileged Visitor. — No Lover Now, but Gambler. — The *Salon* of the Abbaye-aux-Bois. — Madame Vigée-Lebrun.

THE coronation festivities, which were chiefly intended to amuse and dazzle the people, being brought to a close, the court of the old *régime* was now to revive, and, like a phœnix from its own ashes, more resplendent than ever. "A great king again rules France," said obsequious courtiers — "another *Grand Monarque*, in the person of Charles X." Society, therefore, was to be reconstructed after the old model; prodigality was to reign unrestrained as well as undismayed by the sure recurrence of the old *régime* deficits.

The very grand funerals of the Restoration, the public entries, the christening, the coronation, and accompanying *fêtes*, all arranged with utter disregard of the cost, had made heavy demands on the state's coffers. The large contributions towards the expense of pompous ecclesiastical processions had considerably increased the weight of these demands, and, together with the milliard required for the indemnity, had left, wherewith to return to the old order of things, one of its most prominent features, an empty treasury.

In this dilemma recourse could not be had to the old method of levying a new tax and handing it over to the *fermiers généraux* to collect. But M. de Villèle again introduced his project for reducing the five per cent. *rentes* to three. It met with less opposition than before. The bankers now supported it; they had more thoroughly considered the measure, and found it as advantageous to them as to the state. The project, therefore, became law, and an acceptable sum of sixty millions was realised. A rage for financial speculation also set in, and the great wealth of the Rothschilds and other bankers is said to date from this time.

The session closed; hostile speeches, if not hostile feelings, were laid aside for a time; the *beau monde* were retiring to country châteaux or to the seaside. It was necessary to recruit, after the anxiety and fatigues of the great event and its festive celebration, also to prepare for the ensuing winter campaign of pleasure. Madame and her children were *en route* for Dieppe. She was exceedingly popular there, and her arrival was anxiously looked forward to: first, for the sake of her own bright presence, and secondly, because of the increased and increasing prosperity her visits brought to the town.

Madame was extremely fond of theatrical entertainments, and under her patronage a small theatre, called "*Le Théâtre de Madame,*" had been recently erected at Dieppe. It was rarely open except during her stay, when actors of some repute performed there. Ivory-carving and lace-making principally employed those families who were not of the fisher population, and these industries were greatly encouraged and developed under Madame's protection. Thus Dieppe, then little more than a poor fishing village, recommended by Madame's physician for its healthfulness as an occasional brief residence for "*les enfants de France,*" grew into favour and fashion as a seaside watering-place.

But while the court and the aristocracy were inhaling sea-breezes, or complacently, in the quietude and repose of their stately châteaux and wide domains, congratulating themselves on their supposed recent successes, and confidently anticipating future ones, the hand of death was busy among the opponents of despotism and priestcraft. In the course of the autumn several stanch patriots were snatched from their duties — the interposition of Heaven, as the king was very readily persuaded to believe, for the removal of the enemies of the Lord's anointed, and the triumph of religion and vigorous government.

The constant recurrence of stormy and exciting scenes in the Chambers between the ministry, bent on carrying out their views, and the opposition, sternly resolute and strenuous in their efforts to thwart them, had tried both the physical and mental powers of men of ardent temperament. On the 20th of November the death of Général Foy was announced, and consternation spread throughout the country as the disastrous news became generally known.

"The heart of young France," says a contemporary, "beat in that of this great patriot and noble orator, victim of his eloquence and patriotic devotion, and each man felt that in his death he had lost a friend." Suffering from a complaint that retirement for a while from public life might have wholly subdued, or have long retarded its fatal results, he could not be induced to absent himself from the Chamber on any occasion when, as he said, if he could not prevail to prevent the encroachments of the new reign on the liberty and rights of the people, he could at least lift up his voice against them. Yet life was ebbing away while engaged in those violent and exhausting political struggles with the ultra-royalist party.

The desire was unanimous to do honour to the man for whom so much admiration and regret were expressed, who had so steadfastly sought his country's welfare and advocated the cause of the people. His funeral was a remarkable one, wonderfully impressive, though unaccompanied by any gaudy trappings or the ordinary mournful paraphernalia of woe. Old companions in arms, and both political adversaries and friends, surrounded his coffin, which was borne by the students of the military and other colleges to the cemetery of Père-Lachaise; the bearers being changed at short intervals, in order that the much coveted distinction might be shared by as many as possible.

The *cortége* following the coffin in perfect order along the boulevards to the cemetery, numbered upwards of 20,000 persons. All were in deep mourning; strict silence was observed; and all were bareheaded, though rain was falling in torrents. Many carriages of both private and public individuals also attended, driving slowly in the rear of the procession. The carriage of the Duc d'Orléans, with servants in his livery wearing crape, did not escape remark.

M. Casimir Périer, who then was preceptor to the general's three children, was the first speaker at the grave. After dwelling on the great loss the nation had sustained in the death of its zealous defender, and eulogising the general's public and private virtues, he concluded his oration with the suggestion that "France should adopt her champion's children."

Among the vast throng filling and surrounding the cemetery, of course only those who were near the grave could hear these words. But as soon as the sentiment of the speaker was communicated from one to another of the anxiously listening multitude, it was responded to, as with one voice, "The children of Général Foy are henceforth the children of France—*les enfants de la patrie!*"

On that same evening a national subscription was opened for the purpose of erecting a monument to the memory of the illustrious patriot-general, and to provide for his children. The sum subscribed amounted to upwards of a million *francs* (40,000*l.*) in the course of a very few weeks, when it was considered not yet nearly completed in the provinces. It was headed by the Duc d'Orléans with a subscription of 10,000 *francs*.

This should have shown Charles and his favourite advisers that, heavy as was the price they had paid to win over this wily opponent, he still kept his eye on the future, and had not been induced by the liberality of their largesses to abandon his old system of tactics. There was, however, some consolation for them in the death of the general, and in those gaps which soon after occurred in the liberal ranks, and were not readily filled up.

The removal of those eloquent speakers, Camille Jordan, Manuel, Stanislas Girardin, and one or two others who died at about this time, was regarded with satisfaction by the king and his *déplorables* as a lessening of the number of enemies to combat. They seemed to treat with contemptuous indifference the solemn funeral demonstrations which, as those deaths severally occurred, testified to the overwhelming feeling of the country.

M. de Châteaubriand, although a royalist, had been one of the most vehement opponents of his party ever since Louis XVIII. had so abruptly dismissed him from the ministry. In various pamphlets and numerous articles in the *Débats* he vigorously attacked his former colleague — very frequently stinging him to the quick, for with his pen he was a powerful opponent, though practically so weak and unsatisfactory as a statesman. The death of Louis XVIII. induced a pause. The grieved ex-minister laid down his pen, as though sheathing his sword during a truce. Hostilities were, however, immediately renewed when he found that the Villèle or the "*déplorable* ministry" was to continue in power.

Madame Récamier was still with her niece in Italy, when it occurred to her friend, the Duc de Doudeauville, who was one of the ministry, to urge her to return to Paris. The extreme virulence which wounded vanity now imparted to M. de Châteaubriand's natural eloquence, and which was doing much harm to the royalist party, while it was drawing the liberal one around him, might be subdued, he thought, by Madame Récamier's influence, were she on the spot to exert it.

She did not immediately comply with the duke's entreaty. She had imposed a sacrifice on herself, as she considered, for the sake of her own dignity, and sufficient time had not yet elapsed, she feared, for the attainment of her object.

Madame Récamier arrived in Paris only in the following May, returning to the Abbaye-aux-Bois, where she had now a charming apartment, not large, yet very pleasant, the *salon* looking on the convent garden. It was comfortably furnished, too; and though there was no trace of the splendour and luxury of former days, a certain air of graceful propriety prevailed, harmonising with her own simple elegance, and the now subdued *éclat* of the lady's beauty.

Thither hastened M. de Châteaubriand. The cure had been effected. He was in raptures; not a word of reproach; tenderness and respectful attention had taken the place of the former exacting querulousness that had both disturbed and offended her. "From that time," says a friend of Madame Récamier, "his sentiments towards her were unalterable;" and, it may be added, then began that singular intimacy — almost slavery to his whims — which continued until death, twenty-three years after, put an end to it.

Whether she attempted to soften his asperity of tone in his political pamphlets is doubtful, for she

Madame Récamier.
Mezzotint by G. W. H. Ritchie.

believed him to be the victim of his courage in opposing what he could not conscientiously approve. "Dear and ever dearest," wrote M. de Montmorency, "as this is your conviction, it must be so, and I have been wrong in judging otherwise." But her presence alone may have acted as a charm on him.

While waiting to see what course the king and his ministers proposed to take, he wrote a pamphlet sufficiently royalistic in sentiment, called "*Le roi est mort; vive le roi!*" He attended the coronation, too, which, however, as a peer of France, it was his duty to do. He so far shared also in the distribution of honours on that occasion as to be named by the king *chevalier des ordres du roi* — a mere honorary distinction, but with which was associated the possession of the blue riband and badge of the Order of the Saint Esprit, which the king at the same time conferred on him.

The *salon bleu* of the Abbaye-aux-Bois was once more the resort of all who were distinguished in literature, science, and art, in which at this period there was a remarkable reaction, military glory being no longer in the ascendant. Rank and wealth also frequented that modest counterpart of the celebrated *salon bleu* of Rambouillet; though, unlike that famous school of literature and politeness, politics were not altogether excluded.

Yet Madame Récamier was opposed to subjects so disturbing to the serenity of her guests and the harmony she delighted in being warmly discussed in her *salon*. Since M. de Châteaubriand had become one of its most assiduous frequenters it was more exclusive than of old; more royalist in its sentiments, even inclining to ultra-royalism, yet with an occasional dash of liberalism. This was according to the varying mood of the great man now the idol of her *salon*, the "Grand Lama," as some of her friends called him, to please whom and to suit whose tastes Madame Récamier, to the intense mortification of many old danglers, had modified all her habits.

She received none who had not the good fortune to be thoroughly in his good graces. There was, however, this consolation to former friends and adorers, — and relief, one may suppose, to herself, — that it was only at his hour she was restricted to receiving none but his worshippers and friends. This was from three to five. At three they took tea *en tête-à-tête* punctually to the minute, and this daily visit was announced to her every morning by letter.

M. de Châteaubriand had then adopted the habit of favouring his wife with his company at dinner at six precisely. "He preferred," he said, "to dine at seven; Madame de Châteaubriand's appetite was ready for dinner at five; but they had come to an agreement that each should sacrifice an hour and dine together at six." "By this arrangement," he said, as one day he was taking leave of Madame

Récamier and her circle, "we are both much annoyed, which may be called mutual satisfaction. Such is marriage!" After dinner he dozed for an hour in his armchair, while his wife amused herself with a pious book or her embroidery. He then bade her good evening, and retired to his own apartments, to write pamphlets or political articles for the newspapers.

Madame Récamier saw no more of him until the next day. Her general circle, therefore, visited her in the evening. The Duc de Montmorency never failed, though compelled to be late because of the duties of his post of *chevalier d'honneur* to Madame la Dauphine. But the Superior of the Abbaye allowed in his favour — and because he was a sort of influential chief of the Jesuits — the outer convent gate to remain unlocked till midnight; the usual hour of turning the key being eleven.

It was at these evening *réunions*, where always were assembled many more gentlemen than ladies, that, sure of deep sympathy and inviolable secrecy, men of opposite parties and conflicting views often sought to obtain the promise of a quarter or half hour's *tête-à-tête*. When granted, they would pour into Madame Récamier's listening ear the tale of their political hopes and fears, tell her of plots and intrigues, and ask her opinion of their schemes.

Wonderful woman! to have been the depositary of so many domestic and state secrets, and to have kept them all, at the same time consoling, counselling, and sometimes admonishing, as the nature of the communication confided to her safe keeping seemed to require. Some of her contemporaries have said — but it is always a woman's pen that has written such ill-natured things — that all those joys and sorrows, schemes and projects, as they were poured into one ear passed out at the other. She thought only of looking pretty and sympathetic, and had always the same formula ready: "You know how all that concerns you interests me — how rejoiced I am," or "how grieved I am," etc. This must be slander.

M. Benjamin Constant, that once most ardent of despairing lovers, no longer, it appears, frequented her *salon*. Of course the flame of love had long ago died out; and now, unfortunately, all the time not devoted to the exciting political discussions of the Chamber he gave to gambling. Debt and difficulties, therefore, beset him at every turn.

Madame Récamier is now verging on fifty, and those love-lorn slaves who once so earnestly pleaded but for a smile, for one word, even one glance of tenderness, now claim the friendship they formerly rejected. She had then enough to bestow on all; but now, though she has still an ample stock for old friends, it is of a cooler kind. Its warmest rays, they say, are reserved for M. de Châteaubriand to bask in; while they, who may be said to have borne the burden and heat of the day in long years of devoted attentions, now languish like drooping flowers yearning for evening dews and sunshine.

Yet they continue to gather around her; the *salon bleu* of the Abbaye-aux-Bois, until 1830, probably yielding to none in the rank and talent of those who composed its society. The men of *la jeune France*, afterwards so distinguished, were preparing for the downfall of what the ruling powers were then endeavouring to set up. They were studying and writing for that future to which they were looking forward with hope and confidence; but the aristocratic *salons* then ignored them.

M. de Lamartine and Victor Hugo (whom M. de Châteaubriand named *un enfant sublime*) were, as royalists and young poets of the romantic school, favourites in the *salons* of *les grandes dames* — the Princess Bagration, Madame Labriche, the Duchesse de Duras, and others. M. de Villemain also, though but slightly tinctured with royalism, was welcomed with distinction in the most exclusive *salons*. His conversation was considered a most finished specimen of an art which under the old *régime* had been sedulously cultivated as one of the distinctive marks of high birth and breeding.

A series of state balls was arranged for the winter, and Madame assumed the sceptre as queen of the revels. But the reproving presence of Madame la Dauphine was an antidote to gaiety. The pleasantest *salons* were the literary and artistic receptions of the Comte de Chablot; that of Baron Gérard, the great painter, and of Madame Vigée-Lebrun, the once fashionable portrait-painter. She had now grown old, but retained considerable remains of her former great beauty, and was as lively and *spirituelle* as in days of yore.

CHAPTER XII.

Preparing for the Carnival. — The Jesuits an the Colporteurs. — The King a Jesuit Priest. — Talma's Last Part. — Primogeniture. — The "Three Hundred Spartans." — The Decree of the Cour Royale. — Reproving the Judges. — " Move On, Gentlemen." — Madame's New Year's Reception. — Death of the Duc de Montmorency. — A Change in Popular Opinion. — The Czar's Mental Depression. — A Reconciliation. — Death of Madame de Krüdener. — Her Last Words.

RAND state balls were announced, which were to surpass in splendour all former ones, and great preparations were making for a brilliant carnival. Yet the aspect of affairs, whether social or political, was far from being gay. Disturbances were constantly taking place in the churches, and the streets were too frequently the scene of tumults, quelled only with the aid of the military. Throughout the departments the same riotous disposition prevailed, and from the same cause, the preaching of the Jesuit missionaries.

Favoured by the king — who was less solicitous for the security of the crown, whether for himself or his grandson, than for the restoration of ecclesiastical power and the rule of the Jesuits in France — the Congregation sent forth its apostles to preach throughout the length and breadth of the land. But discord and impiety, wherever they appeared, were the sole results of their preaching. Ribald jests and songs hailed the arrival of these unwelcome visitors; while quickly following them came the colporteurs, amply supplied with cheap editions of the most objectionable of Voltaire's works. Tens of thousands of them were put into circulation by means of these itinerant vendors of books, as well as large numbers of those of other philosophical and atheistical writers of the eighteenth century.

Molière's "*Tartufe*" ("Tartufe" and "Jesuit" being considered convertible terms) was always demanded at the provincial theatres when notice was given that the "Fathers of the Faith" were about to preach. Thus "*Tartufe*" was being performed simultaneously in nearly every town and city of France as a protestation against the Jesuits, crowds flocking in to applaud and hiss, the performance often ending in a riot.

For a man to call another a Jesuit was to offer him the greatest of insults, to cast a stigma upon him, which blood must flow to efface. So generally did it become a term of reproach with all classes, that even the urchins of the streets, if a quarrel arose among them, would exasperate each other with the epithet, "Vile Jesuit!" — the sure consequence being blows. Even the king, who was at once their patron and slave, winced under the imputation, which was purposely brought to his knowledge, that he was reputed a Jesuit, and not only a member of the famous society, but an officiating priest.

It was thought advisable generally to prohibit the performance of "*Tartufe.*" But this only made matters worse, especially in some large towns where there was a chronic disposition to revolt, such as Lyons, Avignon, and Rouen. There the prohibition produced an *émeute* that continued for several days. The people determined that the preaching should be prohibited as well as the play; and in carrying this determination into effect several persons were injured, and one or two deaths occurred. The reverend fathers were very unceremoniously dealt with, and, to escape the possibility of further violence, were glad to beat a hasty retreat.

The deep interest excited at this time by the struggle of the Greeks for emancipation from Turkish oppression imparted vigour to the people's struggle for emancipation from priestly rule. Any success on the part of the Greeks kindled the most lively enthusiasm, and a report that the Turks were put to the rout was hailed with acclamations loud as those which greeted the news of the flight of the Jesuit missionaries.

The great success of the tragedy of "*Léonidas*" was in some degree due to this feeling. Its author, M. Pichot, and Talma, who personated the hero, had of course their due share in the triumph it achieved. Léonidas was the last part created by Talma. The tragedy was produced on the 26th of November, 1825, and the great actor died in the following year.

The moment did not seem propitious for plunging into a stream of pleasures and launching out into extravagance. But the Duchesse de Berry had joyously taken that plunge, and had given her first costume ball. It was, indeed, but the prelude to that series of balls to be afterwards developed each into a living and picturesque page of history. But Madame la Dauphine, though she did not withhold her stern, chilling presence from this scene of gaiety, from her reverence for whatever had been customary under the old *régime*, was yet far less fitted to participate in the public life of the court than even the devotee king.

He, like his magnificent ancestor, Louis XIV., had drunk of the cup of pleasure to its very dregs before taking to piety in his declining years. But Charles still sacrificed to the graces. His feelings were not even yet so utterly dead to the world but that — all Jesuit though he was — without much grief to his righteous spirit, without much searchings of heart, he could emerge from his oratory to partake of worldly enjoyments to the moderate extent of appearing all smiles and bows, to receive the homage of admiring ladies at a ball, or, perchance, at a theatre.

A subject, however, of extreme annoyance to both the king and Madame la Dauphine was the rejection of the project to revive at this time the law of primogeniture; and that notwithstanding the utmost efforts of the ministry to produce a contrary result. Had it become law it would have greatly disturbed the existing arrangements under which numberless estates were then held, and have produced much litigation as well as family discord.

Many of the deputies and peers saw that their interests would be prejudiced by its adoption. Numerous defections, therefore, occurred even among the "three hundred Spartans" — as the majority were ironically called — whom places, pensions, and titles had hitherto made the minister's own. In this unexpected defeat of the ministry the people saw a triumph of their now cherished Charter. Accordingly it was celebrated with much exultation, and — like other small mercies that Providence, in spite of the Jesuits, occasionally vouchsafed them — with extravagant demonstrations of joy.

The retrograde propensities of the government, directed and lorded over by the priests of the Congregation, who, in an occult manner, influenced all the movements of society and the state, were so vigorously attacked by the press that the Jesuits instigated proceedings against the popular journals, the *Constitutionnel* and the *Courrier*, which, joined by *la petite presse*, carried on this sort of warfare persistently. They were accused of "provoking hatred of priests in general, and in the name of God blaspheming God and holy things." The complaint was heard before the Cour Royale and was rejected.

The presence of the Jesuits in France was condemned by the decree of the court, as "putting the civil and religious liberties of the nation in peril, their principles being incompatible with the independence of any government whatever, and especially with the constitutional Charter." This memorable decree of the Cour Royale was heard by the Jesuit priests of the Congregation, and by the government, with amazement. But so greatly did it excite popular enthusiasm that the *vivas* which greeted it first in the crowded hall of the tribunal were taken up by an anxiously expectant throng outside, and repeated by more distant groups, until the triumph of the journals being thus telegraphed, as it were, throughout Paris, the whole city resounded with acclamations.

Nor did this suffice to express popular satisfaction with the decree. Many houses were illuminated; bonfires were lighted in different parts of the city, and songs and dances, with *vivas* for the judges of the Cour Royale, alternating with cries of "*À bas les Jésuites!*" testified to the general feeling of joy.

The king heard with astonishment of the riotous delight of the people, and the "audacity of those lawyers of the Cour Royale", whose decree was the cause of it. The duchess received the unwelcome news with a sort of angry grief at the inefficacy of her prayers for the stiff-necked people of France, who could not be brought to bend to the spiritual yoke and the blessing hands of the disciples of Loyola.

It would have been well for Charles had he accepted the decree as a friendly warning voice. But so far was he from doing so that a remonstrance, harshly worded, was conveyed by M. Peyronnet to M. Séguier, the president of the Cour Royale, for neglecting to control the decision of the court, and thus failing to comply with his majesty's known wishes.

"The business of this court, monsieur, is to render decrees, not services," replied the president, haughtily.

But the new year had arrived, and the usual felicitations were to be offered to the king and the several members of his family. M. Séguier and the judges of the Cour Royale must make their appearance at the Tuileries as well as other officials of the various departments of the government. The superciliousness of the assembled grandees, and the stony stare or averted look of courtiers and attendants of every degree, publicly proclaim that the will of a king and a Madame la Dauphine must under no circumstances be with impunity disregarded.

Their congratulations are received by the king with as little courtesy in voice and in manner as possible, his features assuming as stern an air as his expressionless countenance permits; for when not simpering and smiling his face is a blank. A pretty complimentary new year's address has been prepared for Madame la Dauphine's gracious ears. She hears it with evident disgust, but deigns to utter two words of reply; they are: "*Passez, messieurs!*"

"Shall her royal highness's gracious reply be inscribed on our register?" asks the president of his colleagues as, obeying the royal lady's imperious command, the gentlemen "move on."

But another and more gracious royal lady is receiving compliments and felicitations in a more gratified and gratifying manner. If her many pleasing qualities do not altogether atone for the dauphine's utter want of them, they at all events enable her to retain popularity, while that of the rest of the royal family is fast fleeting away. On this new year's day she is in full court costume, wearing splendid jewels, and looking very youthful and charming. She is surrounded by a brilliant *cortége*, ladies of honour and the superior officers of her household.

Her two children are with her, one on either side. Taking note of mamma's gracious words and gracious manner, they, too, dispense smiles and bows. They also occasionally kiss their hands when they recognise an acquaintance in the throng of military officers, the magistracy, the men of letters, celebrated artists, and others who pay their respects to royalty at this new year's reception — a far less prosy affair with Madame and *les enfants de France* than with their elders.

As for the judges of the Cour Royale, their decree involving a stigma on the Congregation, the Jesuits were anxious to cancel it. But Charles would not move further in the matter. To prove, however, that they had lost none of his esteem and confidence, he gave them a public testimony of it by appointing Duc Mathieu de Montmorency, who was the "head and soul of the Congregationist party," to the post of governor of the Duc de Bordeaux.

This appointment afforded an opportunity for the expression of Madame Récamier's sympathetic congratulations. The king's discernment in selecting so excellent a man as her very best friend to preside over the education of the heir to the throne gave her infinite satisfaction. She prophesied that it would have a lasting effect on the happiness of the nation, as the virtues of the governor must necessarily influence the character of his youthful charge. Yet, estimable as he was in private life and as Madame Récamier's dear friend, the ultra-Jacobin, transformed into an ultra-royalist and Jesuit, was a very unfit governor for a young prince destined, as then was supposed, to reign over France.

But Duc Mathieu de Montmorency was permitted to hold his office but for a very short time. Two months after his nomination, when apparently in perfect health, he died, while kneeling in the church of Saint Thomas d'Aquin on Good Friday. His head was observed to sink forward, but he was supposed to be absorbed in prayer, and at first it was feared to disturb him. As he continued motionless, his friends became anxious, and, on approaching him, to their dismay they found he was lifeless. He was deeply mourned by Madame Récamier; so much so that her great veneration for him and the place he ever retained in her memory often caused a jealous pang in the breast of the exacting egoist who succeeded him as the chief of Madame Récamier's best friends — M. de Châteaubriand.

It was singular, as showing how changeful is popular opinion, that Charles X., on addressing the Chambers at the opening of the session of 1826 a few days after the announcement of what was regarded as so objectionable an appointment, should have been considered as wantonly annoying and further braving the nation by speaking in laudatory terms of his "magnanimous friend" Alexander I. The once popular czar had recently died, and it was suspected that he had been poisoned. The French people thought that, if it was so, it was but just retribution on their former favourite for his complicity in the murder of his father, the Emperor Paul; for the foreign coalition against France, for Ste. Helena, and the Holy Alliance.

Alexander had been ill for some time, his illness originating in injury to the muscular membrane of his foot from a fall from his horse. This produced erysipelas and attacks of fever; but he refused to take medicine (perhaps dreading the poisoned cup), preferring to trust to the vigour of his constitution. He was also much influenced by his views on predestination. He had been for some years oppressed by deep melancholy, his thoughts continually reverting to the violent scene of his father's death. It has, however, been asserted, and probably is true, that when unwillingly drawn into complicity with the conspirators, he understood that not death was intended, but merely restraint on Paul's mad acts.

The dreadfully devastating inundations of 1824 he regarded as God's judgment upon him for neglecting to aid his coreligionists in Greece in their struggle for freedom, notwithstanding that the terms of the Holy Alliance forbade him to offer aid. This, with domestic sorrow, the dissatisfaction of his people, the risings of the peasantry, and a vast conspiracy against the throne, preyed on his mind. He was making a tour in his dominions, desiring to acquaint himself with the needs of the people, and also with the idea of abdicating, and leaving to abler hands the remedying of the ills he might discover.

When he left the Crimea he was suffering from intermittent fever. The empress was with him. They had been reconciled after the death, at the age of eighteen, of his natural daughter, Sophia Narishkin, to whom he was devotedly attached, and whose death he believed to be a punishment for his sins. How profoundly he was affected by this and other troubles of his private and public life, his agonised utterances during the last two or three days of his life, when his brain was wandering, clearly prove. He died on the 1st of December. The empress survived him but six months. She was taken ill suddenly, and died, while on her journey back to St. Petersburg in the following May.

Madame de Krüdener's influence, once so great, the czar had long ago cast off. When she returned to Russia in 1818, after having been expelled from all the Swiss and German states, he received her with extreme coldness, and declined further interviews when she sought them. The cause of Greece then became the subject of her preachings. In 1820 she publicly, in a kind of lyrical prayer, asked of God the triumph of the Hellenic cause. She had not foreseen, it appears, that the mysterious pact of the allied sovereigns, which she is supposed to have inspired and definitively revised, was eventually to become an instrument of oppression to the people.

The constant state of excitement in which for some years she had lived, together with the severe ascetic discipline she imposed on herself, at last told on her health. She was very ill in 1823. Her physician recommended her to spend the winter in the South, to abandon her *cilice* or horsehair chemise, and to treat herself less rigorously if she would live to benefit others.

The Princess Galitzin, being desirous of founding a colony in the Crimea, asked Madame de Krüdener to accompany her thither, thinking the climate might be beneficial to her. She consented, though apparently in a most hopeless condition. On descending the Volga, strength so completely failed her that at Karason-Bazar she was carried on shore, and there, a few days after, she died, the Princess Galitzin and Madame de Benkheim remaining with her to the last.

Thus ended the career of this extraordinary woman and singular illusionist, who, while inflicting severe penance on herself for a life of early depravity, doubtless hoped and intended to do good to others by leading them, as she believed, heavenward.

"The good I may have done," she said, "will remain; but what I have done wrong the mercy of my God will blot out."

CHAPTER XIII.

A *Procès* Gained. — Royal Ingratitude. — Loss of Court Favour. — The Savonnerie. — An Ornament Lost to the Court. — The Sin of Light-mindedness. — The Governess and the Governor. — The Bourbon Temperament. — "*Contes à Ma Fille.*" — M. Bouilly Presented to Madame. — Doubting the Pavillon Marsan. — Accepted on One Condition. — A Profession of Faith. — The Young Prince's Studies. — Principles Fraught with Danger. — A Flattering Leave-taking. — Madame's Methodical Habits.

*PROCÈS* had for several months been pending, whose object was to test the legality of the transfer by Louis XVIII. to Madame du Caylu of the Château of St. Ouen, claimed as part of the domain of the crown. This claim, strongly contested on her part, had been recently decided in her favour. It was, of course, no subject for popular enthusiasm; yet as anything serving to thwart or oppose the views and intentions of the king and his ministry was hailed with general satisfaction, so this decree of the Cour Royale met with warm approval far beyond the lady's private circle of friends.

The course pursued towards her by the king and the Duchesse d'Angoulême, or allowed by them to be pursued, had something, it was thought, of ingratitude in it. The countess's influence had been constantly employed to induce the late king to adopt a system of government more in conformity with the views of the royalist immaculates and the chiefs of the Congregation. It is true that, influential as she was, in some respects, she had advanced their views but little. Nevertheless, if she could adroitly introduce politics in the course of her morning *tête-à-tête* with her royal lover, or covertly could drop a word in his ear in favour of any scheme her employers had greatly at heart, she let no opportunity pass without doing so.

The duchess had always looked disapprovingly on her *liaison* with the king. Having, however, no power to put an end to it, she was not unwilling to turn it to account when possible. But scarcely had the king drawn his last breath when an order emanating from an illustrious lady's boudoir, where as much of the business of state was transacted as in the council-chamber, commanded the fair countess to withdraw from the court.

Louis XVIII. had been so unsparing of substantial acknowledgments of his fair friend's apparent devotion to him, that he might well have forborne to add to them the fine domain of St. Ouen. Long promised, it was obtained only when the hand of the royal donor could not, unaided, sign the papers necessary for its transfer. But it was contended that he knew perfectly well what he was signing, and that in the same manner and at the same time he had also signed several state papers.

Ministers who had contrived to enrich themselves while bringing the state into great financial difficulties, and who were menaced in the Chamber with impeachment for embezzling the public funds, were not likely to be credited with much probity or disinterestedness in instituting these proceedings against a lady who had lost favour at court. She was greatly congratulated on her triumph, by those friends from whom, like herself, the smiles of royalty were withdrawn. At once she made the Château her residence, having her two children with her, but still living apart from her husband.

She occupied herself very assiduously with agricultural experiments, and also devoted much time and attention to reviving the fame of the tapestries and carpets of the Savonnerie. This establishment — incorporated with that of the Gobelins in 1826 — is said by Larousse to have been entirely her work. The revival of the prestige of its manufactures may have been due to her; but the foundation of the establishment dates so far back as 1604, when Marie de' Medici gave permission to Pierre Dupont and Simon Bourdet to instal themselves and their looms in the Louvre. Needing more space, they transferred their manufactory to

Chaillot, occupying there a large building erected for soap-making works, whence it obtained the name of the Savonnerie.

After leaving the court, Madame du Cayla was accustomed to preside at the board of management of her favourite establishment. To her success, it appears, in obtaining by cross-breeding a race of sheep with long silky fleeces, the perfection of the carpets produced after the method of the Savonnerie is due — the softness and fineness of the wool rendering them superior to those of Persian manufacture, both in the strength of the tissue and in its velvety appearance.

Madame la Duchesse de Berry, who took great interest in all artistic and useful pursuits, visited the countess's establishment — the countess playing cicerone, and explaining to the princess the various processes of the manufacture. On another occasion she surprised Madame du Cayla by her unexpected appearance at St. Ouen with Madame de Gontaut and her children — her own two, and the two of her adoption, for Madame had faithfully carried out the promise she made to her dying husband to be the protectress of his two natural daughters.

The visit of this family party was for the purpose of showing the children Madame du Cayla's long-haired sheep, Madame being as much delighted as her children with the model flock that wandered at will in the park and grounds of St.

Ouen, and of which the little duke claimed two, "to eat the grass," he said, "at Rosny."

At the instance of some friends of the countess, who thought that her banishment from the court circle deprived it of one of its ornaments, she was no longer actually restrained from paying her respects to the stern dauphine and to Madame. But the freezing reception she met with from the former effectually extinguished any smouldering hopes she may have had of her eventual reinstatement. Madame, however, welcomed her cordially; and this, with her subsequent visits to the Savonnerie and St. Ouen, though each had its distinct object, gave Madame la Dauphine an opportunity of commenting severely on the sin of light-mindedness.

By the laws of France, the mother of the king, or heir-apparent to the throne, in his minority, is prohibited from any interference in state affairs, unless named regent. Madame was fully aware of this; but the restriction in no way troubled her. She was far more disposed to enjoy the passing hour, and to use the influence her position gave her, in accordance with her own tastes and fancies, than in meddling openly or secretly with the concerns of government.

She gave no heed to such matters. Yet by that very circumstance she seemed at times to be acting in opposition to the views and wishes of the dauphine and the king, and his, or their, ministry.

She had her own ideas, as before observed, respecting the education of her children; and they were not altogether in harmony with those that prevailed in the ultra-royalist court circle.

The time had now arrived when the Duc de Bordeaux, being six years old, was to pass from the care of a governess — as was customary for French princes — to that of a governor and preceptor. The Duc de Montmorency had been appointed prospectively to the former office — Madame de Gontaut's charge of the royal children having then several months to continue. The duke's successor was the Marquis de Rivière, captain of the king's *garde du corps*. He is described as "a Jesuit of the worst type; fanatical, and destitute of intelligence." The Abbé Tharin, Bishop of Strasburg, — another devoted partisan of the Jesuits, — was named by the king to assist the marquis in his arduous duties, in quality of preceptor.

The Comtesse de Gontaut appears to have fulfilled her trust very conscientiously. The youthful prince was delivered by his governess into the charge of his governor with a kind of slight ceremonial. A very long written statement was handed to him describing the character of her pupil — the method the countess had adopted for developing those excellent qualities of mind and disposition she discerned in him, and which, carefully trained, would lead, she believed, to the happiest results. The elementary instruction he had received was also fully entered into.

The young gentleman's domestic household would have been appointed at that time, but that when the Duc de Berry was assassinated a promise was made by the duchess to the servants of his establishment that, if she gave birth to a son, they were to pass at once nominally into his service, though forming part of her household, until the young prince's separate one should be named.

Madame had perceived some two years before that her son was disposed to give way to fits of rage on receiving the slightest check to his whims — that he had inherited, in fact, the Bourbon temperament. She was desirous of curing this defect, which in a child so flattered, so caressed, so obsequiously obeyed, was likely to become unendurable if not promptly restrained. He was fond of his sister, but disposed to tyrannise over her. This, too, was a fault that might develop into a vice, therefore the sooner it was eradicated the better; and Madame believed that both children, though so young, were sufficiently intelligent to be worked upon by the means she proposed to adopt.

During her girlhood she had been both greatly interested and greatly influenced, it appears, by the works of that prolific writer of charming tales for childhood and adolescence, the dramatic author

J. Nicolas Bouilly. His well-known "*Contes à ma fille*" was written expressly for his daughter. But when afterwards he was induced to publish this collection of tales, it obtained immense popularity, and was followed by many works of similar character. It is doubtful whether they have been equalled, either in the interest of the stories or the great charm of the style in which they are narrated, by any works of the kind which may have succeeded them; surpassed they hardly can have been.

The royal children were scarcely five and four years of age when the Duchesse de Berry, conversing with her first lady of honour, the Duchesse de Reggio, expressed a wish to become acquainted with the author of "*Contes à ma fille*." M. Bouilly being known to Madame de Reggio, she was desired to inform him that the Duchesse de Berry had read his works, that she admired them, and greatly wished to know their author. She had also a particular request to make to him.

Of course he was much flattered, and expressed himself deeply sensible of the honour done him. A letter of admission was forwarded to him for the Duchesse de Berry's reception after mass on the following Sunday, and the Duchesse de Reggio was to present him. Punctual to the moment he made his appearance at the Tuileries. The duchess, accompanied by many ladies and gentlemen of distinction, was returning from the chapel, and a brilliant circle waited her arrival in the *salons*. All were in full court dress, or uniform, M. Bouilly being conspicuous, as he says, amidst this gay throng by his plain black coat, unadorned by cross or mark of distinction of any kind.

As soon as his name was announced, Madame de Reggio advanced and led him to the duchess. Gazing fixedly at him, she said, with what M. Bouilly, who was *très galant*, describes as an enchanting smile, "When reading your works I have often tried to imagine your form and features. I now find you exactly like what I supposed the writer of these delightful stories for young girls to be. Will you," she continued, "be willing to contribute towards forming the hearts and minds of my children?"

M. Bouilly replied that they were already in the hands of persons too able and too experienced for him to presume to coöperate in so important a matter. "I could not pretend," he said, "to be their instructor."

"But you have especially the gift of impressing the youthful mind with the happiest and most excellent ideas, while simply offering them as amusement," replied the duchess. "I ask of you a series of tales which, while serving for my children's recreation, may imperceptibly guide them in the path that leads to happiness of life. In a word, do for them what you have done for your daughter — a most amiable and accomplished young woman, I am told."

But M. Bouilly was far from being anxious to accede to the duchess's proposal. He piqued himself on being one of "the old founders of equal rights in France," and in that character he doubted whether his interference in the education of *les enfants de France* would be favourably viewed by the Pavillon Marsan.

He therefore replied that, although as a father he had sought to impress on his child's mind the ideas and moral sentiments suited to her modest social position, by means of simple tales that amused and interested her, yet the children of kings having in their elevated sphere other and higher duties in life, it would perhaps be desirable to set before them less lowly examples of conduct, and in a less simple style than he had adopted as story-teller to his own daughter and children of similar condition.

"The qualities you name as objections," exclaimed the princess, with eager delight (she was always so enthusiastic), "are precisely those which have induced my request to you. Too many will seek to excite the imagination of my son and daughter with ideas of grandeur, power, and royal etiquette. But you, while sporting with and amusing them, will teach them how to gain the love of the people, to enter into their feelings, to study their manners, to become acquainted with their habits, and by that means to learn and know how to contribute to their happiness."

"If that, Madame, is really the mission you would confide to me," he replied, "I trust I should be found equal to it; and if the freedom of my language may be pardoned, on one condition I accept it."

"Granted before 'tis named," exclaimed the princess.

M. Bouilly's one condition was that for the series of tales he proposed to write for the royal children, no remuneration should be offered him. Severally, as they were written, he was himself to read them, and, the series completed, to be permitted to present it to the duchess as an offering for the amusement of *les enfants de France*. In that way only, he declared, could he preserve his freedom of manner and language as a writer of moral tales, and the independence of mind that should prevent him from becoming a mere flatterer.

He regarded this announcement as a sort of profession of faith. But he observed that, while some who were present obsequiously followed the example of the royal lady and smiled benignantly upon him, a dark cloud passed over the faces of others. The duchess herself listened approvingly, and replied, "I was perfectly convinced while reading your works that you were a man of honour," which probably meant that she believed he would inculcate no sentiments opposed to those of the "right divine," instilled into the minds of those royal babes from their very cradle.

M. Bouilly seems to have been very successful as writer and reader of stories to M. le Duc de Bordeaux and Mademoiselle de France; and charming and appropriate tales they were for the amusement and moral instruction of children. This sort of teaching and training continued for two years, with great satisfaction to the duchess, who, with some slight additional authority in such matters, became Madame, by the death of Louis XVIII. within a month after her arrangement with M. Bouilly.

Her son, having attained the ripe age of six years, passed, as before mentioned, from the hands of his governess into those of the Marquis de Rivière and the Jesuit priest, his preceptor. But as their duties were almost nominal — for the young prince was not troubled with much study at this early age, and was not yet actually emancipated from female control — Madame was desirous that he should continue to share with his sister the lessons and conversation that gave to both so much pleasure.

M. Bouilly's arrival with a new story was looked forward to with much delight; the minute questioning he was subjected to as to where he had heard all those things, and the further particulars that were eagerly demanded of the heroes or heroines of his tales, appear to have amused and interested Madame almost as much as her children. But this state of things was not to continue. Many became jealous of the high esteem with which Madame regarded him, and the attachment he had inspired in her children.

"This old liberal," said the royalist courtiers, "this old dotard, has presumed to put himself on a level with those high personages to whom the king has confided the education of his grandchildren. He has endeavoured to imbue their minds with principles fraught with danger. In one or more of his drivelling tales he has made royal birth a secondary matter compared with what it pleases him to call the dignity of manhood. 'It is a great error,' he writes, 'to suppose that all must yield to the whim or the will of one who is born a prince. Royal blood alone will not secure him the love of the people if he is wanting in other and higher qualities.' It is inconceivable that Madame should tolerate such writings, and allow their author free access to the heir to the throne. She should be told that the whole court entirely disapproves them."

Much more of the same sort of disparagement of his work and his character continually assailed him; but Madame defended and supported him to the end. When, finally, other engagements, together with a conviction that his efforts to carry out Madame's wishes were neutralised by the insidious acts of the enemies he had unwittingly raised up against him, compelled him to withdraw from the court, she took leave of him at one of her receptions with many expressions of good-will.

M. Bouilly on this occasion was, like the rest of the company, in full court dress. "I have great pleasure, monsieur," said Madame, "in publicly thanking you in the presence of this numerous circle for the two volumes of interesting tales you have written for my children. They are still too young to understand how much they are indebted to you. But some years hence, when the Duc de Bordeaux shall have more fully profited by them, he will in person pay you a visit to express his thanks for them."

"Yes, yes!" exclaimed the young prince; "they are beautiful books. I shall read them very often, and keep them all my life."

But the seeds of liberalism which M. Bouilly was supposed to have implanted in the mind of the youthful Duc de Bordeaux were destined to bear no fruit. Very different were the ideas instilled into his mind by the instructors who afterwards had charge of him, and formed, or dimmed, his understanding in those later years of adolescence when separated from his mother. Yet certain anecdotes related of him during the four or five years following 1826 would seem to indicate that some traces of the "old liberal's" moral tales remained yet unobliterated.

This may have been owing to Madame's habit of talking with and questioning her children for an hour every morning on subjects she was anxious to impress on their memory. Afterwards she was present at the morning lessons of her two adopted daughters. She was an early riser; summer and winter she was up at six, and her day marked out in a methodical manner scarcely to have been looked for in one reputed so thoughtless, and so fond of gaiety and pleasure.

CHAPTER XIV.

A Crusade against the Jesuits. — Slaying the Hydra. — A Rigorous Law. — "They Shall Repent of It!" — Busy; Building and Improving. — Justice and Love. — The Faithful Three Hundred. — "The *Canaille* Must be Coerced." — A Mark of Royal Favour. — Not a *Vivat* Greets Him. — What Is the Reason? — False Hopes. — Two Great Events.

WHILE Madame, in her ambition to train up a king in the way he should go, — one worthy, she hoped, to sit on the throne of France, — was using the small influence she possessed in the matter in furtherance of her plan, Charles X. and his ministry were doing their best to bring that tottering throne to the ground.

The ascetic Comte de Montlosier's menacing crusade against the Jesuits, in pamphlets, speeches, addresses to the people, and appeals to the courts, requiring that "the proscribed Society of Jesus be excluded from France," had greatly irritated that body, concealed under the name of Fathers of the Congregation. No less sorely annoyed were the king and his ministry by the vehement and continually increasing opposition with which the government measures were met by those liberal journals regarded as the exponents of public opinion.

To imprison and fine an editor, and now and then, as a warning to others, to suppress a pamphlet or journal more than usually virulent in tone or sarcastically eloquent, was found to be useless. Instantly another arose to take its place. It was like attempting to slay the Hydra by cutting off one of his heads. The press, like that mythical many-headed monster, to be slain effectually, must be slain at one fell blow. The priests and the king and his "deplorables" were fully agreed that this was the only sure course to pursue. To prevent the abuse of the liberty of the press, that liberty, without delay, must at once and forever be taken from it.

"Ah!" exclaimed Charles, exultingly, — repeating that favourite phrase with which he hailed every new scheme that seemed to offer him a chance of putting his foot on the neck of the rebellious nation, — "they shall suffer for it, the rebels!"

"France at that epoch" — to use the words of a French writer * — "regarded that intelligent and indefatigable purveyor of her political emotions, Journalism, with the feelings of a young lover. To strike the press was to stab France to the heart." When, therefore, M. Peyronnet, on the 30th of December, 1826, had the effrontery to lay before the Chamber of Deputies his "*projet de loi* for preserving the liberty of the

* Étienne Malpertuy.

press from its own excesses," it was received with an explosion of anger and wrathful reproach — which was echoed throughout the country — such as even the "deplorable ministry," so often violently opposed, had never before encountered.

By the excessive rigour of this law, writers, printers, and booksellers were henceforth at the mercy of the government, and consequently of the Jesuits of the Congregation. It rendered the emission of thought by means of the press impossible. "As well," exclaimed Casimir Périer, "announce that printing is suppressed in France for the benefit of Belgium."

M. Peyronnet, deprecating, in the *Moniteur*, the outcry against his perfidious law, spoke of it as a "law of justice and love." This singular epithet was at once taken up and applied to it in derision. "The perfidious *loi Peyronnet*" formed the one subject of conversation in the *salons*, the *cafés*, the workshops, the colleges. It affected not only the journalists and the printing and bookselling trades, but all the material interests of France, theatres, banking-houses, business establishments; and even the French Academy joined in the chorus of malediction.

MM. de Châteaubriand, Villemain, Lacretelle, and Michaud, as a deputation from the academic body, waited on the king to present an address on the subject, praying that so important a measure as the abolition of the liberty of the press might be reconsidered. But his gracious majesty sent them word by the first gentleman of the chamber that he would receive neither the deputation nor their address; while the three last-named academicians, who held appointments in the government, in the course of that day were informed of their dismissal. "They shall suffer for it!" he cried again, elated with the idea of the great things he was, as his ministers told him, about to accomplish by "acting with so much vigour."

"Justice and love" deprived the Carnival of much of its gaiety. There was certainly dancing enough at the Tuileries; and at the Palais Royal the festive gatherings were unusually numerous. But they were said to veil an immense deal of intrigue. For there was a desire on the part of many, who thought no change could possibly be a change for the worse, to urge on the Duc d'Orléans towards the throne, by inducing him at this crisis to play the part of "first citizen of France, and openly declare himself at the head of the liberal party."

But La Fayette's place in a republic was not that he was watching and waiting for, and he was far too wary to risk the attainment of his object by any inopportune demonstration against the king and the government. The people must fight out this battle of the liberty of the press for themselves. He was busy; building and improving, adding estate to estate, and providing for his numerous family.

Scarcely did the siege of Missolonghi, and the terrible cruelties that followed it, obtain more than a passing notice, deeply as the French had sympathised with the Greeks in their struggle with their Turkish masters. But what in ordinary times would have caused profound emotion faded into nothingness before the absorbing question of the "law of justice and love." A state of passionate excitement seemed to prevail throughout society. Even the people who were unable to read were as angry and outrageous on the subject as the journalists themselves, and their *vivas* for the liberty of the press were among the loudest with which the streets of Paris and every town in the kingdom echoed from morning till night.

Of course epigram, *chanson*, and play had each its part in this feud. Operas and dramas that should have received attention met with disapprobation if they contained no prominent allusion to the subject uppermost in every one's thoughts. Rossini produced at this time his "Siege of Corinth;" but its reception was by no means flattering. Even the drama, "*Le dernier jour de Missolonghi*," had not nearly the success anticipated.

The play in request was the "*Mariage de Figaro*," and that for the sake of Figaro's ironical definition of the liberty of the press. This passage of the play was prohibited, but demanded by the audience with so much persistency that, to prevent a serious riot, it was given. But once was not enough. It was encored, and, from the riotous enthusiasm that followed, one would have thought, says M. Muret, that the audience in the pit was solely composed of journalists and men of letters, restrained from giving expression to their thoughts in print.*

However, this law that occasioned so much commotion in the country, so much heated discussion in the Chamber, by the aid of the faithful three hundred, who at a glance from the minister voted as one man, was accepted by the deputies. Opposition became more strenuous and violent than before; for those who did not habitually oppose the government now raised their voices in condemnation of this measure. Petitions to the king flowed in from all parts,— there being a desire to separate him from his ministers; to show him that the confidence withheld from them was placed in him, and that they looked to his sense of "justice and love" towards his people to repair his ministers' abuse of those terms, by withdraw-

* The following was the suppressed passage of Figaro's speech; "the law of justice and love" would seem to have been founded upon it: "Pourvu que je ne parle pas en mes écrits, ni de l'autorité, ni du culte, ni de la politique, ni de la morale, ni des gens en place, ni des corps en crédit, ni de l'opéra, ni des autres spectacles, ni de personne qui tienne à quelque chose, je puis tout imprimer librement, sous l'inspection de deux ou trois censeurs."

ing the odious project to which they had applied them.

But Charles refrained from taking the vigorous step suggested to him, of which he was to have had the whole credit. His idea of vigour, derived from his favourite, the Marquis de Rivière, — who appears to have been his governor as well as his grandson's, — was coercion. "The *canaille* must be coerced," said the marquis; "and seeing that nothing is left for them but to obey, obey they will."

It, however, began to be whispered about that the Chamber of Peers viewed the new law with much disfavour. They saw revolution advancing behind it, and were determined on its rejection when brought before them. In the mean time, by way of turning the thoughts of the people from this all-engrossing subject, and parading their king before them in awe-inspiring splendour, it was determined to celebrate with *éclat* his first entry into Paris as Comte d'Artois on the 12th of April, 1814.

It happened that the 12th fell on Wednesday in the Holy Week; consequently, the grand *fête* was adjourned, but only until the following Sunday,— a day even less appropriate, one would have thought. The Jesuits were of a different opinion. The restoration of the monarchy by right divine in France being celebrated conjointly with the Saviour's resurrection would give more significance to the former great event and to the twofold rejoicings.

The national guard were to receive on this auspicious occasion an especial mark of royal favour. The guarding of the Tuileries was to be exclusively confided to them for the whole of that day. This honour, they were told, was in acknowledgment of the monarchical devotion of which they had given so overwhelming a proof in 1814. This flattering announcement was not responded to by any of the signs of grateful joy which were expected to hail it. Thirteen years had elapsed, and in the course of them many changes had occurred in the ranks of the citizen soldiers; and whatever may have been the general feeling among them in 1814, monarchical devotion seemed to have died out in 1827,— unless perchance it was too profound for utterance.

On the morning of the 16th, the king, wearing the uniform of a colonel-general of the corps he delighted that day to honour, after receiving the felicitations of the great officers of state, the Chambers, and the magistracy, proceeded to the Place du Carrousel, a brilliant staff accompanying him. There, Madame la Dauphine, Madame and her children, the duchess and the princesses of Orléans, and a group of ladies of the court, were assembled to witness the parade and the relief of the guards on duty at the Château.

But the attitude assumed by the national guard

threw a damp on the spirit of this gay assemblage. The *vrai chevalier* advances as usual on his favourite prancing, curveting steed, bowing and smiling in his most gracious manner, and expecting that his condescension towards his *bourgeois* troops would be acknowledged by an enthusiastic reception. He loved popularity, and felt assured that he well deserved it. But the national guard, stiff and stern, which gives them a more soldier-like appearance than usual, receive their colonel-general in solemn silence. Bows and smiles avail him naught. Not a *vivat* greets him! Of course it is a concerted plan.

Astonishment, consternation, fire the breasts of the indignant monarch and his royal and courtly *entourage;* for not only is this gloomy silence maintained in the ranks of the national guard, but the gaping and generally noisy throng assembled to see the parade have, in their amazement at the funereal solemnity that prevails, also lost their voices.

Have the police, too, joined in the plot? — and what has become of their paid leaders of applause? Have they omitted to fulfil their customary duty of skilfully distributing them amongst the crowd? But, whatever the reason, the national guard went through the business of the parade like a set of automata, and the king and his *cortége* withdrew without a single voice having been raised for a *vivat*.

In dismay, he questions his courtiers as to the reason of this terribly chilling reception. Most of them know, but prefer to suggest that the Duc d'Orléans is not unconnected with it. Charles rejects the idea. But there is one among his grand officers — the Duc de Doudeauville — who has the frankness and the courage to whisper in his royal master's ear, "Justice and love."

Forthwith the ministers are summoned to his presence, and the king informs them of his *bon plaisir* to withdraw the law of "justice and love." Of course they regard this decision as involving the forfeiture of their *portefeuilles*. But it is not so. His majesty desires that they will retain them. He approves their vigorous policy, and will shortly put a curb on the licentious press as effectual as the law he withdraws. On M. Peyronnet, who has so recently spoken in glowing terms of eulogy of his law of justice and love, it now devolves to inform the Chambers that by the king's command it is withdrawn. Thinking, probably, that the less said about it the better, he mounts to the tribune, and, without preamble or comment, merely states the fact, and retires.

That same evening Paris was aglow with light from the many-coloured rays of the tens of thousands of lamps employed in the general illumination. This was repeated, as the welcome news spread, in every town in the kingdom, — the joy of the people being expressed in the usual exuberant and emotional fashion. This was partly owing to the belief that with the end of the obnoxious project there was also an end to the "deplorables," whose probable successors were already named and openly announced.

But they were not so ready to relinquish place and power, however strong the manifestation of public feeling might be against them. A fortnight elapsed. Still they held their places, and murmurs were again beginning to be heard, when the national guard were informed by the Duc de Reggio (Maréchal Oudinot) that the king proposed, as a further mark of his favour, to pass them in review on Sunday, the 30th of April. This was, of course, to afford them an opportunity, by an enthusiastic reception of his majesty, of making the *amende honorable* for their moody silence on the combined anniversary of those two great events, the Restoration of the Bourbons and the Resurrection of the Saviour.

CHAPTER XV.

An Eventful Day. — " Homage, Not Lessons ! " — A Change of Mind. — " What Would Louis XIV. Have Done ? " — " An Act of Vigour. " — Extinguished Forever. — Refusal to Pray for the King. — The Old Revolutionist. — " What if They Are *Canaille !* " — Grand *Fête* of the Jubilee. — Victory of Navarino. — A Sign from Heaven. — The End of the " Deplorables." — A Riot and a Massacre. — A Hint to the New President.

BRIGHTLY beamed the morning of this eventful April day, and very early all Paris turned out to secure an advantageous position whence to witness the interesting spectacle of thirteen legions of citizen soldiers reviewed by their king, presenting an effective force of from 19,000 to 20,000 men. They were ranged in the Champ de Mars, the dense crowd of spectators occupying the surrounding slopes and the heights of Chaillot. The king was accompanied by the Duc d'Angoulême, the Duc d'Orléans, and the Duc de Chartres, and attended by his *aides-de-camp* and the officers of his household. As at the parade, the princesses and ladies of the court were present in carriages.

The tide of popular favour having turned, a hearty chorus of *vivas* gratifyingly salute the royal ear. But presently, like bitter drops mingled in a cup of sweets, were heard the unwelcome sounds of "*Vive la Charte!*" and "*Vive la liberté de la presse!*" Charles had not expected this. It was no part of the programme. He, however, strove to bear it with a heedless air, and to ride smilingly along the lines. But when he and his gay *cortége* came in front of the seventh legion, he was unmistakably made to comprehend that he had not yet satisfied the expectations of the people.

Vociferous cries of "*À bas les ministres! À bas les Jésuites!*" issued from the ranks. Suddenly the king stopped, and, with extreme irritation and his face flushed with anger, he exclaimed in a loud voice, "I came here to receive homage, not lessons!" But this outburst of temper did not secure the homage even of a cessation of the offensive cries. Those who raised them seemed to follow the lead of some secret prompter, and as the royal party passed on, louder than ever the king and his son were assailed by them. The Duchesse d'Angoulême received her full share of these marks of the people's displeasure, while mingling with them were heard *vivas* for Madame and for the Orléans family; which, under the circumstances, could scarcely have given much pleasure.

The review ended, it was thought prudent to take some precautions against a probable riot in the evening. None, however, occurred. But the illumination was so general, and in so many instances in the form of large transparencies representing in a very flattering manner the Comte d'Artois's entry into Paris, that the king, on hearing this, was disposed to let the occurrence of the morning pass without further notice. "There are factious spirits among the national guard," he said, "but as a body they are perhaps not disloyal. Let them know," he continued, addressing Maréchal Oudinot, "that on the whole I am satisfied with their general efficiency."

On the morrow the marshal brought the order of the day for signature. He is informed that in the interval the king has changed his mind. The national guards have insulted his confidential ministers. Marching into Paris, — with all the exultation of a conquering host, — they had slackened pace for a moment while passing the hôtel of the Ministry of Finance at the corner of the Rue Castiglione, in order to serenade M. de Villèle by a more vociferous shouting of their obnoxious cries. Again in the Place Vendôme they had committed a similar outrage before the hôtel of the Minister of Justice, M. de Peyronnet.

These trusted advisers of the crown instantly hastened to St. Cloud to proffer their resignation. The king declined to accept it, and immediately summoned a council. "What," said M. de Rivière, that profound admirer of the *Grand Mo-*

narque, " would the great Louis XIV. have done in such a case ? " All were silent. He therefore replied to his own question, " Disbanded the rebels, doubtless." The idea of so high-handed an act of royal prerogative greatly pleased the king. The dilemma he had been in to devise a punishment for so considerable a body of men — for one and all had apparently more or less shared in the offence — vanished at once. The national guard was of revolutionary origin, and wholly incompatible with the monarchy by right divine; its abolition was therefore in every sense welcome to him. It was a step in the right direction, a backward one.

But the opinion of the council respecting it was not unanimous. Even the Jesuit Bishop of Hermopolis — the king's grand almoner — thought it "a dangerous step to take, and, at the least, inopportune."

The Duc de Doudeauville declared that it would be nothing less than an act of insanity; if adopted, he begged to resign his office of Controller of the Household.

" An act of vigour," replied the marquis, correcting him. " Vigorous measures are needed."

The king was of the same opinion; consequently the ordinance was signed that night and despatched to the *Moniteur.* In the morning it appeared. It struck Paris with stupor, which was succeeded by general indignation and the proposal of an armed protest against it. Other counsels, however, prevailed, perhaps suggested by the partisans of those who were watching and waiting; for it was clearly seen whither the king's impolitic acts were leading him. The citizen soldiers, individually and collectively, although they felt themselves bitterly aggrieved by the blow now aimed at them, yet by some means arrived at a tacit but general understanding that no resistance should be made and no seditious cry raised.

Their guns and their uniforms were not demanded. Those souvenirs of their days of military glory were therefore carefully put aside with the tricoloured cockade and banner, until the arrival of an event now looming distinctly on the political horizon should bring them into use again. Their reappearance in the July days had probably considerable influence on the course of the revolution. Now, however, the courtiers congratulate the king on the act of vigour which so quietly and effectually has extinguished them forever.

Blinded by what he believed to be the success of his *coup-d'état* and the consolidation of his ministry, Charles, on the 12th of June, issued another royal ordinance, reëstablishing the censure and imposing restrictions on the press as stringent as those laid upon it by the law so recently withdrawn. It was reported also that, believing he might now dare everything he chose, he proposed to authorise, simply by an ordinance, the reinstatement of the Jesuits in France, with the same powers and privileges they possessed before their banishment in 1762.

The Duchesse d'Angoulême had expatiated at some length on the desirableness, nay necessity, of their reinstatement. For until the training of the people was again in their hands, there was evidently no hope of reclaiming the nation from the error of its ways, or of the realisation of that earnest hope so devoutly prayed for by the king — that France should purge herself of her revolutionary errors, and seek peace and pardon in the bosom of the Church.

The pious duchess, who was always overflowing with Christian pity for Madame, her light-minded sister-in-law, had now an example to point to of the evil results of her thoughtlessness and want of Christian care in the early education of her children. The little Duc de Bordeaux had of late obstinately refused to say his prayers — not prayers generally, but to include in them any petition for a benediction on his governor and the king. This being communicated to Charles, threw him into a terrible state of mind, though, not to grieve him too deeply, it was withheld from him that it was on himself and his favourite marquis that the child declined, and very peremptorily too, to invoke the blessing of Heaven.

For some time he would give no reason for it;

but being greatly pressed by his mother, he at last, bursting into tears, exclaimed, "My friends! my friends! they have sent away my friends." These friends were the national guards, of whom a certain number, accustomed to mount guard at La Bagatelle (a favourite residence of Madame after her husband's death), stood high, it appeared, in the young prince's favour. He had noticed their continued absence, and an attendant, to whom he was also attached, explained to him the cause. Hence the young gentleman's resolve to withhold from its authors the benefit of his prayers.

The marquis reminded the king of M. Bouilly, "the old revolutionist, who boasted, as he was told, of being a 'founder of liberty and equal rights in France,' and whom Madame had imprudently employed for two or three years as writer and reader of moral tales to the royal children."

"Very imprudent, indeed," remarked the king; "but the children are so young, and the stories Madame brought to me were amusing and apparently harmless."

"'Tis in early youth that the deepest impressions are made on the mind," replied the learned governor, with the air of a philosopher who has given utterance to a profound and original thought.

He then informed the king that he had talked with Monseigneur the Duc de Bordeaux that morning, and had rallied him on his tears and his grief, which he thought more judicious than reproving him for his sympathy with such people. "They are no soldiers," he had told him; "but cobblers and tailors and small shopkeepers. Why should your royal highness condescend to fret about such *canaille?*"

"What of that!" cried the prince. "There are noble qualities in men of all classes." "A remarkable reply for so young a child, but showing that the old revolutionist's teaching had taken effect. It was, in fact, what Bouilly called the moral of his tale, 'The Ring-doves' Nest,' a tale inculcating sentiments that had excited the indignation of the whole court, but which," the marquis regretted to say, "Madame had found unobjectionable."

"I commend my grandson to your watchful care," said the king. "If sentiments of a dangerous tendency have been implanted in his young mind, I confide in your proved loyalty and ability to eradicate them."

The marquis bowed low and kissed his gracious sovereign's extended hand, in acknowledgment of this mark of his favour and confidence; and with the casual remark that the sooner those able teachers of youth, the Society of Jesus, were restored to their former position in the state the better for it, the conversation closed.

But Charles, after passing an hour or two in his

oratory, sought counsel of the Archbishop of Paris concerning the project he had so much at heart. The archbishop advised a preliminary measure, to prepare the people for the reëstablishment of the Jesuits. This was a repetition of the grand *fête* of the Jubilee, an affair of much ecclesiastical pomp, lasting several days, with processions, sermons, stations, collections, and all those exciting religious exaggerations so attractive to the faithful, ending with abundance of plenary indulgences from Rome.

The king and his family, in May, 1826, had followed these processions on foot. But the people, led by curiosity to gaze on these strange sights, had looked on the part their sovereign played in them with indignation, even derision — not, as was expected, with the reverence due to an act of saintly humility. The concluding ceremony of that Jubilee was the benediction and laying of the first stone of an expiatory monument to the memory of Louis XVI. on the Place de la Concorde. Thus, these Bourbons, who came back professing forgetfulness of the past, were always devising some means of keeping alive its most painful memories.

However, the threatened repetition of the Jubilee mummeries, and the reëstablishment of the Jesuits, appear to have so unfavourably affected the funds that it was thought better to set them aside, together with other acts of vigour meditated by the king, until a more convenient season. People had begun to ask, "What next?" and to inquire if the king was insane. "He never had much sense to boast of," said others; "but he seems to have lost even that small portion which nature did vouchsafe to him."

Happily the victory of Navarino occurred about this time, and the enthusiasm inspired by the deliverance of the Greeks, and the share of the French in effecting it, diverted for a while the thoughts of the people from their own troubles and the follies of their infatuated king.

The successful naval contest was celebrated with great *éclat*. But the hated ministry were held to have no part in its glory. Just a slight reflex of the great honour awarded to the French navy was allowed to rest on the king by those who still wished to separate him from his ministers and to throw on them the chief blame of his acts.

Charles was present at the *Te Deum* at Notre-Dame. In the discourse which followed it, the archbishop told him that the successful part borne by the French in the naval victory was a sign from Heaven that divine support was afforded to their sovereign, and that he was encouraged to continue to trust in it. Charles believed this; it gave him fresh vigour; and, nerving himself to new efforts, he was determined, he said, to "strangle the revolution in both Chambers."

Forthwith seventy-six good men and true were created peers; the deputies were dissolved, and measures taken for the election of a new Chamber of the ministry's nomination.

But here divine support changed sides. An overwhelming liberal majority was the result. "The three hundred," who ate M. de Peyronnet's good dinners and paid him with their votes, were defeated, and with their masters, the "deplorables," must now take flight,—a moment, too, when Charles, confiding in Archbishop Quélen, was gleefully singing, "They shall suffer for it, the rebels!"

What a triumph! One burst of enthusiasm rang throughout the city; every part of it was illuminated. Wherever, perchance, a window was perceived unlighted, a shower of stones instantly smashed every pane in it. This was unfortunate, as it led to disturbance and the interference of the *gendarmerie*, who were pelted with mud and stones. The *réverbères* were broken; sticks and stones were used, swords were drawn, and blood was shed. *Vivas* resounded on all sides for "*l'Empereur Napoléon II.!*" "*La république!*" "*La Charte!*" and timidly here and there for "*le Duc d'Orléans!*" As for the king, none cried "God bless him!"—he was associated with "*À bas les Jésuites!*"

But the tumult soon became general, and there was desperate fighting in the Rue St. Denis.

The streets were unpaved, and furniture of all kinds was brought from the houses or thrown out of windows to raise barricades. The troops were drawn out, and, by order, it was reported, of Maréchal Marmont, fired on the people and into the houses, wounding women and children. Shrieks of rage and anguish mingled with cries of "*À bas le traître!*" "*Vive Napoléon II.!*" and "*Vive la garde nationale!*" When towards evening the tumult partly subsided, from twenty to thirty persons lay bleeding in the Rue St. Denis, the greater number dead.

On the following day, towards evening, the disturbances were renewed. An order had been issued to the inhabitants to light up the windows of their houses, all the *réverbères* being destroyed, and the city in darkness. The garrison of Paris was brought out to intimidate the rioters, and as the people began to assemble in large numbers they were dispersed and pursued by the cavalry through the intricate web of winding and tortuous streets still existing in Paris. Many peaceable persons were thus thrown down, wounded and killed by the trampling of the cavalry horses. The police were active too, and made innumerable arrests.

It was, however, remarked that suddenly, and as at a given signal, order was generally restored. This gave rise to a strong suspicion that this very serious *émeute* — which the people named "the massacre of the Rue St. Denis"—was an organised one,—a parting service of the deplorable ministry to their sovereign, affording him a pretext for plausibly urging on their successors the necessity of adopting stringent measures.

On the 4th of February, 1828, this ministry, which M. de Villèle, its most able member, had persistently kept in office for upwards of seven years, came to an end, and was succeeded, greatly to the monarch's dissatisfaction, by a liberal one.

"You know," said Charles to M. de Martignac, who took M. de Villèle's place as president of the Council, "that I have not willingly separated myself from your predecessor. His system is mine, and I trust you will conform to it."

CHAPTER XVI.

Disappointed Expectations. — Anything to Get Rid of Him. — An Exchange of Embassies. — To Rome He Went. — A Damaging Blow with a Fan. — A Visit of Condolence. — Royalty *en Voyage*. — The Chateâu de Chambord.— Threatened with Demolition. — Bought by the Nation. — Ungraciously Accepted. — Some Sketches of Chambord. — Deceived and Undeceived. — A Long Deferred Journey. — Delighted with Chambord. — An Enthusiastic Welcome.— A Successful Expedition.— Saintly, Popular, and Powerful.

NONE had more powerfully contributed towards the overthrow of the "deplorables" than M. de Châteaubriand. Wounded vanity imparted peculiar acrimony to his attacks on M. de Villèle, whom he further despised as a man who had enriched himself by extensive frauds on the state. With the advent of M. de Martignac to power, he expected his majesty would invite him also to take his seat in the Cabinet; for, as was remarked by a member of Madame Récamier's council-chamber, he could never see, what was so clear to others, how cordially he was detested both by Louis XVIII. and Charles X. Charles was indignant at the name of *"ce vieux révolutionnaire"* being even mentioned to him.

Though a professed and, indeed, firm supporter

of legitimacy, yet he had declared, speaking from his place in the Chamber of Peers, that he had no faith in divine right; and who, it was asked, had blown louder "trumpet blasts" (his pamphlets were so called) than he, in denunciation of restraints on the liberty of the press — otherwise, the crippling of his own seditious pen.

However, M. de Martignac hoped to persuade the king to appoint him Minister of Public Instruction, as bringing him less frequently in contact, or rather collision, with his majesty than would some other posts in the government. But M. de Châteaubriand, hearing of this project, disdainfully rejected the appointment before it was really offered. The *portefeuille* of Foreign Affairs, or the embassy to Rome, regarded the first in dignity, he would alone accept.

Glad to get him out of Paris, the king named him ambassador to the court of Vienna, the Roman embassy being already satisfactorily filled by the Duc de Laval. Before he had absolutely refused it, as, very curtly, he was about to do, Madame Récamier — who was, of course, in the confidence of all concerned in this matter, and who herself may have been not unwilling to find relief for a time from the monotony of her exacting friend's daily visits and the details of his political vexations — begged him to await the result of a letter she was about to write to the duke on the subject.

The Duc de Laval was one of her very numerous dearest friends and earliest devoted admirers. He was also the cousin of Duc Mathieu de Montmorency, whom both had so much loved, whose memory they tenderly cherished, and regarded as another bond of their own friendly union. The duke replies, yielding to the wishes of his "dearest friend," while confessing that his position at the papal court is in every respect congenial to him; also that he entirely disapproves M. de Châteaubriand's political conduct. Nevertheless, as a tribute to the warm and sincere friendship so long subsisting between him and the lady who pleads for the irritable viscount, he will exchange embassies with him.

M. de Châteaubriand selfishly accepted this generous sacrifice on the part of the duke. He, however, may not have known — Madame Récamier being a skilful diplomatist — that the surrender, made so readily and with so much gallantry, was a tribute to old friendship, whose origin had been young love. He would rather, in his immense egotism, ascribe it to the duke's sense of the superior abilities of the great political writer, statesman, and diplomatist to whom he yielded place. At all events, to Rome he went, and remained there eighteen months.*

---

* His letters to Madame Récamier during that period have never, it appears, been published; for, although containing many interesting particulars respecting the events of his embassy, dur-

Besides these matters, there occurred at this time (April, 1828) that event, slight indeed in itself, being but the indiscreet act of an Arab in a fit of anger, which eventually gave France her colony of Algiers. Hussein Dey was complaining bitterly to M. Deval, the French consul, in the presence of the consular agents of other European countries, of the conduct of France towards him. Especially he dwelt on the injustice of withholding payment of the large sums of money he claimed for supplies of wheat, etc., to the Republican government, and at last worked himself into a passion. The dey and his grievances were probably treated with some superciliousness by M. Deval, for he struck the consul a blow with his fan (a damaging blow to himself alone), and ordered his slaves to drive him from his presence.

The deaths of several public men also, who had played a more or less prominent part in affairs under the empire, and since the Restoration, had taken place during the past year or two. To some of them, in quieter times, the honour of a public funeral would have been decreed. But they passed away almost unnoticed, owing to the extreme and continual state of agitation in which

ing which one Pope died (Leo XII.) and another was elected, with details concerning the social life of the Rome of that day, Madame Le Normant thought them too numerous. The greater part, too, contained long and reiterated complaints of his health, the expenses of his embassy, so ruinous to him, and the perversity of people who did not in all things agree with him, etc.

the king's unwise and vexatious acts had so long kept the minds of his people. Among those who were adherents of Napoleon, the arch-chancellor Cambacérès, M. Caulaincourt, Duc de Vicenza, and the astronomer Laplace, may be mentioned.

The king, too, had to lament the sudden removal by death of a chief favourite, his evil counsellor, the Marquis de Rivière. He died on the 21st of April, cut to the heart by the ill success of those "acts of vigour" he had so urgently recommended. Duc Jules de Polignac, who was then ambassador to the court of St. James's, hastened over to console his sovereign; and great and general was the alarm his arrival occasioned. But after a few days' stay he returned to London, his visit proving to be merely one of condolence, though probably arrangements for events that were to follow were then secretly entered into between him and the king.

Soon after the accession of M. de Martignac to power, it was thought advisable, during the lull of political strife which ensued, that the king and his family should seek popularity by showing themselves to the people of the provinces. Charles and his son, accompanied by M. de Martignac, went eastward, enthusiastic receptions and hearty welcomes being arranged beforehand by official programme; M. de Martignac's favour with the people being looked to to supply any deficiency in the display of exuberant popular feeling there might possibly be towards the monarch.

The Duchesse d'Angoulême was already in the South, lending the support of her presence to the teaching and preaching of the missionary fathers or Jesuits. They, in return for the advantage derived from the light of her countenance beaming upon them, paid her great homage, and received her with much ecclesiastical pomp and parade. Where the people showed but little hostility to these priestly doings, they evinced great curiosity respecting the duchess, and assembled in crowds to see her go through her public devotions; at other places, where opposition was encountered, she was frequently saluted with many insulting cries.

Madame, holding entirely aloof from these religious and political squabbles, had a much longer journey and varied programme before her. The propagation of royalism was doubtless in some measure connected with it; and, so far as regarded the extending of her own popularity, she was likely to be the most successful of the royal party. She was to pass through Tourraine and visit Chambord — a project of long standing, and, with her, the main object of her journey. Thence she was to proceed to Anjou, Vendée, Poitou, and through the southern provinces to Bordeaux.

The ancient château and wide domain of Chambord, with which Louis XV. recompensed the military services that the great Maréchal Saxe rendered to France in the course of his reign, had escaped the fate which, during the destructive fury of the revolutionary times, fell on many historic and royal residences. It was built for François I. under the direction of the Italian sculptor and architect Primatrice, and had occupied 1,800 workmen nearly thirteen years to complete. It was the sole nearly perfect specimen in France of a royal château of the Renaissance period. For this reason Comte Étienne de Calonne — formerly of the household of the Duc de Berry — suggested its purchase, as the nation's offering to Henri Dieudonné, the new-born heir of its ancient line of kings.

But the nation's offering appears to have given Louis XVIII. and his brother more dissatisfaction than pleasure. When the revolution was succeeded by the empire, the château of François I. became the property of "the usurper," who bestowed it on Maréchal Berthier, Prince de Neufchatel and Wagram, on condition that the endowment granted with it should be applied to the restoration of the château and the keeping up in good order of the magnificent gardens and park surrounding it.

Berthier, "even Berthier," as was said at the time, after slinking away uneasy in conscience from Fontainebleau, — for the faithful Berthier was about to turn traitor, — retained by his desertion of Napoleon both his empty titles and the substantial gifts which had accompanied them. But his enjoyment of them — if he felt any — was short-lived. Berthier died in 1815. Some four or five years later, his widow, finding that for her the domain of Chambord was but a burdensome possession, applied to Louis XVIII. for permission to sell it; and permission was granted.

No offers appear to have been forthcoming for the whole estate, and the fine old historic château was thus threatened with demolition. Some portions of its sculpture, magnificent mantelpieces, doors, and cornices, — the *chefs-d'œuvre* of Primatrice and his assistants, — all in excellent preservation, would have been purchased for removal elsewhere; while the park and extensive forest were already marked out in lots of so many *arpents* and *ares*,* and the sale announced for the early part of October. On the 29th of September the "child of miracle," the God-given heir to the throne of France, made his appearance, and it then occurred to M. de Calonne that this auspicious event afforded an opportunity of rescuing the Chateau de Chambord from destruction.

So anxious was he to save it that he instantly wrote to Madame Berthier, urging her to defer the sale for six months. She consented; and the municipalities of the kingdom being communicated

---

* An *are* is 100 square metres; an *arpent*, 51 ares.

with, the idea was generally approved, and the subscription opened. On the 5th of March following, M. de Calonne, as the agent of the four thousand municipalities of France, was able to make an offer for the domain of Chambord, which was adjudicated to him for 1,542,000 *francs* (between 60,000*l.* and 70,000*l.*), which appears to have been a very moderate price.

In the interval, the Minister of the Interior, Comte Siméon, presented a statement to the king against a subscription then proceeding for the purpose of purchasing Chambord. The party most eager for it was that which had compelled the retirement of M. Decazes; therefore their project was looked on with much displeasure by the king. The opposition ridiculed the idea of the old Château de Chambord being offered as an appanage to the young prince, the eloquent Louis Paul Courrier making a long sarcastic speech against it.

The Comte d'Artois would not have been opposed to the subscription; but to throw it away in the purchase of Chambord was intolerable. Courtiers exclaimed deprecatingly that all attached to the court would be compelled to make a journey of forty leagues when royalty was in residence there. One of these grumblers was despatched to Chambord — so little was known of the old royal château — to look at "the ancient dungeon keep," and to bring back some trustworthy account of it. The report of this gentleman, who did not like journeying forty leagues on a road no longer a royal one, was simply that Chambord was partly in ruins; that he had seen what was formerly called the *cabinet du roi*, and that it was far too small to contain the *grandes entrées* of the present.

Yet, in spite of the domestic cabal of the Tuileries, and the political one of the ministry and the Chambers, the people who subscribed the money considered that the manner of its expenditure was for their own decision. Chambord was bought with the people's general approval, and offered in the name of the nation. It was not received with much graciousness, and seems to have been long left to the charge of its enthusiastic admirer, M. de Calonne. The people of Chambord, however, celebrated its restoration to a royal owner with great rejoicings and many village *fêtes*.

Nearly a twelvemonth after, when the youthful heir had been publicly, at Notre-Dame, christened Henri Dieudonné (the first name expressing political hopes, the second the sentiment of religious gratitude for Heaven's gift), M. Merle, the dramatic writer, returned to Paris from an artistic ramble in Brittany, bringing with him many sketches of places he had visited, and among them several of Chambord, its château and surrounding scenery. This being reported to the Duchesse de Berry, she expressed a wish to see them, and M.

Merle accordingly brought his drawings for her inspection.

A year and a half had elapsed since the assassination of her husband. Depression of spirit could not last nearly so long in one of so vivacious a temperament; but romantic feeling still survived. "She wore," says M. Merle, "deep mourning, and her apartment was entirely draped with black. The two daughters the duke bequeathed to her were with her, as well as her own two children. She was teaching music to the former, and the whole party seemed lively enough, but all were in black."

M. Merle's drawings (they appear to have been water-colours) being placed before her on a music-stand, after looking long and attentively at them she said, "Are these really faithful representations of Chambord, taken on the spot?"

He assured her that they were. "Then I have been greatly deceived," she exclaimed. "I was told it was a mere heap of ruins."

Entering at once with deep interest into all that M. Merle could tell her from his notes concerning Chambord, and from information gathered from the people of the neighbourhood, she became quite enthusiastic. Some tracings he showed her of the wonderful sculpture of the oratory charmed her; and it was a happy coincidence, she thought, that the oratory itself had been placed under the protection of the archangel Michael. With the drawings of the interior and exterior of the château before her, she desired M. Merle to point out and explain as much of them as was possible. Louis XIV., he told her, had held his court at Chambord, and there for the first time Molière's "*Bourgeois Gentilhomme*" was performed, and did not then meet with the *Grand Monarque's* approval.

In one wing of the spacious edifice King Stanislaus had lived; and there Maréchal Saxe had died. Many of the earlier events connected with the château were also mentioned, and, so far as was known, her inquiries answered respecting the artists who had assisted Primatrice in its decoration.

"I have been greatly deceived," she exclaimed again. "Chambord is a great historical monument."

"The inhabitants would be greatly delighted to receive a visit from the mother of their prince," said M. Merle.

"I will go there," she answered. "If you return, you can tell them so; and that it will be for me, as well as for them, *un jour de fête*."

The prejudices of Louis XVIII. and the Comte d'Artois, though arising from different motives, were alike difficult to overcome, and Madame's visit had consequently to be long deferred. Charles, as king, had at last been convinced that Chambord was something more than a heap of ruins; but, until M. de Martignac took office, no favourable opportunity had occurred for Madame's visit.

On the 16th of June, 1828, Madame, accompanied by the Duchesse de Reggio, and attended by a very small suite, set out in high spirits for Chambord. She stopped two nights on the road at the châteaux of the Duc de Bellune and the Duc d'Avarey, and courageously crossed the Loire in a storm. All Chambord assembled in holiday attire to greet her. That she might converse with as many as possible of the people, she went on foot as far as Nonant. Flowers were strewed in the pathway before her, and bouquets innumerable presented; the villagers, with whom as she walked along she smilingly chatted, forming her escort. They would not hear of guards; the people represented France, they said, Madame represented her son, and guards, both agreed, were not needed.

Of course she charmed all hearts, and was herself no less charmed with Chambord and its inhabitants. Her first view of the château, with its picturesque *façade*, its terraces and terraced Italian gardens, its domes and numerous turrets, — giving it in the distance the appearance of a city more than a palace, — drew forth many expressions of surprise and delight. M. de Calonne was there to receive her, to read an address of welcome, and to conduct her over the château. She visited it throughout, mounting to its very highest point to enjoy the magnificent perspective, and inscribing her name, "Marie Caroline," on the wall of the double spiral staircase — said to be the first of the kind constructed, and remarkable also for the quaint carvings enriching it.

The park was then in full beauty, and its long, broad avenues of wide-spreading trees were fully clad with the tender green foliage of early summer. Grassy banks sloped gently down to the Loire, which passes through the lower part of the park — its blue waters, but a day or two before so turbulent, then with soft murmurs gliding peacefully onward.

Having gained golden opinions from all sorts of people, Madame, charmed with the hearty spontaneousness of the reception she had met with, left Chambord, with a promise to repeat her visit at no distant day, and to bring her son with her.

From one triumph she proceeded to another. La Vendée welcomed her with enthusiasm, it being understood that it was not a state visit or in any way connected with official objects. Extraordinary preparations were made to receive her at Blaye, where so different a scene was by and by to be enacted. Church bells were ringing, volleys of musketry continually firing, such being the custom of La Vendée, and dancing was going on in the open air — an amusement in which Madame joined as gleefully as the rest.

She made several long excursions, and went mountaineering on foot. The roads being all but impassable for carriages, she rode one of the sturdy little ponies of La Vendée; for she "was determined," she said, "to traverse the bad roads of the country like a Vendéenne." Passing from one excitement to another, she concluded her adventurous expedition by visiting the château of Pau, to see the room where Henri IV. was born, who, as she flattered herself, was to live again — with perhaps a vice or two the less, and a virtue or two the more — in the God-given Henri V.

On the 1st of October, Madame arrived in Paris, greatly elated, and pardonably so, with the successful result of her journey. She attributed to royalist sentiments what was wholly due to her personal popularity and the evanescent joyousness of feeling during a continual round of provincial gaieties.

But it was strange that Charles — also returned — should have made the mistake of ascribing to the enthusiasm of popular favour those demonstrations he knew to have been officially arranged and prepared for at every stage of his journey. It appears, however, that he did persuade himself that the army and the people of the provinces were devoted to him — "that he was venerated even as the saintly Louis IX.; was popular as Henri IV.; powerful as Louis XIV.; that he had but to persevere in *his system*, and the clouds which seemed to have been gathering round his dynasty would prove to be only mists that the first favourable wind would disperse."

CHAPTER XVII.

The Annual Visit to Dieppe. — Courtier and *Fiancé*. — Concession to the People. — Astonishing the Chambers. — Madame's Costume Balls. — *La Mode* Suppressed. — "*La Muette de Portici*." — Advancing without Walking. — Home Occupations. — Shopping in Paris. — Opposed on All Sides. — A Terrible Blow. — "*Le Mouton Enragé*." — Radiant with Joy. — A Careful Guardian.

MADAME had been absent nearly four months from her family, who were staying at Rosny, but with whom she still purposed, though later than usual, to make the annual visit to Dieppe. For Dieppe had now its fashionable season; but, lacking the inspiring presence of Madame, it had been this year as gloomy as a season without sunshine.

She was accompanied, as on former occasions, by the Duc d'Orléans's eldest son, the Duc de Chartres. Of her numerous cousins d'Orléans the young duke was considered chief favourite; and his very humbly submissive manners and obsequious behaviour towards her were the subject of general remark, even amongst those who themselves were well disposed to cringe and fawn in the august presence of royalty. Many of his *bon bourgeois* father's partisans were confounded at seeing this youth of eighteen, this scion of a liberal and patriotic house, brought up to rough it with youthful fellow citizens at the Henri Quatre College, play the finished courtier so outrageously as to outdo and put to the blush not a few old stagers of "right divine" views.

But it was possible, or rather very probable, that, in so well-ordered a family as that of Louis Philippe d'Orléans, the model husband and father would supplement his son's public school training by a course of home lessons in worldly wisdom and virtue. Then, the young duke was the affianced husband of Mademoiselle de France, a lively, intelligent child, now eight years old. There remained still just a chance that marriage would eventually follow their betrothal; for Louis Philippe's hopes, now raised, now depressed, had latterly sunk lower than at any time since Charles began his unfortunate reign.

The throne of France was doubtless in jeopardy; yet it depended on the monarch to firmly establish or overthrow it. Since his return to St. Cloud, deputations had arrived in Paris from several departments to thank him for the dismissal of his former detested ministry and the nomination of a liberal one. He had recently held a camp at St. Omer, and although the enthusiasm was officially ordered, yet no seditious cries were raised, and the same may be said of the demonstrations that so pleased him during his tour with M. de Martignac.

As he was almost childishly delighted with any outburst expressive of popular favour, he had now the opportunity offered him of gaining the applause of the nation, by justifying those hopes which the new political arrangements naturally gave rise to. Charles, dissembling his real intentions, seemed actually about to do so. Yielding — Madame la Dauphine being still absent — to the strongly expressed disapprobation of the people, both he and his son abstained this year from accompanying the procession of the Virgin, bareheaded and on foot, in celebration of Louis XIII.'s vow.

But to the general surprise, — and the Duc d'Orléans's chances seemed for a moment to tremble in the balance, — when in 1829 the Chambers assembled, Charles, surrounded by his new ministers, delivered a speech in which the language and sentiments of M. de Martignac were clearly recognised. Several measures, intended, as it seemed, to meet the views of the constitutional party, were also promised, the irrepressible satisfaction it occasioned on the liberal side resulting in loud cries of "*Vive le roi!*" The ultra-royalists displayed a like enthusiasm; while to the further amazement of the Chambers, Duc Jules de Polignac, who had crossed over from England apparently for the sole pleasure of witnessing this scene, followed up the king's speech by a long eulogy of the Charter. He in fact announced his constitutional conversion. On the morrow he was again on his way to his embassy, equivocally remarking, as he bade a smiling adieu to the Duchesse d'Escars — whose *salon* was famous for political intrigue — that the time had not yet quite arrived for his ministry.

It, however, was not far distant. Meanwhile, the Parisians, consoled for past disappointments by the expectation of a good time coming, entered heart and soul into the grand dispute between the Classicists and Romanticists. The quarrel was no less vehement than when the partisans of Rameau and Lulli contended for the preëminence of their respective favourite composer; or the later struggle, which was made almost an affair of state, between the admirers and patrons of the rival musicians, Gluck and Piccini.

"Rococo!" exclaimed the Romanticists when Racine was mentioned; "*Perruque, archi-perruque! à bas* the Greeks and the Romans! away with their chlamys and togas! and hurrah for the shoes *à la poulaine*,* the halbert, morion, brassart, and cuish!" It was then that Madame gave one of her most brilliant and successful costume balls — balls that were long in preparation; the costumes of the period represented being reproduced with scrupulous fidelity.

The ball in question personified the court of François II. The Duchesse de Berry appeared

---

* Pointed and turned up toes, resembling the *poulaine*, or prow of a ship.

as the young queen Mary Stuart; the Duc de Chartres as François. Around them were grouped the most prominent characters of the court of the old Louvre, and the ladies and gentlemen forming their household. Prince Metternich mentions this ball, and sends his wife a programme of the quadrilles; remarking that he is surprised Madame should have chosen the *rôle* of Mary Stuart. When these balls took place it was Madame's custom to send 12,000 *francs* to be distributed among the poor. She derived so much enjoyment from these and other court gaieties that she deemed it incumbent on her to seek at the same time to mitigate sorrow, as, in some sort, a sanctification of her pleasures.

It was singular that, when recently so many restrictions were laid on the press, a small journal of fashion and gossip, *La Mode*,— in which the above-named costumes were given, and which, if not exactly edited by Madame, was under her control and immediate patronage,— was suppressed for infringing the law. In its chit-chat pages an allusion to political affairs had been noticed, and Madame's journal appeared no more. This vexed her greatly. "I have a mind," she said, "to turn *révolutionnaire.*"

The costume balls of the Tuileries had a favourable influence on stage costume. For although the reform initiated by Le Kain and Mdlle. Clairon, and carried so much further by Talma, Mdlle.

Duchenois, and other actors and actresses of note, had done much towards correcting the many glaring anomalies of former days, there was still, in historic costume, something left to desire. The two plays, "*Louis Onze*" and "*Henri Trois*," produced at about this time by M. Mély Janin, are said to have been given with greater fidelity of costume than any previously represented on the French stage. The fever of Classicism and Romanticism was then at its height.

"Strange period," remarks a French writer, "when the gravest of public interests and questions of literature and the arts were debated with equal ardour and acrimony."

In the musical world, and with the public generally, enthusiasm was raised to its highest pitch by Auber's opera, "*La Muette de Portici.*" Its popularity was so great, that when, soon after, Rossini produced his "*Guillaume Tell,*" it made little or no impression. Naturally this mortified the composer exceedingly. But the success it afterwards achieved amply atoned for the first indifferent reception. As Masaniello, Adolphe Nourrit is said to have far surpassed his father, and to have sung the charming music of this inspiring piece with wonderful *verve*. Mdlle. Taglioni, then in high repute, added not a little by her representation of the dumb girl to the attractions of this favourite opera.

Meanwhile, public affairs, in the opinion prevailing at the court, were not proceeding satisfactorily. Charles, while warning M. de Martignac that his system was opposed to his views, yet consented that it should be tried. So far it had brought him the applause of the people; and, as this was as sweet music to the royal ears, the ultra-royalist party took fright. He might find sailing with the wind pleasanter than the vigorous efforts to make head against it, and what evils might not result from such a system!

The Duc d'Orléans, too, — though for different reasons, — was not free from alarm. Yet, while keeping the chances of a revolution steadfastly in view, and neglecting no opportunity of secretly strengthening his political interests, he appeared to live so entirely in the bosom of his family, and to be so absorbed in making provision for their material welfare and augmenting his immense possessions, that no suspicion of other motives could attach to him. "He was advancing without walking (*Il avançait sans marcher*)," as Louis XVIII. was accustomed to say of him. The young duke, his son, became more than ever assiduous in his attentions to Madame. Prudent paternal counsels had shown him how the next turn of fortune's wheel might make him either a king's son or the son-in-law of Madame. It was expedient, then, while the father kept well in view the former chance, that the son should take care of the latter.

At Dieppe, at La Bagatelle, or the Tuileries, he

seemed to have taken upon himself the office of Madame's *chevalier d'honneur.* He also shared in her pursuits and amusements, though doubtless not wholly from calculation. There must have been a charm in one of so bright a temperament, so enthusiastic and intelligent; and her society may well have been attractive to a youth of nineteen. She was always so fully occupied, too; either taking lessons herself, teaching music and drawing to her children, or regulating the expenditure of her income. This she managed very methodically, paying everything monthly, and, unlike Bourbon royalty generally, keeping wholly free from debt.

Her income, from all sources, was 1,730,000 *francs*, between sixty and seventy thousand pounds a year; with which she contrived to be both charitable and munificent. A certain hour twice a week was devoted to the receiving of petitions, and giving audience to poor people desirous, for any particular object, of securing her interest or aid for themselves or others. From one of her remarks, it may be inferred that her ladies, or other persons about her, often found these audiences more wearisome than pleasant. "I am not at all tired, but very much pleased," she said, "to hear all these poor people tell me of their affairs. I find it far more interesting than the novels that the ladies of the court pass their time in reading."

As he accompanied her when driving and walking in Paris, which was her custom daily when at the Tuileries, a glimmer of her popularity may have been reflected on the young Duc de Chartres. The entry of Madame into any shop, workroom, or artistic *atelier*, caused quite a flutter. What she bought or gave orders for was almost sure to be for a while the fashion, or much in request. She was sometimes petitioned to aid the waning fortunes of an establishment less in vogue than others, by allowing her carriage to draw up at the door, while she condescended to enter the house and inspect the goods. If she purchased, or only admired, forthwith the article so honoured was "*à la Duchesse de Berry*," or "*à la Madame*," and customers came to buy it.

Thus the mother of the Comte de Chambord sought to supply towards the court and all classes of society Madame la Dauphine's neglect of the requirements of her position. To revive a taste for *les belles lettres* and the arts was her constant aim, and while banishing from her *salon* the exaggerated restraints and stiffness of the old rigid court etiquette, she personally set an example of manners at once easy and polite, and of liveliness without too much mirth.

But what avails the popularity of Madame, when that of the king, which for a brief space promised to be again in the ascendant, has once more fallen to zero? M. de Martignac and his colleagues have resigned, finding themselves opposed on all sides, and the king secretly caballing against them.

The ultramontane party had cried aloud against "the abomination of desolation, and the desecration of the sanctuary," when MM. Guizot, Villemain, and Victor Cousin were restored by M. de Martignac to their professorial chairs. The true faith was declared to be in mourning. Worse still, under pressure from M. de Portalis, the king had consented, though greatly against the grain, to inquiry being made into the nature of the instruction given in the secondary ecclesiastical schools.

As soon as this reached the ears of Madame la Dauphine, "she hastened to Paris to recall the king to his senses." The act he had sanctioned was, as it were, a blow aimed at her efforts to stimulate and support the reverend fathers of the Congregationist propaganda. There was no difficulty in convincing him of the sinfulness of this act; but, happily, it served to open the way to the speedy dissolution of the uncongenial ministry. He withdrew his consent. The ministry resigned, and Charles again breathed freely.

When M. de Martignac and his colleagues presented themselves officially to take leave of their gracious sovereign, he replied to their respectful address in the language of disdain. They had shown no respect to "his system;" and he intended to plunge a moral dagger into their hearts when he let them know, individually and collectively, that he was glad to get rid of them.* Duc Jules de Polignac was recalled from his embassy to form an absolutist ministry, and royalist fanatics sang a song of victory.

The *Figaro* announced next morning that "the celebrated Dr. Roux had been summoned to perform an operation for cataract on the eyes of a very great personage." This announcement cost the editor six months' imprisonment. It, however, did not deter the author of the play, "*Jeanne, la folle*," from publishing in the journal *L'Album* a cutting satire on Charles X., entitled "*Le mouton enragé.*" The author was a young man named Fontan, said to have been not more than twenty years of age. Compelled to leave Paris, he fled with his unfinished play to Poissy, in the neighbourhood of Versailles.

There he was arrested, and was condemned to five years' imprisonment in the loathsome gaol of Poissy, and a further five years of deprivation of civil rights, besides a fine of 10,000 *francs*. It was thought that if he would sign a paper, to be presented to the king, expressive of his regret, that, his youth being taken into consideration, his sentence might be remitted, or the term of impris-

---

* One *souvenir* remained of the Martignac ministry, and was not interfered with — the popular creation of *sergents de ville*, due to M. Bellegarde, Minister of Police.

onment shortened. Jules Janin and Frédéric Soulié, much interested in Fontan, prepared the document, and pressed him to sign it. He positively refused, and would acknowledge no fault. He was a Breton, self-willed, and strong in his political antipathy. The July days released him. His play, then finished, was produced, and greeted with unbounded enthusiasm, Mademoiselle Georges playing the heroine, and Ligier the hero.*

Several other arrests and imprisonments for offences of this kind took place at the same time. But at length, on the 9th of August, the *Moniteur* announced that the able Duc Jules had formed his ministry. In the words of a contemporary, "Charles and the Duchesse d'Angoulême were radiant with joy." She drove about Paris, a defiant smile on her countenance when saluted by "*À bas Polignac!*" and "*À bas les Jésuites!*" Charles was unusually elated, and went out hunting every day, so happy was he in the belief that he was now truly King of France by the grace of God, and his crown in the safe-keeping of a royalist and absolutist ministry.

The situation in some respects resembled that of 1789, when the queen and her Polignac coterie urged Louis XVI. to adopt coercive measures to put down the revolutionary movement. Now, the daughter of that ill-fated queen, and the son of her intimate friend, like the blind leading the

* Théodore Muret.

blind, were guiding the weak-minded Charles to his own ruin — ruin involving the loss of that crown which Louis XVIII. on his death-bed bade him be careful to guard for his grandson — *Que Charles Dix ménage bien la couronne de cet enfant.*

CHAPTER XVIII.

Seeking Repose. — Sinister Forebodings. — Political Tours. — A Sad Disappointment. — Patiently Biding His Time. — A Very Gay Season. — Incendiary Fires. — A Fearful Example. — Reliques of Saint Vincent de Paul. — Absolving the King. — Ministers in Council. — Torturing the Sealing-wax. — The Sentiment for Glory. — Mortified Exceedingly. — A Dreary State of Things. — Preparing for Royal Guests.

M DE CHÂTEAUBRIAND is in the Pyrenees at the baths of Cauterets, seeking repose after the fatigues and vexations of politics and diplomacy. Daily he writes to Madame Récamier of his aches and pains, his many expenses, his scanty income, his overwhelming *ennui*. Sometimes he fancies he is dying; then he is miserably conscious of growing old — a very distressing communication to make to his fair friend, who liked that unpleasant process no better than he. Suddenly, however, his whims and fancies are dispelled. The news reaches him that the Martignac ministry has given place to a purely absolutist one, and that the incapable Jules de Polignac presides in the Cabinet. Without a moment's avoidable delay, he sets out for Paris, and requests, on his arrival, an audience of the king. Very different motives have been

assigned for this act, by those who believed in him and those who did not. His object, however, was stated to be an earnest desire to warn Charles that he stood on the brink of an abyss, and to implore him to retire, ere dragged to destruction by his obstinate and short-sighted advisers. But Charles had never sought his counsels, and now, holding him in the utmost antipathy, he refuses to see him.

In the *Journal des Débats*, the organ of the viscount's party, an article attacking Polignac and his colleagues forthwith appears. Sinister, indeed, are its forebodings concerning the destiny of the Bourbon monarchy, and the conclusion is "Unhappy France! unfortunate king!" M. Bertin-ainé, the editor of the journal, is cited to appear before the Correctional Court, and is sentenced to six months' imprisonment, and fined 500 *francs*. Articles, more or less vehemently denouncing the government and expressive of the danger to which the institutions of the country are exposed, appear in several other journals, and their editors are similarly treated.

Numerous resignations are sent in from functionaries in various departments of the state, and all are joyfully accepted. M. de Châteaubriand did not resign until the following spring. He was under the delusion that he could yet serve royalty. But the days of the Polignac ministry glided on —no *coup-d'état* had yet signalised it; and, his leave of absence being expired, he gave up the embassy, and resumed the pen to make war on the ministry.

The people and government were indeed preparing for a struggle *à outrance*. Général La Fayette was making a political tour through the provinces, to ascertain the feeling of the people; for he and the Republican party were for rising in arms in the name of the Charter and the public rights and liberties. Everywhere a popular ovation awaited the "champion of liberty," — the hearty spontaneousness of his reception contrasting remarkably with the official ones prepared for the Duc d'Angoulême, who was on a provincial tour at the same time, in the vain quest of popularity.

The elderly dauphin caused much surprise to many of the simple country folk, some of whom journeyed a league or two to look at him, and felt themselves poorly rewarded for their pains. The dauphin was associated in their minds with the idea of youth, and they had expected to see a child, perhaps the little Duc de Bordeaux, or at least a very young man. A fat, elderly graybeard of between fifty and sixty was in their eyes but a sorry specimen of a dauphin; so turning away in disgust, many avenged themselves on him for the disappointment he had caused by shouting in his ears, in spite of the police who were on the *qui vive*, "*Vive la liberté! Vive La Fayette!*"

All knew La Fayette — at least by name, which seemed to have been known and venerated from father to son for three or four generations, so early had the veteran general begun his career in the cause of liberty and independence. At the period in question he was in his seventy-second or seventy-third year, and as ardent as ever for freedom and the rights of the people; therefore "*Vive la liberté! Vive La Fayette!*" greeted him wherever he went; his popularity having, perhaps, never been greater than at this time.

The wary Duc d'Orléans feared to put himself in rivalry with it. Silent and motionless, holding himself aloof from the Tuileries, and carefully avoiding — as counselled by the wily old Prince Talleyrand — all contact with the ministers, he was biding his time.

But he was quite in readiness for whatever might happen when that revolution, now awaiting its hour and its day, should take place. "The interval," as a French writer (Paul Lacroix) remarks, "he was turning to good account, managing his enormous fortune and extensive possessions with as much diligence and ability as though he had appointed himself his own steward."

The Chambers were not opened, as usual, at the close of the year; and at the new year's receptions the king, in a haughty tone, openly reproached the judges of the royal courts of justice, he being again greatly dissatisfied with their lenient decrees concerning the press prosecutions.

"Magistrates," he said, "I would have you bear more constantly in mind the importance of your duties, and that for the real welfare of my subjects you strive to render yourselves more worthy of the marks of confidence you have received from your king." They bowed and passed on, to pay their respects to that gracious royal lady, Madame la Dauphine, who frowned them her usual reply.

During the fifteen years of the Restoration no winter had been so wholly devoted to court gaieties as that of 1829-30. It would almost seem that the opening of the Chambers was deferred until the middle of March, to prevent the annoyance of heated party discussions from interrupting the unwonted round of festivities in which this revived court of Louis XIV. had determined to indulge. Never had there been such brilliant balls, such splendid *toilettes*, so dazzling a display of diamonds and other precious gems; or, since the Louis Quinze days — which for picturesqueness of *toilette* had the preference to the grand-wig period of the *Grand Monarque* — had the gentlemen worn so much embroidery, satin, jewelry, and lace. Again the stately *menuet de la cour* was introduced, and the somewhat less grave *gavotte* — Madame and the Duc de Chartres, say letters of that date, "figuring to great advantage in them." Masquerades, — another innovation at this pious court of **Charles Dix** and the dauphine, — concerts, and theatricals followed each other in quick succession.

Charles, with the Duchesse de Berry and his son, visited the Théâtre Français for the last time on the 5th of January. The reception he met with was as freezing as the weather appears to have been, and he cared not to encounter it again. The sombre attitude of the people, far more menacing than the noisy outbursts that sometimes occurred, caused no disquietude, however, to the king or his ministers. They regarded it as submissiveness, forced, perhaps, but still submissiveness, — the natural result of the vigorous acts of so strong and resolute a government.

But frightful distress prevailed in the provinces. The farmers and the peasantry were ruined and reduced to beggary by the incendiarism which raged unchecked throughout the country. The people accused the Jesuits of these fearful acts; they, in their turn, accused the liberals, whom they termed Jacobins, Bonapartists, and Protestants. The crops were fired, farm-buildings destroyed, the cattle often perishing in the flames; yet who were the perpetrators of these heinous deeds none could tell. Subscriptions were set on foot to relieve the distress of the sufferers from these terrible calamities. But so wide-spread was the misery that, although large sums were collected, the relief afforded was but partial.

Nevertheless, the festive ardour was not restrained in court circles — the Palais Royal vying with St. Cloud and the Tuileries in fêting its own particular set of adherents. But as, alas! all that's bright must fade, so this gay carnival came at last to an end, and the season of penitence, fasting, and prayer set in. After such a round of festivities, enjoyed with so much zest, it is to be feared that to some of the votaries of pleasure this sudden turn from gaiety to devotion must have proved irksome, weary work. It was, indeed, rumoured that a certain royal lady had not been able wholly to subdue the natural petulance of her character when gently, but firmly, reproved by the more sternly pious dauphine for the brevity of her private orisons. "The short time, she was told, spent in her oratory must both grieve and offend the truly devout; while to the less heavenly-minded it was a fearful example."

There was, however, an especial reason for this reproof. As the carnival of 1830 was distinguished beyond those preceding it by its unwonted joyousness, so the following Lenten season was to be rendered remarkable by a grand ecclesiastical spectacle of peculiar religious gravity. It had been for some time in preparation, and it was needful that those who were to assist at this solemnity should chasten their minds by longer and more frequent devotional exercises, more rigid fasting and mortifying penances.

It was a ceremony intended to awe the multitude, and — the system, as it was termed, of Charles X. being more religious than political — was destined to be the prelude to a royal ordinance reëstablishing the Jesuits in France. This was the first sure step, as MM. de Polignac, de Bourdonnaie, and de Bourmont told the king, — knowing it was what he had long wished to be told, — "towards finally closing the revolutionary gulf opened in 1789, after having cast into its seething depths the demoniacal Charter that had issued from it."

The *reliques* of one of the greatest patrons of Jesuitism, Saint Vincent de Paul, were to be borne in solemn procession through the streets of Paris, and with all the pomp of the olden time when the Church reigned supreme. The shrine, or *reliquaire*, was of massive silver, richly wrought and gilded. Its contents were a statuette in wax, a slip of wood, said to be a piece of the true cross, and some fragments of human bones, those of the saint, as asserted. But it was perfectly well known that the bones of Vincent de Paul had long years ago mingled with the dust of the earth, to which, nearly two centuries before, they had, with little ceremony or care for their preservation, been consigned.* The revival of ecclesiastical

* In those days, when the plague so often raged in the dirty,

pageants and ceremonies, so utterly unsuited to the age, was severely criticised, and vehemently protested against as bringing religion into contempt rather than exciting reverential feelings.

So strongly were these views expressed that it was feared some indignity might be offered to the king,— such was the irritation of popular feeling, — should he and his son persist in their intention of following the procession on foot. The archbishop, therefore, thought it prudent to absolve the king and the dauphin from the obligation they were under to pay this homage to the *reliques* of the old Jesuit priest. Consequently they joined the procession only as it entered the church. The presumption of the people in thus censuring the acts of their pious sovereign served, however, but to convince him that there must be no relaxation of either vigour or rigour on his part. That still yawning revolutionary gulf must be speedily stopped up, and, if possible, hermetically sealed. Yet he was graciously pleased, before adopting

---

crooked streets and lanes and alleys of old Paris, Vincent de Paul was a good friend to the sick and poor. He had rather an eccentric style of preaching, which, as he was accustomed mirthfully to say, brought the crowns out of the ladies' pockets. It was chiefly ladies who went to hear him during those periods devoted to piety after a course of excessive pleasure or depravity. He alarmed the consciences of the fair penitents, and when excitement was at its highest pitch, he himself went round with his bag. Those not provided with crowns, for very shame tore off earrings, rings, or other jewels, and threw them into the wily priest's *sac*.

extreme measures, to propose in council to seek to awaken enthusiasm by a concession to the national sentiment for glory.

Charles, during the Polignac ministry, held his Cabinet councils on Sundays and Wednesdays, the singular part of them being (as described by M. Nettement, the royalist author of "*L'Histoire de la Restauration*") that, on assembling, its members, including the king, sat down, mechanically as it seemed, to a sort of occupation, which each pursued persistently during the two or three hours the council lasted: Charles with scissors cut paper to pieces, often in very droll forms; the Duc d'Angoulême had always a military annual open before him, and backwards and forwards he turned the leaves, with pencil in hand, as if about to make notes.

The Duc de Polignac and M. de Montbel made, as if vying with each other, endless designs with their pens on the paper supplied for their use. M. de Chabrol — considered to be more attentive than the rest to any question under discussion — invariably, as he took his seat, took up the sealing-wax and a sort of bodkin for passing a string through the papers. As the discussion became warm or languid, so would the sealing-wax be more or less tortured by the bodkin; and when M. de Chabrol, delivering his own opinion with a little more than usual energy, would lean with greater force on the bodkin, the sealing-wax often resented it, and scattered itself in atoms about the room.

This gave a cheerful turn to proceedings so strangely conducted, and the Council enjoyed the relief of a hearty laugh. So drowsy was the atmosphere of the Cabinet, that, in spite of his best efforts to keep his eyes open in the presence of royalty, a minister would sometimes drop into an uneasy doze, and from a doze into snoring sleep. Charles would not have him disturbed; but when, in great confusion, the sleeper opened his eyes to find that tired nature had triumphed over etiquette, the king handed him his snuff-box, and again king and councillors enjoyed a laugh.

Louis XVIII. was by no means so tolerant in his council-chamber. Affairs of state were conducted there in a different, though not more businesslike fashion. His fondness for quoting Latin, and the high idea he had of his talents and attainments, made him require that attention should be wholly centred on himself. Charles is said to have shown some superiority in his views when diplomacy was the subject treated. But, like Louis XV., whom in some points of character he resembled, he did not enforce them, either from self-distrust or indolence.

Preparations were then making on an extensive scale for the despatch of a fleet to Algiers. When the king opened the Chambers in March he announced this in grandly sonorous Louis-Quatorze style. "I am about," he said, "to take signal vengeance on the Algerian corsair chief, who has had the temerity to insult my people, my kingdom, my banner, my throne." This was the expedition whose announcement was to send a thrill of enthusiasm through France, and to be received by the Chambers with exuberant joy.

Some indications of disapproval were, however, the only marks of attention the proposed hostile enterprise met with. The nation was too intently occupied with its own internal affairs to take an interest in this question, further than to condemn the course pursued by the government towards the dey. His ports had been blockaded for the past two years, which, with the great provocation he had received for his indignant outburst against France, and the blow with his fan to her consul, was thought to be punishment far exceeding the heinousness of his offence. Consequently, no sympathy whatever was felt with the objects of the expedition.

The tone of the address mortified the king exceedingly. It was prepared chiefly as suggested by M. de Châteaubriand, and was a complete protest against the ministry; while every word dealt a blow at what was termed the royal prerogative. Two hundred and twenty-one deputies gave it their votes; and M. Guizot, who edited the address, appears at the opening of this session to have forsaken the royalist benches as a deputy, and to have taken his seat amongst extreme liberals. On the same occasion, the eminent barrister, M. Berryer, made his oratorical *début* in defence of the monarchy by right divine.

On the 19th of March, the day following the presentation of the address, which was received by the king in the most severe and chilling manner, the rebellious Chambers were dissolved, and the opening of the session prorogued by royal ordinance until the 1st of September, the new elections being appointed to take place on the 29th of June and 3d of July.

Meanwhile, another brief period of festivity was shortly to vary and, to many persons, no doubt, enliven the then dreary state of things, both political and social. For frightful poverty prevailed, the result of the incendiary fires which still continued to devastate the departments. Whole families were begging from door to door, driven to desperation by the great calamities that had fallen on them. When their needs were not supplied, they threatened to fire the premises of those from whom they implored charity, that they, too, might share the misery they either refused, or were unable, to relieve.

These mysterious nightly recurring conflagrations were now attributed to the emissaries of the Duc d'Orléans. But, however ungenerous and treacherous his conduct may have been towards the elder Bourbons, one cannot for a moment credit him with deliberately sanctioning deeds so revolting to humanity, even while remembering that he was the son of Louis Philippe Joseph Égalité. At this particular juncture the Palais Royal was preparing to worthily entertain Neapolitan relatives. The Tuileries was similarly occupied ; and Madame la Duchesse de Berry was *en route* to meet and welcome her parents on their journey from Madrid to Paris.

CHAPTER XIX.

A High-handed Despot. — Royal Visit to the Opera. — An Exciting Opera. — The Tuileries Eclipsed. — An Unmindful Host. — Placed in a Dilemma. — A Lovely Night. — Seized with Sudden Frenzy. — Dancing on a Volcano. — " They Shall Suffer for It, the Rebels! " — Nothing New Intended. — Playing a Winning Game. — " God Preserve France and the King! "

THE coming guest of France, Francis I. of Naples, was a man after Charles's own heart — a very high-handed despot. It was his disbandment of the national guard of his kingdom that was said to have given the Marquis de Rivière the idea of suggesting a similar course to Charles, and to have mainly influenced him to adopt it. Francis and his queen were returning from Spain, whither they had conducted their daughter, the Princesse Marie Christine, to marry her to Ferdinand VII.

They arrived in Paris in May, and were royally received at the Tuileries, and entertained with exceeding splendour. All the forms and etiquette that had prevailed in court ceremonies in the grand reign of the *Grand Monarque* were religiously observed, even to the smallest punctilio. Unhappily, the Marquis de Dreux-Brézé, whose heart would have so rejoiced, whose spirit would have leaped with gladness, at this revival of the bygone glories of France, had recently, alas! been gathered to his fathers. His office, however, was hereditary. There was, therefore, this consolation for his family, that the honour snatched by the hand of death from the head of les Dreux-Brézé descended on a scion of that noble house.

The royal visit to the opera was a brilliant affair — state carriages, numerous cavalry escort, and double line of troops in the streets: partly a precautionary measure. For, although the Parisians generally were amused during this visit by the display of old-world pomp and parade, there were ardent spirits in the capital who, on very slight cause for excitement, might have turned this pompous revelry into a scene of bloodshed. The exterior of the Opera-house was brilliantly illuminated, and a vast crowd was attracted by it. The Minister of Police, Maugin, one of the most infamous that had ever held the office, had distributed an ample number of his staff in various disguises among the throngs of people. Any attempt, therefore, to raise a seditious cry was speedily repressed, and the offender, to his surprise, arrested by one of the crowd, one of his fellows, as he may have fancied, to whom, perhaps, he had unintentionally opened his mind on the state of things around him.

The opera selected for the amusement of Neapolitan royalty was the immensely popular "*Muette de Portici."* Scarcely an appropriate one, it would seem; the triumph of revolt could hardly please two sovereigns so determined to play the despot as Charles X. of France and Francis I. of Naples. Three months later, this exciting opera so powerfully spurred a Brussels audience to action that it led to the outbreak of the revolution that had for some time been imminent there.

It might, too, have reminded Charles — for he could not be wholly ignorant of it — that the most strenuous efforts were making throughout France to obtain a sweeping liberal majority in the new Chamber, in order to put down his ministry; and, if not exactly to overthrow him (for many would have spared him, had it been possible), at least to bring him to his senses. But with his absolutists, and his old friend Jules at the head of them, what should he fear? — so he thought.

It is to be hoped that the music of "*La Muette*" gave pleasure to the royal party, if the subject of the opera was less satisfactory. That another Masaniello should arise and expel the Bourbon dynasty from their Neapolitan throne was a thought not likely to cross the mind of Francis I. Disturb it, it need not — for when the second Masaniello, in the person of Garibaldi, accomplished that feat, Francis had for many years lain in his grave; he was then, indeed, on the very brink of it, as he died in 1830, shortly after returning to his kingdom.

Had Francis been the most powerful potentate on earth, greater efforts to do him honour could hardly have been made; and the Duc d'Orléans on this occasion eclipsed the Tuileries. Knowing, prudent man that he was, that there is a time for all things, a time to make money and a time to spend it, he opened wide his purse-strings, and showed that he also could play the host in kingly fashion, and on fitting occasions be lavish in expenditure. Especially he launched out to a great extent in preparations for the grand banquet, ball, and Neapolitan *fête* given to his brother-in-law on the 31st of May, exactly two months before the votes of the deputies placed him on the throne as King of the French.

Charles X. was present; also the Duc and Duchesse d'Angoulême, the latter greatly against her will; for she abhorred the Duc d'Orléans, and entered the Palais Royal with a shudder. The Duchesse de Berry, on the contrary, was delighted at so much homage being paid to her parents by her dear aunt and uncle. "He is so good," she said, "so pleased with our admiration of the fairy scene prepared for our surprise in the gardens." Charles, it appears, had not been aware how extensive were the improvements at the Palais Royal. The fine galleries erected in the place of the old wooden ones particularly struck him.

But, pleased as he was with the alterations and improvements in the palace and gardens, he was both surprised and shocked when he became conscious of how unmindful his cousin had been of his and their royal guests' feelings when issuing his invitations for this *fête*. The leading men of the liberal and constitutional "factions" — so Charles termed them — were assembled in full force that evening in the newly renovated splendid *salons* of the future king; and not only were they there *par tolérance*, but as distinguished guests, profanely elbowing, if the term be permitted, the pious and immaculate supporters of priestcraft and absolutism. It was almost a breach of the law of sacrilege; certainly it was a breach of good taste.

But how could the princely host have avoided it? Had he abstained from fêting his royal relatives, or have fêted them less lavishly, the parsimony with which he was credited would have been inconveniently conspicuous, considering his views. To have banished his political friends from this grand festive scene would have been an open renunciation of the tacitly conceded and accepted leadership of the liberal party, and the ruin of his hopes. Dark, threatening clouds, too, were then gathering so thickly around the throne, that a thoughtful family man like the Duc d'Orléans might well choose to set aside scruples likely to interfere with his, and his wife and children's, safety during the fury of the coming storm.

The pretender to his throne, one would have

thought, must have stood plainly revealed before Charles that evening. But he chose to shut his eyes to the painful fact; and a certain nobility of sentiment, which, notwithstanding his lamentable failure as a ruler, he possessed and the duke did not, forbade him to believe in his cousin's baseness; while, unhappily, it induced him to confide in the counsels of his old friend, the brainless Jules Polignac. Otherwise, it was not yet too late to thwart his *rusé*, treacherous relative's plans.

It was a lovely night that 31st of May, soft and warm, with a gentle breeze that just lightly stirred the foliage, and, the windows being widely opened, tempered the heat of the brilliantly lighted ballroom and perfumed its atmosphere with the fragrance of the sweet-smelling flowers that filled the balconies. Dancing was proceeding with great animation to the inspiring strains of two full bands which played alternately, when Charles, with one of the gentlemen in attendance upon him, stepped out on the balcony looking on the garden. He remarked on the beauty of the night, and expressed much pleasure that the breeze, light as it was, was favourable for his fleet, and, as he hoped, then wafting it, with full sails, towards Algeria.

A vast crowd had assembled in the gardens, and in the course of the evening there had been many *vivas* for the Duc d'Orléans. No particular attention was given to them; and if seditious cries had mingled with them, they were lost in the vigorous performance of the bands, the hum of conversation, and the sound of revelry generally. But some one or more among the crowd recognised the unfortunate king; and, as the fact of his presence became known, a fearful clamour arose. Amidst a chorus of hisses and denunciations of the hated ministry, the king withdrew. It was an embarrassing moment, even for the Duc d'Orléans. He felt, or feigned, regret, and would rather the unseemly *fracas* had not taken place.

The mob, on seeing the king standing before them, were seized with a sudden frenzy, and vociferated their "*À bas*" for the ministry individually and collectively with a sort of savage glee, mingling with them *vivas* no less turbulent for "*Liberté!*" "*La Charte!*" "*La Fayette!*" "*La République!*" "*Napoléon II.!*" "*La Presse!*" and "*Le Duc d'Orléans!*" but none for the king. The uproar was so great that a serious disturbance seemed inevitable; but, as often had happened during this agitated reign, the sudden and menacing outburst was as suddenly quelled. Justly or not, suspicion then, as at other times, rested on the emissaries of the Duc d'Orléans.

It was on the occasion of this famous *fête*, when the noisy demonstration in the gardens was at its height, that the Comte Salvandi, — who was in the suite of the King of Naples, — addressing his host, said: "Monseigneur, it is truly a real Neapolitan *fête* you have given us. We dance on a volcano."

There was some slight dissension in the royalist camp after the scene in the Palais Royal gardens. A disposition was evinced to advise Charles to abate his pretensions to a certain extent, at all events for a time. But, supported in his views by Polignac, he saw in what had occurred only a reason for more speedy action and yet more vigour. Polignac could not comprehend the situation, or the necessity of following the course prescribed by Louis XVIII. — "putting the ship of the state on another tack when she encountered a contrary wind." M. la Bourdonnaie, though a fierce ultra-royalist, then resigned, and Charles filled up his place by recalling the very unpopular M. Peyronnet, of the "deplorables," to his counsels.

Silently, but menacingly, the court awaited the result of the 29th of June and 3d of July, when the elections were to take place. The kingdom from one end to the other was agitated by the feverish excitement of this political contest. So preoccupied was the public mind with the determination to overthrow the ministry that, in the interval, the announcement of the complete victory over the dey, the taking of Algiers, the capture of treasure and spoils of war of immense value, did but momentarily divert attention from the efforts making to obtain a victory over the government. A day was given to illuminations and *Te Deums;* but the great festive celebration of the defeat of "the corsair chief" was reserved for the end of July.

The result of the elections was a strong opposition majority. The king, exasperated by this fresh instance of the nation's rebellious spirit, burst forth into violent expressions of anger, continually repeating his usual threat, "They shall suffer for it, the rebels!"

In secret council the king and his ministers determined to call to their aid a *coup-d'état*. On Saturday, the 24th of July, the ordinances were decided on; but they were kept secret, and not signed until the following day, for the sake of profitable speculation on the Bourse. The king was at St. Cloud, which he preferred as a residence to the Tuileries, where he saw and heard too much of his good people of Paris. He was in joyous spirits on Sunday, the 25th, and after his devotions went out hunting with the Duc d'Angoulême and Duc de Luxembourg, — a rather fatiguing pastime in that exceptionally hot summer. But the hunting season appears to have been all the year round in the France of the old *régime*.

There was not the slightest buzz in the household of any extraordinary measures in preparation; indeed, M. de Peyronnet declared in the course of the day, to a newly elected royalist deputy, — a M. Royer, who had been invited to dine at the household table, at which the Comtesse de Cossé presided, — that there was nothing new, and nothing new intended; the Chambers would assemble on the 3d of August. Even Duc Armand de Polignac, the brother of Duc Jules, had not been told that a thunderbolt was about to be launched on the party of resistance — a party composed of men of various shades of political sentiment, who had merged their differences, and under that name combined to resist the attempted infringement of their public rights.

But "walls have ears," says the proverb, and those of the royal council-chamber appear to have been no exception to this rule; for on the 24th Madame Bondy, the wife of a deputy, conveyed to the Duc d'Orléans full information respecting the ordinances. She further made known to him that his arrest had been proposed; and that friends bade him beware of the snares of St. Cloud, although the king had not favoured the proposal, refusing to doubt his cousin's loyalty.

The Duchesse d'Angoulême was at Vichy, but her return expected, Madame in her absence remaining at St. Cloud, to preside in the king's *salon*, and to be his partner at whist. He sat down to his rubber with a much less languid air than usual that eventful evening. He had done the deed. He had signed the ordinances, and already, in imagination, he saw the rebels brought to their knees. Madame remarked that they were playing a winning game, due to the unaccustomed spirit of her partner's play.

M. de Peyronnet was then on his way to Paris, the bearer of those valuable documents, in the natural and moral effect of which Charles had such entire confidence that he would not admit a doubt of their result being all he and his ministry desired. These ordinances reëstablished absolutism. At once and forever they put an end to the liberty of the press; dissolved the Chamber of Deputies before it had assembled; entirely changed the electoral law, and reconstructed the Council of State. They were delivered personally by M. de Peyronnet to the chief editor of the *Moniteur*, who, after looking them over, exclaimed: "May God preserve France and the king!" M. de Peyronnet smiled, and repeated the loyal words, as confident that his ordinances secured the safety of both, as the former that they fatally endangered it — that they were, in fact, the death-warrant of the monarchy.

So morally blind were both the king and his ministry to the real state of affairs, so satisfied that these ordinances would put down all resistance to their views, that the moment was thought opportune for the Algerian rejoicings.

Thanksgivings, *fêtes*, illuminations, theatrical performances, and other festive doings were announced on a grand scale. But, unhappily for Charles and his advisers, the people, — not altogether happily for themselves, — instead of celebrating the conquest of Algiers, substituted their victory of the July days.

CHAPTER XX.

A Thunderbolt. — The King Has Violated the Charter. — A Flag of Truce. — A Check to Court Gaiety. — " What News in Paris, Marshal ? " — Strong in His Divine Right. — " Down with the Traitor ! " — An Attempt to Buy Marmont. — Listeners in the Closet. — Whist and *Écarté* at St. Cloud. — Barricading in Paris. — Pleading Etiquette. — Unchanged and Unchangeable. — The Hôtel Laffitte. — War in Paris, Peace at St. Cloud. — The Battle Still Rages. — Cockade, Musket, and Uniform. — " *Drapeau Tricolore, Relève-toi*." — Injudicious Play. — " She Is the Friend of the People." — Ready to Set Out for Dieppe. — " Yesterday It Was possible." — France and the King.

WHEN the royal ordinances appeared in the *Moniteur* of the 26th of July they were received by the Parisian public, as Charles and his ministers expected and desired, with surprise and terror — a momentary sensation of stupor, such as a thunderbolt suddenly falling in their midst might create. But this feeling soon gave way to indignation, to amazement at the reckless audacity of the ministers and the exceeding blindness of the king. It was too clearly apparent to all that revolution was imminent. Speedily the sinister news spread throughout the city. Groups of people assembled in the streets. The greater part had not read the ordinances, but from those who had they learned that "the king had violated the Charter which secured to the nation its rights and liberties."

This sufficed for the mass of the people; but what the ordinances really aimed at was known only to the few, while still fewer took the trouble to read the long article appended to them in their justification. It set forth that the spirit if not the letter of the 14th article of the Charter fully justified the measure adopted by the king and his ministers. However, all were agreed that they were arbitrary measures, which must be resolutely resisted, though without exactly knowing at the moment what form resistance should take.

This occurred at an early hour; but as the morning advanced the usual busy life of the city was suspended, and shops recently opened again were closed; public affairs alone were thought of, and excitement increased as the streets became densely thronged. It seemed to be only in the streets that a question which concerned all classes of the community could be discussed, and all went into the streets to discuss it, some with the *Moniteur* in hand, to read aloud to the people. By and by all offices, workshops, and manufactories were closed, and clerks, workmen, and shopmen went forth to swell the throng.

The chiefs of the republican and Orléanist parties — Général de La Fayette and the wealthy banker Laffitte — being both absent from Paris, intelligence of what had occurred was instantly despatched to them. Not a moment did they delay to present themselves on the scene of action, nor did they spare either energy or money to turn to account the occasion that had arisen for the accomplishment of their respective long cherished views. But in the brief interval a flag of truce was held out to the king. The Chambers, legally advised, determined to assemble, and the journals were issued as usual. But a protest was signed, declaring that "the ordinances, being contrary to the terms of the Charter, could not be obligatory, either on the sacred and inviolable person of the king, or on the citizens whose rights they attacked." It was hoped — and by a few sincerely hoped — that on their thus separating him from his ministry Charles would open his eyes to the danger threatening his crown, and be induced to avail himself of the chance of saving it thus afforded him at the eleventh hour — that he would, in short, withdraw his ordinances and change his ministry, before menaced revolt became open revolution.

Though the crowd was for some time very orderly, yet a large body of men, suddenly freed from their daily occupations to lounge idly in the streets, soon found employment in mischief. Stones were thrown at the *réverbères*, but frequently struck the people. Some blows with the flat of the sabre were also given by a detachment of cavalry that had been rather fiercely assailed while merely passing, it appears, to their barracks. But as yet, though angry feelings were beginning to show themselves, no blood was shed.

At St. Cloud the officers of the guard and gentlemen-in-waiting received their first information of the ordinances from the *Moniteur*, brought in at the *déjeuner à la fourchette*, and a sort of vague fear of evil consequences checked the lively flow of conversation that usually enlivened the court breakfasts and dinners of the ladies and gentlemen of the household. The king, having heard mass, had already left St. Cloud for Rambouillet, Polignac being with him, and both in excellent spirits. The king, with his son, did not return until eleven at night.

As he alighted from his carriage, he asked carelessly of Maréchal Marmont, who was in attendance, if he had been to Paris, and what was the news there.

"Sire," he replied, "there is great alarm among the people, great consternation, and much despondency. There is also a heavy fall in the funds."

The king made no reply; but the dauphin, who followed, said: "How much have they fallen?"

"Four per cent., Monseigneur."

"Ah, well, they will soon go up again," he replied, and passed on.*

But Polignac, who had secretly been to Paris,

* *Mémoires du Maréchal Marmont.*

fearing that the protest of the journalists, together with secret attempts to shake the king's determination to enforce his ordinances, might induce him to waver in his resolve, returned forthwith to St. Cloud, and there awaited his majesty's arrival. He informed him that a little agitation had followed the publication of the ordinances, but no signs of an *émeute*. As for the forty-four journalists who had presumed to sign a protest against them, the king, on hearing of this act of *lèse-majesté*, at once ordered their arrest and the seizure of the printing-presses of the journals they were connected with. For the rest, he assured his able adviser that he and his colleagues had his fullest confidence; that he would do nothing, listen to nothing, but through their intervention; and should further and more stringent measures become necessary, he depended on them to take them.

Invested with these high powers, Duc Jules thought himself equal to putting down any opposition the ordinances might in the first moment of alarm encounter. The king on his part, strong in his divine right, and his trust in the doughty champions of Throne and Altar with whom he had surrounded himself, quietly sought his couch, unaware that the disquietude of his household had induced secret precautions to be taken to prevent a possible attack on him, perhaps by an assassin's hand.

On the 27th, after mass and private devotions, the king sent for Marmont. News had just been brought in that the police dared not arrest the journalists, and that the attempt to forcibly enter the printing-houses and put the seals of the police on the presses had resulted in terrible scenes of violence. The police had had very much the worst of the fray. But the seriousness of this encounter between the police and the people — which made matters more difficult for the ministry — was very much toned down to meet the royal ear.

"Marshal," said the king, when Marmont entered, "there seems to be some uneasiness among the people of Paris. I would have you go there and take the command of the first military division, calling first to consult with Prince Polignac. Quietude being restored, you can return here in the evening."

"Declare the capital in a state of siege," was Polignac's order; for the people were unpaving the streets for barricades, and sending showers of mud and stones on the *gendarmerie*, who replied with their muskets. But to select Marmont to quell this revolt was to make the worst choice that could possibly have been made. His very name exasperated the people, and, with intensest rage, they hailed him with "*À bas le traître!*" — the betrayer of the emperor and of France, the man who surrendered the capital to a foreign army. He, indeed, would gladly have declined the command now thrust on him, for he shared the popular feeling of disapprobation of both ordinances and ministry, and unwillingly acted in their defence.

Nevertheless, though declining to attempt the arrest of the chiefs of the liberal party, declaring that it was worse than useless, he ordered the troops to leave their barracks, and took steps to put down the riot that now reigned throughout the city. Cannon were pointed and seven regiments in position at 5 P.M. Several men were killed, and many thrown down and trampled upon in the Rue St. Honoré and the Rue Feydeau, where vast crowds had assembled. But the people having taken possession of the Hôtel de Ville, Général de La Fayette, who had arrived in the course of the day, at once made it his headquarters.

Laffitte was scattering money on all sides, and supplying provisions to the hungry troops, for whom no rations were provided, thus winning over partisans for the duke, then in *cachette*, waiting to be urged to come forward. A million, he thought, would buy Marmont's defection and put an end to the civil war then raging in the streets, the people attacking the soldiery with any sort of weapon they could find and fighting desperately. A deputation, consisting of MM. Casimir Périer, Laffitte, Général Sebastiani, and one or two others, waited

Casimir Périer.
Photo-etching after the painting by Hersent.

on Marmont, who was naturally considerably embarrassed when, with as much delicacy as such a subject could be treated, Laffitte exclaimed, on entering:

"Marshal, we come to entreat you to stay this sad sacrifice of life. Our fellow citizens implore you to let these terrible hostilities be put an end to."

But Marmont did not yield to the indirect offers of his tempter—the wealthy banker, then so lavish of his wealth, so ardent in his efforts to promote a cause for whose success, a few years afterwards, on his last appearance in the Chamber, and almost with his dying breath, he implored pardon from God and man for having contributed to.

The marshal spoke in extenuation of the severity of his attitude towards the people, of the positiveness of his orders; but promised to write to the king for less stringent ones, that the unnecessary effusion of blood might be stayed. He, however, was almost prevailed on to arrest Polignac.

But in a closet adjoining the apartment where Marmont had received the deputation, MM. de Polignac and de Peyronnet were concealed, listening to what passed between Marmont and these chiefs of the party of resistance. Finding that their own personal safety was in jeopardy, they changed their official coats for plain ones, left the Tuileries by a private door, and reached St. Cloud in a *fiacre*. "All was going on well," they assured the king. "Perseverance, and all would speedily be settled, the people seeing that obedience was the only course left to them." The king reminded these confident gentlemen that he had given his promise to remain firm. And, thus comforting and comforted, he sat calmly down to his nightly rubber.

The *salons* were opened that evening for a reception, and the *jeu du roi* began. The *écarté* tables were also set out, and playing and betting were going on apparently with as much spirit as usual. Yet many stood around whose preoccupied air seemed to denote that their thoughts were concerned with the events of the day far more than with the incidents of the card-table.

The 28th was still an anxious day of hopes and fears. It was difficult for the recognised chiefs of the movement to restrain the people, who were running up barricades eight or nine feet in height, cutting down trees, overturning vehicles, and with the aid of paving-stones, and furniture recklessly thrown from the windows, rapidly constructing formidable defences. The whole population was in arms, and every house, as if by magic, had become a fortress, every window a loophole, the firing from them defending the barricades. The attempt to destroy them had made matters worse, the people and the soldiery thus coming into collision; while two or three regiments, after refusing to fire on the insurgents, fraternised with them.

The streets of Paris might again be stained with the blood of its people, but it was evident that, without the immediate withdrawal of the ordinances, resistance so determined, so thoroughly organised, it was vain to attempt by force to overcome. Yet there was a pause. All was ready for action, and skirmishing was going on around; but, with more consideration than he really deserved, the infatuated monarch's reply to Marmont's urgent despatch, sent off at an early hour, was awaited by the deputies, who were assembled *en permanence*. Several of the more influential and honourable men among them still desired a reconciliation with the king, and clung to the hope that some concession on his part would open the way to it.

Far more time than necessary had elapsed for the return of the messenger. At last he came; the delay was explained. No one could be found to deliver the marshal's despatch. The Duc de Duras, replying to the entreaty of the bearer, pleaded etiquette, and said that he dared not intrude on his majesty unsummoned. He believed, too, that he was then in his oratory. For nearly two hours this despatch, on the reply to which a throne depended, lay on a table outside the anteroom leading to the king's apartment. At last M. Weyler de Novas, an officer of the household troop, having an appointment with the king, and knowing that the state of affairs was perilous, ventured to deliver the marshal's despatch, and even to tell his majesty that the agitation and excitement in Paris were so serious that they were likely to imperil his throne.

The king smiled. "Your attachment to me leads you to exaggerate the danger," he replied.

"Not so, Sire; the danger, unfortunately, is too real," was the rejoinder of this old royalist officer, whose attachment to his sovereign bade him speak frankly.

But Charles was not convinced. MM. de Polignac and de Peyronnet told him a different tale, and the former suggested the reply to Marmont's despatch; assuring the king that with vigour the *émeute* would be put down that night. One of Marmont's aides-de-camp was charged with the unwelcome duty of informing the deputies of the substance of the reply. Submit his orders to them in full he dared not. But they were given to understand that the king, at all risks, — even of the sacrifice of the capital, — was determined to maintain his ordinances, unmodified, unchanged, and unchangeable as the laws of the Medes and Persians; that Marmont was to hold his ground firmly, to assemble his troops on the Place du Carrousel and Place Louis Quinze, and keep the populace in check.

A burst of indignation rang through the Salle. "To arms! to arms!" they cried. "Unfurl the tricoloured banner! Appoint a provisional government!"

The Duchesse de Berry was with the king when the answer to Marmont's despatch was decided upon. Anxious and restless, she remained standing at a window of the château, where a mounted telescope was placed. Gazing continually through it she sought to ascertain something of what was taking place at Paris. Suddenly she utters an exclamation. She sees the *tricolor* hoisted above the towers of Notre-Dame.* The king is informed of this. It produces an angry exclamation, and the despatch of an officer to Marmont to repeat his orders of the morning, and to declare Paris in a state of siege.

But at that same moment steps were being taken to put the city in a more perfect state of defence, — men, women, and children labouring with extraordinary diligence, under the glowing sun of those July days, to raise up fresh barricades. The students of the École Polytechnique, and, in some instances, old engineer officers, both directed their operations and worked with them. As many as 6,000 of those defences are said to have been constructed before day dawned on the 29th, when every street had become a stronghold. On the evening of the 28th arms and ammunition were distributed at the hôtel Laffitte; provisions also, and linen for the use of the ambulances, with money amounting to many tens of thousands of *francs*.

* Nettement.

The maledictions of the whole city were heaped on the head of Marmont. His position was certainly a difficult and unenviable one. His troops were wavering between neutrality and defection — their sympathies being with the people. Everywhere, while giving orders for the slight defence, which was all he attempted, necessary for the Louvre and the Tuileries, already fortified to bear a regular siege, the epithet "infamous traitor" continually met his ear. He was very roughly handled by the mob, and when, surrounded by his officers, a false report was spread that he was dead, it was received with deafening shouts of exultation.

But what was passing at St. Cloud, while this terrible battle of Paris was being fought, while Frenchmen were slaying each other, and side by side with the dying and the dead lay many who had sunk from sheer exhaustion, burning thirst, and maddening excitement from long exposure to the almost tropical heat of that year?

To the sultry summer day has succeeded a brilliant night. A faint rosy glow still lingers in the western sky, which is traversed occasionally by flashes of pale summer lightning. Innumerable glittering stars light up the deep sapphire blue of the heavens, and soft zephyrs gently stir the draperies of the *grand salon* of the Château of St. Cloud, the windows of which are widely opened to admit the refreshing evening breeze. The royal whist and the *écarté* tables again form the evening's amusement. But light as is the breeze, it wafts distinctly to the ears of the card-players the rolling volleys of musketry and the dull distant roar of the cannon.

The dauphin is deeply absorbed in a game of chess with a general officer, who seems to be listening to those sounds of fearful strife with more attention than he gives to his royal adversary's hesitating moves. The king betrays no emotion, or rather he is stoically insensible; for he is not deaf. He hears those sounds that announce the execution of his orders, and knows that the battle still rages, though day has drawn in. Night it can hardly be called, so cloudless the sky, so clear the atmosphere; and what a contrast its serenely peaceful beauty presents to the mind to the sanguinary scenes and savage conflicts indicated by the sudden rushing sound of the fusillade and the long-drawn echoing mutterings following the discharge of cannon — cannon now mowing down by hundreds those presumptuous, rebellious Parisians who persist in asserting themselves as knowing better what is good for them than even a son of Saint Louis.

M. de Peyronnet is announced. The shades of evening have enabled him to make his way out of Paris unrecognised, luckily for himself. But he comes to keep up his sovereign's courage and firmness. "There is nothing more to fear. The lull now noticed in the firing is the end of the contest. The insurgents have given in;" so he smilingly reports.

A lurid glow, as of flames rising and sinking, is seen spreading over Paris. It is the burning of the barracks, which the people have taken by assault. Want of ammunition has, however, adjourned the continuance of the battle until the morrow's dawn. But the *tricolor* is unfurled, and with it have reappeared the cockade, musket, and uniform of the national guard. Again the citizen soldiers are reorganised, under Général de La Fayette, to whom all this turmoil and the cries echoing around him of " *Vive la république !* " are as the trumpet-call reawakening the energy of the old war-horse. With all the fervour of 1789, when he created and headed the national guard at the taking of the Bastille, the old general now sees their ranks re-formed under his command, and declares that it is with his full consent that his name is placed at the head of this insurrectionary movement. On unfurling the old banner, they said :

> " Drapeau tricolore,
> Viens, relève-toi :
> Je suis libre encore ! "

It was not M. de Peyronnet who disturbed his majesty's righteous spirit with these unpleasant particulars. They were narrated by Colonel Romarowsky, Marmont's aide-de-camp, at the court dinner, which the Comtesse de Cossé had invited him to join while waiting to see the king, to whom he had brought despatches and a confidential verbal communication from the marshal.

His majesty cared so little for the news the colonel brought him that for a considerable time he neither read the despatches nor summoned their bearer to his presence. The consequence was that the colonel, who was voraciously hungry, — no provision having been made for supplies to either officers or men, — got a good dinner, and, in reply to the questions with which he was overwhelmed, undeceived the household as to the state of things in Paris. He advised that the guard should be doubled at St. Cloud, which was done that night without consulting the king or the dauphin.

His majesty's countenance was anxiously watched that evening after the marshal's despatches had been read to him. Surely, it was thought, his eyes must now be opened to his danger. Yet his expressionless features showed no sign of inward agitation or restrained emotion. His play was not so strictly in rule as usual. In a moment of distraction he had probably forgotten how the game was proceeding. In general he played his cards readily, without hesitation; but on this occasion he appeared puzzled, doubtful, and after more than once changing his mind, he laid down the king of trumps — injudicious play, it appears. But Madame in her turn betrayed that her thoughts were further away from the card-table than even his majesty's by placing the ace of trumps on her partner's king,

An angry flush passed over Charles's face, but no remark whatever was made; and Madame, with a mind intent on other things, played on all unconscious of her crime. This little incident of the *jeu du roi* did not, however, pass quite unnoticed. It was mentioned on the morrow by more than one member of the household, and was recorded in at least one private letter, for the information of distant friends who took a deep interest in the events of that agitated period.

Madame had that day urged the king to allow her to go to Paris, and to take her son with her; but he absolutely forbade it. The word "abdication" had already been uttered, but silenced as soon as uttered. It was considered premature even by those who believed that eventually it must come to that. Madame fancied that with her popularity her appearance in Paris would have a calming influence on the people. She was probably in error; yet when, with a sort of savage glee, the *fleur-de-lys* was torn down and destroyed wherever met with, the arms of Madame placed over the doors of her tradespeople were respected. "Leave them, leave them," they cried; "she encouraged trade; she is the friend of the people."

And it was certainly entirely owing to the Duchesse de Berry that France in 1828 and 1829 had again a real court at the Tuileries; that the Théâtre Francais and the Opéra were more frequently attended, if not by royalty itself, — except in her own person, — yet by the court circle. Following her example, music was more generally cultivated, literature and the arts more liberally patronised. The king, who was every day becoming more of a devotee, and at last was consenting to grow old, cared not for the revelry and dancing in which Madame delighted. He could bear nothing more exciting than his rubber after his daily hunt.

The Duchesse d'Angoulême was alone intent on the revival of processions, fastings, penances, and enough and to spare of sermons; also the refurbishing of the faded reputation of certain miracle-working saints, — the restoration, in fact, of the court of Louis Quatorze in its decadence and days of hypocritical piety. But for the sprightly temperament of Madame la Duchesse de Berry the court epidemic of false piety and *ennui* would have killed the younger nobility.

On the 29th of July her travelling-carriages were ready, all preparations made, and she and her children waiting only the hourly expected arrival of the dauphine from her religious tour, to set off for their annual visit to Dieppe.

Doubtless the crown of France was then irrecoverably lost to Charles and his son. But a chance still remained open to the Duc de Bordeaux. If that morning, instead of going down to the gardens of St. Cloud with the king, — who chose to while away an hour or two in reviewing the young gentlemen of St. Cyr who came with their cannon to offer their services to his majesty, — the Duchesse de Berry had acted on the impulse that bade her present herself with her son before the assembled deputies, Henri V., perchance, might have reigned.

It was M. Laffitte who said so when, at an interview with the governor of the Tuileries, M. Glandevès, being urged by him to preserve the crown for the Duc de Bordeaux, who should be brought up, he said, in constitutional principles, he replied, "Yesterday (29th) the regency was possible; but," he added, "if Madame had led in her son with one hand, in the other she must have carried the *tricolor.*"* But would she have carried a flag that to the Bourbons was the symbol of every crime? It is doubtful, yet not impossible, that as that much-lauded heretic Henri IV. thought Paris worth a mass, so the Duchesse de Berry, had she known of this chance, might have thought that to preserve the crown for Henri V. it was worth while even to brandish the *tricolor*, really the symbol of loyalty and patriotism — the national colours crossing the Bourbon banner representing France and the king.

* C. H. Marchal, "*La famille d'Orléans.*"

CHAPTER XXI.

Seen with a Shudder. — Sack of the Louvre and Tuileries. — *"Mort aux Voleurs!"* — Beginning to Grow Serious. — The Great Warrior in a Rage. — " Ah, Marmont, *Embrassons-nous!*" — " No Concession; Go on, Persist!" — Again, " Too Late, Too Late." — The Republic or Napoleon II.? — " Not a Bourbon, but a Valois." — " A Crown, or a Passport." — Saving the City from Anarchy. — Pleading in Vain. — Paris after Its Triumph. — Citizens Who Died for Liberty. — A Stifling Embrace. — A Treacherous Memory. — A Delightful Piece of News. — Tears and Tenderness. — The Civic Coronation. — Not a *Vivat* for La Fayette?

NOT only on the towers of Notre-Dame is the *tricolor* now unfurled; it has displaced the white banner of the Bourbons, and floats in its stead over the clock pavilion of the Tuileries. If the anxiously watchful eyes of Madame have discovered this, it has been seen also with a shudder by most of the denizens of the Château of St. Cloud. They have heard, too, the deep booming sound of the single cannon pointed and fired by Marmont, who with his troops had been carried across the Tuileries gardens by the irresistible pressure of an overwhelming and advancing mob, causing a general breaking up of the ranks. Bareheaded, his uniform torn, and at some distance from his men, this cannon being close at hand, he fires it, sweeps back the crowd then entering the palace, re-forms his scattered forces under the great trees of the avenue, and retreats in the direction of St. Cloud, shouts of execration attending his departure.

The Louvre and the Tuileries are in the power of the people. The galleries and apartments swarm with a no less turbulent, savage, and fiendish herd than that which sacked the royal dwelling on the 10th of August, 1792. There is among them a considerable sprinkling of thieves, just liberated by the mob from the Conciergerie and other prisons. They break open the chests and presses, and abstract jewels of the value of two or three millions. The pictures and statuary of the old museum alone are safe from their depredations. The more fiendish and fanatical tear down the tapestry hangings, break the costly furniture and throw it out of the windows, and smash the magnificent porcelain vases, and the very beautiful clock and chimney ornaments. They strip the paper from the walls, open the drawers and wardrobes, tear and trample on the clothing, destroy the toilet accessories, and continue the work of destruction generally, accompanied with peals of laughter, oaths and imprecations, and snatches of ribald song.

In the confusion occasioned by this havoc and wanton mischief, some person, or persons, contrived to secrete and carry off, undetected, considerable sums of money in gold and notes. Several small cabinet pictures, rare gems, and other artistic objects were also stolen. No attempt was made to check the destruction of the most priceless *objets d'art;* but, as on former and more recent revolutionary movements, the sovereign people tolerated no theft. The cry of "*On vole ici,*" therefore, raised a shout of indignation. The penalty of death was pronounced on the offenders, and "*Mort aux voleurs!*" chalked in large letters on the walls.

Several men detected with stolen articles in their possession were instantly shot. The horrible idea occurred in one instance to place on the throne the bleeding body of one of them, a poor ragged wretch, in his blood-stained garments, the furious rabble, women as well as men, dancing frantically around him decked out with the orders and crosses belonging to the king and grand officers, and with the Herbault hats worn at the costume balls of the François I. period.

While this saturnalia was proceeding, Charles X.'s trusted ministers, having escaped from Paris in disguise, arrived, pale with alarm, at St. Cloud, to inform their sovereign that the *émeute* had now assumed a really serious aspect. They no longer counselled vigour and persistence, but were willing to resign, that, with a new ministry, the king might withdraw his ordinances, and restore order in the capital. On Charles also the idea began to dawn that matters were growing serious. For Marmont and his troops had reached the Château earlier than the ministers, and that scene of violence had occurred between him and the dauphin, in which the latter displayed a brutality of temper which the marshal, who had witnessed Napoleon's fierce explosions of dissatisfaction with his officers, had never seen equalled.

Fearing an attack on St. Cloud, Marmont had addressed his men in an order of the day, and, as they were famishing and urgently demanding bread, he had ordered 20,000 rations for them, the commissary officer replying that he had but 200 rolls, and that they were needed for the household.

The dauphin, rushing in, in a furious passion, exclaimed: "So you have dared to give an order of the day, traitor, without consulting me! You would betray us, then, as you did *that other!* Your sword!" he screeched.

But the marshal declined to render his sword, and in a violent scuffle to take it from him the dauphin's hands were cut. "*À moi! à moi!*" he raved; "seize this traitor!" and, the guard entering, Marmont was put under arrest.

But it was a very inopportune time for such a scene; and as soon as the king heard of it he sent the Duc de Luxembourg to restore the marshal's sword, and to bring him from the guard-room.

"You were wrong, marshal," he said, "to address the troops. Never talk politics to soldiers. My son has been rather too hasty; but go to him, acknowledge your error, and he will admit his."

"Never!" said the marshal. "Should a man of honour and sixteen years of faithful service be treated with such indignity?"

"Go to Monseigneur le Dauphin," repeated the king, rather more loftily, not liking the marshal's tone.

"Never!" reiterated the marshal. "This, then, is the reward of the sacrifices I have made, the recompense of my devotedness. My attachment to your majesty admits of no doubt; but your son, Sire, inspires me with horror, and henceforth there is a wall of brass between us."

Commands being useless, persuasion must now be tried. "*Mon cher maréchal*," said the king, "do not add to our misfortunes by separating yourself from us." Then rising from his seat and putting his arms round the marshal, he drew him towards the door. The Duc de Guiche and the guard of honour were in the adjoining room. "Duke," said the king, "conduct Maréchal Marmont to my son."

Still he rebels, exclaiming, " Heaven forbid that France should ever fall into the hands of such a man!"

However, the king's wishes and the circumstances of the moment at last prevail. The duke announces the marshal.

"Ah, Marmont," said the dauphin, advancing towards him. "*Embrassons-nous!* Let us forget the past. See how I am punished for it," showing his bandaged hands.

The marshal, rigid as the wall of brass that was henceforth to interpose between him and the dauphin, received without returning his not very hearty embrace. Expressing his regret that his sword, which was destined to defend France, should have been stained by the dauphin's blood, he made Monseigneur a haughty bow, and withdrew.*

Afterwards, being summoned to the council, the dauphin was vehement in opposing the withdrawal of the ordinances. "No concession, no concession; go on, persist," was his advice. But messengers were on their way, promising concession. "Well," he said, "the king is absolute master; but I am utterly opposed to any concession."

The old Duc de Bourbon-Condé had sent the Comte de Cholet that morning to express his deep sympathy with the king. But no one arrived on the part of the Duc d'Orléans, whose absence was attributed to fear of risking his popularity. He was, however, still affecting concealment in disguise at Raincy; and though quite willing to accept the crown, prudence and pusillanimity forbade him to step forward and take it. As to defending the rights of Charles X., whom he so

* *Mémoires du Maréchal Marmont.*

often and so recently had overwhelmed with his protestations of devotedness to him, he never for one moment entertained an idea so contrary to his views and his own and his family's interests.

The messengers sent by the king to announce the withdrawal of the ordinances were received at midnight by Général de La Fayette at the Hôtel de Ville. "Too late, too late," was the response. Royalist desertion had set in, and these gentlemen returned to their sovereign no more. A proclamation announcing that Charles X. had ceased to reign was being placarded on the walls of Paris, and was generally approved and applauded, when other negotiators arrived from St. Cloud with the names of the new ministry. The Duc de Mortemart, not very willingly, was named President of the Cabinet, and the names of Casimir Périer and one or two other of the more moderate liberals appeared in it.

The proclamation was accompanied by a royal ordinance annulling the objectionable ones. The king had thus done all that was demanded of him; but he had done it two days too late, and after Paris, by his order, had been put in a state of siege and some thousands of its citizens slain. La Fayette — surrounded by a number of ardent young men, whose enthusiasm he excited by his souvenirs of the glorious revolution of 1789 and of the American republic — reads the king's ordinance aloud. "What is the answer?" he inquires.

"*Pas de transaction!*" is the general response. "You hear," says La Fayette, addressing the bearer of the king's message; "this comes too late." Already the proposal is made to proclaim the republic; but the Bonapartists raise the cry of "*Vive Napoleon II.!*" and the magic name of the emperor creates so much enthusiasm that La Fayette and his republicans restrain their own cry in order to restrain the spread of the one that accords so ill with their separate views.

But there is nothing to fear from the hapless youth who once bore the name of Napoleon. Both mentally and physically weak, he is almost at that very moment lamenting that the Emperor Francis cannot entrust him with the command of an Austrian force to march to the aid of Charles X.

Then, for the first time, it is asserted, did M. Laffitte openly put forward the name of the Duc d'Orléans. The Orléanist faction, of which he was the indefatigable head, was but a small one. They had, however, worked vigorously for their prince. M. Thiers had published his panegyric in the *National*, of which he was chief editor, and from the lavish hand of M. Laffitte money had passed without stint into those of the enthusiasts who lauded the Duc d'Orléans in the streets, and diligently circulated among the groups gathered around the Hôtel de Ville the tale of the patriotic virtues of the prince who had embraced the cause of the people — "a prince who was not a Bourbon, but a Valois."

This announcement was due to the indiscreet zeal of a youthful supporter. Neither he nor his more sagacious partisans desired to invite the investigation of such a claim. It was his professed ultra-liberal opinions they were anxious to parade before the eyes of the people, as a counterbalance to the great popularity of Général de La Fayette. But it was high time that he should personally appear on the scene. M. Thiers was already in quest of him; while a few deputies and peers, hastily assembled at the Palais Bourbon, were content, without being warm supporters, to accept him as a *pis aller* by the title of lieutenant-general of the kingdom — in order to escape from the "veteran of liberty" and the republic. M. Odilon Barrot at the same time declared, though few agreed with him, that "the Duc d'Orléans was the best of republics." *

Assured by Laffitte — who, by virtue of his well-filled money-bags, had with impunity seized on the prerogatives of power, and reigned *pro tem.* in Paris — that the title offered would with brief delay be superseded by that which he coveted, the duke still affected hesitation. But one of the leading men who favoured his candidature, tired of this farce, settled the question by sending to him an ultimatum thus expressed: " A

* *Famille d'Orléans.*

crown, or a passport." Thus urged, he consented to tear himself from the peaceful joys of domestic bliss, to be offered up as a sacrifice to the public weal, and to come forward, at the call of his fellow citizens, "to save the capital from anarchy."

Overcome by strong emotion, he returned to Neuilly to seek consolation. But in the course of the night he stole into Paris in disguise, for a secret interview with the Duc de Mortemart at the Palais Royal.

"Duc de Mortemart," he said, "if you see the king before I do, tell him I was forcibly brought to Paris; but that I will be cut in pieces (*me ferai mettre en pièces*) rather than allow the crown to be placed on my head! The king, my master," he continued, "has done too much for me, to allow me ever to forget what I owe him."

M. de Mortemart reminded him of the manner in which his name was paraded about the city; the significant cries it elicited, and which certainly referred to him.

"No matter," he replied; "I will save the city from anarchy; but, I repeat, I will never be its king."

The interview ended, the duke returned to St. Cloud, the bearer, it is asserted, of a letter concealed in his cravat from the Duc d'Orléans to Charles X., full of protestations of his attachment to him and his family. The lieutenant-general on the following day issued his proclamation, congratulating the people on their resumption of the glorious colours which he himself had long worn; promising liberty, the reign of law and justice, and concluding with the words, "The Charter shall henceforth be a reality."

It was at this time that M. de Châteaubriand arrived in Paris to speak a last word for the monarch who had so lightly esteemed his counsels and disregarded his warnings. He was at Dieppe, recruiting his health, when, on the evening of the 27th, news of what was occurring in Paris was received there. Madame Récamier — who was now a widow, her husband having died in January at the Abbaye-aux-Bois, full of gaiety and admiration of his wife to the last — had also arrived with a party of friends for the season. A very gay one was anticipated, and *fêtes* were in preparation to welcome the Duchesse de Berry, whose advent was eagerly expected. The fashionable visitors soon fled; all were anxious about their property or their friends, and Dieppe was doomed to a season of solitude and gloom and the loss of its early patroness.

M. de Châteaubriand was recognised as, on the morning of the 30th, he was passing to the Luxembourg, where the peers were then assembling, and whither the people in their enthusiasm bore him in triumph. But this tribute of applause was paid to the distinguished writer rather than to the statesman. His long and very eloquent address to the peers, in which he appealed to the sentiments of loyalty and honour, awakened no corresponding echoes in the hearts of his hearers. He pleaded for the Duc de Bordeaux; but the king's and the Duc d'Angoulême's abdication had not then arrived, or possibly he might not have pleaded in vain, for the pretensions of the Duc d'Orléans met with very little disinterested support. His speech has been termed "the funeral oration of divine right."

Terrified at what might possibly happen to M. de Châteaubriand, and alarmed also for the safety of her niece, Madame Récamier left Dieppe on the 28th, accompanied by her maid, and escorted by M. Ballanche and M. Ampère. They arrived on the 30th, but their carriage was not allowed to enter the town. They were obliged to make their way as best they could on foot, from the end of the Faubourg St. Denis, — traversing near three miles of barricades, narrow, crooked, unpaved, muddy streets full of deep holes, and crowded with a ragged, turbulent set of excited women and men, who eyed them rather suspiciously. All the shops were closed, and apparently all the windows were broken.

Yet Paris, after its triumph, was calming down, and had that day buried the victims of the revolt. A deep, broad trench was dug in front of the Louvre, and filled with the bodies of the slain, with the exception of the *garde royale,* who were buried in the Champ de Mars. Quicklime was abundantly thrown over them, and earth then covered the ghastly spectacle from view. The burial service was impressively performed by the vicar of St. Germain-l'Auxerrois — the crowd surrounding this common grave of the "citizens who died for liberty" appearing to be deeply affected.

The Hôtel Dieu and hospitals generally were filled to overflowing with the wounded; intense heat and excitement, and the want of the necessary surgical appliances, occasioning much suffering and more deaths than the actual wounds.

On the 31st the Duc d'Orléans was proclaimed by the Chambers lieutenant-general of the kingdom. At the same time Général de La Fayette at the Hôtel de Ville was organising a commune, after the pattern of that of republican memory. Three times the new lieutenant-general wrote to him; but the old republican gave no heed to his letters. He determined then to go to him, on horseback and alone. But the deputies would not hear of this; and proposed themselves to form his *cortège*. He was also followed by a noisy crowd, in high spirits after the good eating and drinking they had enjoyed at M. Laffitte's hospitable table, free to all comers. The republicans who filled the Place de Grève frowned on the duke's joyous followers. But the emissaries of Laffitte were on the *qui vive* to communicate their enthusiasm to others, and succeeded in raising the cry of " *Vive le lieutenant-général !* "

As afterwards related to Prince Metternich by Général Belliard * (sent to Vienna to obtain the recognition of Louis Philippe by that court as king) the lieutenant-general, on dismounting, proceeded to La Fayette's council-chamber, and taking him by the arm, drew him, though rather unwillingly, towards the balcony, where, in the sight of the people, he embraced him. "This," he continued, "put an end to the republic." "This fact," said the prince, interrupting him, "is a proof that the Duc d'Orléans" (he abstained from calling him king) "has great confidence in himself. An embrace is but a slight thing to stifle a revolution. Do you think that you may in future attribute the same powerful effect to all his embraces? Do you ascribe to them the value of guarantees of the stability of his government?" The general laughed, and with this their discussion ended, the prince afterwards recording in his diary, "A revolution of the worst kind has triumphed."

On the 3d of August the lieutenant-general opened the legislative session. About 60 peers and 240 deputies were present; all were in undress. He was surrounded by his family. It created an effect; for "a fine family," sings the poet, "is a very fine thing," and doubtless it was

* *Metternich Mémoires.*

with no little pride of feeling that the lieutenant-general presented himself as the father of one. It seemed to give a greater promise of the stability of his government than even his embraces of La Fayette. He spoke of securing the power of the Charter forever — drew a fascinating picture of peace, prosperity, and liberty to be enjoyed by France in the future, and concluded by announcing the double abdication of Charles X. and his son, dated August the 1st, and received on the previous day from Rambouillet.

But he omitted to mention — probably he forgot it — that Charles had written that, "relying on his professions of sincere attachment, he confirmed his cousin d'Orléans in his title of lieutenant-general of the kingdom; that he charged him to proclaim his grandson as Henri V., and appointed him regent during his minority." The bearer of the letter was Général Foissac-Latour, who was deputed by the king to consult with the Duc d'Orléans respecting the arrangements which this change made necessary, and to return with the reply to Rambouillet, where he would await it. But the duke made frivolous excuses to avoid seeing him. The general therefore, having found a friend to deliver his letter into the hands of his future majesty, returned to the deposed one — whose deposition was already made known to him — without the expected reply.

It was deemed prudent to hasten the work of

making the king and remodelling the Charter. Therefore, with more haste than solemnity, "the Chambers, by 219 votes out of 252, declared Louis Philippe d'Orléans and his male descendants called to the throne by the title of King of the French." Laffitte communicated this delightful piece of news to the *rusé* son of Philippe Égalité. He had said a day or two before that "old republican instincts bade him reject a crown." Now he seizes his friend's hands in his irrepressible joy, and, with tears streaming down his face and voice broken by emotion, speechifies thus:

"Devoid of ambition, and accustomed to the tranquillity of private life in the bosom of my family, I cannot conceal from you the sentiments that now agitate my breast. One sentiment, however, dominates the rest — it is the love of my country."

His emotion, it appears, was shared by all present at this affecting scene at the Hôtel de Ville. They wept with their king — all save the old general, who was again dragged to the balcony, to be warmly, however unwillingly, embraced in the sight of the sovereign people, who fancied the republic was being proclaimed. This scene of tears and tenderness within the council-chamber was followed by one of wailing and gnashing of teeth without in the crowded corridor, where indignant republicans lamented the betrayal of their cause, as they considered, even by the champion of liberty himself.

On the 9th of August the new king's first royal *séance* was held. It was like the former ones, with this difference, — not a slight one, — that the *tricolor* flaunted itself everywhere, while the *fleur-de-lys* and the arms of France had hidden themselves out of sight altogether.

The Duc de Chartres (now d'Orléans) and the Duc de Nemours were with their father. The oath was taken; promises and protestations enough to satisfy the most exacting of his adherents were profusely made. At their conclusion the whole assembly rose; the king uncovered, and the hall of the Luxembourg rang with acclamations and cries of "*Vive le roi — le roi des Français! Vive Philippe VII. — Vive Philippe I.!*" The *Moniteur* had, however, proclaimed the new king by the title of Louis Philippe I., as the head of a new dynasty.

He was now king *de facto*; but he had not yet sat on the throne. The Chamber of Deputies had made their king, but thought it necessary to complete their work and make assurance doubly sure by a sort of civic coronation.

Seated on a stool before the vacant throne, with his sons on either side of him, he was presented with the insignia of royalty by four marshals of France, three of them formerly of the empire: the crown by the Duc de Tarente (Macdonald), the sceptre by the Duc de Reggio (Oudinot), the sword by the Duc de Trevise (Mortier), and the hand of justice by Maréchal Molitor. After this ceremony, the declaration of the 7th and the formula of the oath of the 9th were signed. Louis Philippe then rose from his seat, and "firmly and rapidly ascended the steps of the throne." Loud applause followed.

When it ceased, he said, assuming an air of majesty: "I am here to consecrate a great act. I feel profoundly the important duties it imposes on me. I have the consciousness that I shall fulfil them." Again great applause; and, the signal being given, a salvo of 300 guns informed Paris that the deputies had completed their work — they had given the French a king. Forth he comes in triumph, escorted by the national guard. Who of this frantic multitude shall have first the great honour of shaking hands with him? "*Vive le roi!*" Is there not a *vivat* for La Fayette? No — the republicans hold aloof; moody and disappointed by this sudden blow to their hopes, they seek the solitude of their secret societies to devise schemes for better success in, as they hope, the not-far-off future.

CHAPTER XXII.

Urging Charles Out of France. — The Cows of the Royal Dairy. — Madame in Male Attire. — An Embarrassing Position. — The Double Abdication. — Henri V. and Mademoiselle. — The Crown Jewels Demanded. — Unfavourably Received at Dijon. — Ready Cash for the King. — Sympathetic Sorrow. — Madame Soon Weary of Holyrood. — Migrating to Bohemia.

WHILE Charles X. remained in France, the King of the French did not feel securely seated on that throne which, by successful intrigue, he had usurped. It was necessary, therefore, to hasten his departure. Vessels were already chartered to be in waiting at Cherbourg to receive the fallen monarch and his family, and to conduct him whithersoever he would — Jersey and Guernsey, and Belgian ports, excepted. But the royal party moved on slowly, so numerous was the accompanying retinue, civil and military; so long the train of domestics, encumbered, too, with cases and packages, which the fifteen cooks and all other servants of the royal establishment thought it necessary to take with them. They had also a reserve of guns and ammunition, but scarcely any provisions.

They were, however, not yet thinking of exile,

only of moving from St. Cloud to Trianon, *en route* for Rambouillet. This was on the night of the 31st of July, the movement being suggested by the possibility of an attack on St. Cloud; but how matters were generally going on in Paris, the king appears to have informed himself as little as though it in no way concerned him. No orders were given for regulating the orderly progress of this numerous party, or providing for their or their horses' sustenance; or, if given, no one seems to have been charged to see them carried out. All was left to chance; so that when, after a night journey, because of the great heat of the weather, they arrived at Trianon, no supplies were forthcoming, and the only resource was to slaughter the cows of the royal dairy.

A little forage was found in the hunting establishment, and the *fourgons* were sent out that the guns with which they were filled might be thrown into the great lake of Versailles, and supplies of oats brought back. Kitchen utensils were sent from Versailles, and, after a slight breakfast of probably not very tender steaks, etc., from the freshly killed cows, but to which hunger may have added an appetising *sauce piquante*, the king and his retinue, now joined by the dauphin and his attendants, moved on towards Rambouillet.

The king was on horseback, the Duchesse de Berry in a carriage with her children. She still desired to proceed to Paris with her son; but

Charles would not consent. She wore male attire, and wished thus to present herself to the people and to the Chambers. Her dress consisted of "green cloth pantaloons and greatcoat; a black vest and boots, and a coloured silk handkerchief as a cravat;" some sort of hat, of course; but the *tout ensemble* does not give one the idea of a picturesque or becoming costume, and, thus attired, she would probably have excited more mirth than sympathy. Her motive for arraying herself in this manly fashion on her journey was to enable her the better, as she imagined, to defend her children should their safety be in any way menaced.

At ten in the evening the royal party and their retinue arrived at Rambouillet. No courier had been sent to announce them, and, as they were not expected, no preparations had been made to receive them. Other domestics from St. Cloud, with the officers and servants of the royal stables, had followed, adding to the already inconvenient quantity of packages by bringing with them everything connected with their several departments. Twelve state carriages, with all their trappings and appurtenances, and 130 horses now swelled the *cortège*; besides these, 100 saddle-horses, as well as those of the hunting establishment, and a number of vehicles for various uses.

Again, forage and provisions had not been thought of, and there was no money to buy them.

The king had sent from St. Cloud to the Tuileries for money; but none was forthcoming. The Duc de Luxembourg had with him 16,000 *francs* in notes, which he advanced to the famishing *garde du corps* to enable them to purchase supplies. But not a single note could they get changed for gold or silver, at any rate of discount, a report having been spread that the bank had been pillaged. In this dilemma means were in some way found of disposing of a part of the silver plate, and permission was given to shoot the game in the royal preserves.

The king's small army was now considerably diminished. Two whole regiments returned without orders to the garrison of Meaux, whence they had been summoned, declaring that neither they nor their horses could bear starvation any longer. There was a general dearth of ordinary necessaries, with an overwhelming abundance of superfluities. It was at Rambouillet that Charles learned from Général de Girardin, who came direct from Paris, the real state of affairs; and it was then he determined to abdicate, and prevailed on his son, who was by no means willing, to do the same.

The king always wore a very splendid uniform, more or less embroidered, according to the occasion, but invariably with heavy gold epaulets, surmounted by the crown in precious stones. Having signed and sent off the double abdication and the Duc d'Orléans's appointment as regent, he exchanged his uniform for a plain blue frock, and laid aside his orders and other insignia of royalty. Taking his grandson by the hand, and accompanied by two or three of the officers in waiting, he went down to the bivouac of the *garde du corps*, and there presented Henri V. to the listless and dissatisfied soldiers. The child was as much surprised as they were, and far less indifferent. The announcement inspired no enthusiasm in the weary, starving men; but they cried with eagerness, "*Du pain, Sire ! du pain !*" the little duke at the same time protesting against being made a king.

He was afterwards proclaimed, as it were, in the presence of the officers and other members of the household. For a day everything was done in his name, and the poor boy pestered and annoyed with homage and etiquette, doubly ridiculous under the circumstances. His vexation found expression in tears; and at last, escaping from the troublesome attentions of his courtiers, this unwilling king, who in his tenth year was also a colonel of the *garde royale* and wore the uniform, sought his sister. Gallantly offering his arm, " Let us go and play, *ma sœur*," he said, and gleefully they ran off together.

The Duchesse de Berry was rather unduly elated by the elevation, as it was termed, of her son to the throne. That he would eventually be called to sit on it she entertained not a doubt. But on the evening of that same day the news that it was occupied, at all events for the present, by a "King of the French," checked the exuberance of her feelings, and mortified the king by the announcement of his deposition. Four commissioners, among them M. Odilon Barrot, wearing tricoloured cockades, and their horses decked out with tricoloured ribands and streamers, arrived at Rambouillet, charged by Louis Philippe to see his *bon cousin* out of the kingdom. He was very sorry for what had happened; but, "to save France from anarchy," patriotic feelings had induced him to sacrifice the serene joys of domestic life for the weighty cares of a crown.

Charles was required to dismiss his troops, which he did not then do, and to deliver up such of the crown jewels as were in his possession. A King of the French set up by the Chamber of Deputies he would not recognise; but withdrew his abdication, resumed his brilliant uniform and the insignia of supreme power, his officers and *entourage* generally again paying him those honours with which for a few hours the Duc de Bordeaux had been tormented. The commissioners did not remain with the king; they went before to distribute cockades and scarfs and set up the *tricolor* in every town and village on the route to Cherbourg. Now and then they reappeared, when the country people, whom they had incited to offensive demonstrations, were too outrageously insulting. Then M. Odilon Barrot harangued the ignorant peasantry, and bade them be respectful towards royalty in misfortune.

The Duchesse d'Angoulême arrived at Rambouillet on the 1st of August. She had heard of the unfavourable effect of the ordinances at Dijon. Contrary to urgent advice, she appeared at the theatre, and was received with hisses, "*À bas les plumes!*" and many other unwelcome cries. A detachment of lancers escorted her out of the town. The rest of the journey was made by a circuitous route and in disguise. From Rambouillet the king and family then moved on to Dreux, and thence to Maintenon, where the Duc de Noailles received the king. He had prepared for his use the apartment and oratory that had once or twice been sanctified by the *Grand Monarque's* occupation of them, when extensive alterations were in progress in the château of Madame de Maintenon and its surrounding domain.

At last the weary journey was ended, and exiled royalty embarked. Marmont and a small escort accompanied the king to Cherbourg. There Charles presented the marshal with his sword, as a parting gift, and with a short letter in acknowledgment of his fidelity and devotedness to him and his family during the past sixteen years. Just when the vessels were about to weigh anchor, messengers from Louis Philippe arrived with some bags of specie to deliver to the king. They contained 600,000 *francs*, — 24,000*l*. — in gold, and had been brought in one of Napoleon's double-floored carriages for the conveyance of treasure to his armies.

From Maintenon this carriage had kept as closely as it well could in the rear of the royal *cortège;* but strict orders had been given to deliver the specie only after all the party had embarked. It appears that this vehicle attracted more attention at the inns than those in charge of it desired. It was not large, and apparently was lightly constructed; its great weight, therefore, occasioned much surprise and drew forth many remarks. Fortunately, however, the real cause of the surprising weight was not discovered.

Many persons had assembled to witness the embarkation and departure of the royal exiles. It is said to have been a very affecting scene; feelings of deep sympathy were exhibited, and, in many instances, much emotion. The two vessels that bore the deposed monarch and his family from the shores of France were accompanied by a French corvette and small store-ship. They were anxiously watched until fairly out of sight. The crowd then gradually dispersed, silent and saddened, and many women were in tears.

Charles X. could be received in England, M. de Choiseul was informed, only as a private person, M. de Talleyrand, in reply to his question, "Would the English government recognise the Duc d'Orléans as king should he accept the crown?" having been answered in the affirmative. Holyrood was, however, placed at Charles's disposal, it being difficult to find a residence sufficiently spacious to receive his very numerous retinue. Some repairs were made in the gloomy abode, and a little furniture put in to make it habitable for the king. Two furnished houses and all the apartments in the neighbourhood were engaged for the Duchesse d'Angoulême, the Duchesse de Berry and family, and their suites.

Charles seems to have had the reputation of a saint — almost that of a miracle-working one — among the poor around Holyrood. They came there to be cured of all sorts of maladies, actually by his medical attendants, but under the power of his influence. The army of priests he had with him may have contributed towards spreading the idea of the great sanctity of his character and his possession of the divine power of healing the afflicted, whether their ailments were of the body or the mind. The needy also seemed to imagine that he possessed an exhaustless purse.

The manner of life was almost cloistral. The distractions of their former position being wanting, the royal party seem to have had no other resource but additional fasting, penance, and prayer. The ardent Italian temperament and adventurous disposition of the Duchesse de Berry rebelled against the dreary monotony of day after day spent in the chapel and the oratory. More than ever she and the Duchesse d'Angoulême became aware of the utter absence of sympathy in their tastes, feelings, and pursuits.

Leaving her children, therefore, in her sister-in-law's care, she left Scotland, as Comtesse de Sagana, for London. Her intention had always been to return to France to assert her son's rights, and in London she carried on an active correspondence, with that view, with friends and royalist partisans. Eventually she returned to Italy, Charles having given her a written authority to call herself regent during her son's minority.

Scotch mists, if not the gloom of Holyrood, proved too trying for Charles to venture on facing them a second winter. He and his family accordingly took up their abode in Bohemia, Charles taking the title of Comte de Ponthieu; the Duc d'Angoulême and his wife that of Comte and Comtesse de Marne; the little duke, Comte de Chambord, and his sister, Mademoiselle de Rosny. Charles afterwards sought permission to reside in the Austrian dominions. The emperor and Prince Metternich were both much annoyed and embarrassed by the request. It, however, was granted. Metternich suggested Austerlitz as a residence;

but Charles preferred Gratz, in Styria. He had thought of retiring to a monastery when the Duc de Bordeaux came of age — as king. But, because of his years and failing health, the Duchesse d'Angoulême was opposed to it.

CHAPTER XXIII.

Welcome News. — Taking His Walks Abroad. — **Royal Hospitality.** — A Mysterious Death. — Madame de Feuchères. — Flattering Proposals. — Flatteringly Received. — The Ruling Passion. — Not to Be Tempted. — Death of Benjamin Constant. — Quelling a Tumult. — M. Thiers's *Début* in the Chambers. — "*Chacun Chez Soi, Chacun Pour Soi.*" — Prince Talleyrand Dozing.

WHEN the telegraph announced that Charles X. and his family had left the shores of France, then Louis Philippe breathed freely. Until this welcome news arrived he had not enjoyed his great popularity, which lasted full a fortnight or three weeks after his civic enthronement. He seemed to divide the popular favour with Général de La Fayette; for the people fancied that their new king had adopted the extreme liberal opinions of the "champion of liberty," who had said to him at the Hôtel de Ville, "France needs a popular throne, surrounded by republican institutions." Louis Philippe replied: "It is in that sense I understand the present situation and accept it with its responsibilities." Hence the deep sympathy with which the people at first regarded their citizen king and his family.

When with his queen he sat in the balcony, she

plainly attired, the young ladies around her in simple muslin frocks, with the younger young gentlemen just come in from college, his faithful lieges went into hysterics of delight. When, in *habit bourgeois*, he took his walks abroad, his queen on one arm, his gingham umbrella under the other, they gazed with profound admiration. When, condescendingly, he mixed with the crowd, though they pressed round him they treated him with the utmost respect, even addressing him in terms of affection. He, in return for these gratifying demonstrations of his people's love, was most friendly in manner, — *très sympathetique*, as the French say, — very lavish of kindly expressions, and willing heartily to shake any grimy hand thrust forth for the honour of thus greeting him.

From early morn till dewy eve the Palais Royal was full of all sorts and conditions of men — national guards, military and naval officers, provincial mayors and magistrates, young students from the various public schools, delegates from the departments, with a throng of others too numerous separately to mention. All were decorated with tri-coloured scarfs or streamers, and with one or more cockades. It was these outward and visible signs of constitutional principles that gave the right of *entrée*, and secured the welcome which all received, as well as entertainment at the king's table.

But Louis Philippe soon discovered that this royal open-house hospitality, and the importunate familiarities it led to, though tolerated, even encouraged for a time, when he sang the "Marseillaise" with them and for them, to serve a purpose, must be gradually but firmly checked. He must free himself, before the attentions of his enthusiastic admirers had grown to a pass that would make it difficult to do so. It was not the hurrahs of a mob he most anxiously sought to secure, but admission into the brotherhood of kings.

His countrymen have accused him of caring naught for the people, naught for the interests of France, but of having availed himself of the handsome present of a crown to further, first and before all other considerations, the material interests of his very fine family. His vast possessions certainly did not, as hitherto had been the rule with his predecessors, pass into the domain of the crown; but when he had quite overcome his hesitation to accept that present — "being determined to save France from anarchy" — they were already transferred to his children.

The events of the July days and those of the no less eventful month of August still agitated the public mind, when it was startled by that tragic episode of the revolution of 1830, the mysterious death of the old Duc de Bourbon-Condé, father of the unfortunate Duc d'Enghien.

On the morning of the 31st of August he was found by his valet hanging to the fastening of one of the windows of his bedroom, suspended by two handkerchiefs. He was quite dead. His knees were bent, his feet dragging on the carpet. The position struck all who saw him; none believed for a moment in suicide; and, in the manner his assassins would seem to have had suicide supposed, it was proved that he could not have destroyed himself.

Suspicion fell on Madame de Feuchères, an Englishwoman, the wife of Baron Adrien de Feuchères, and a much-favoured frequenter of the court of the Palais Royal. The baron had married her in England, believing her to be a young widow and the duke's natural daughter, born in exile. Discovering afterwards that he had married the duke's mistress, he immediately left the Palais Bourbon. A separation ensued, and he also resigned his post of aide-de-camp to the duke. This woman, who was of exceedingly low origin, but remarkably handsome and insinuating, it appears, had at one time exercised extraordinary influence over the old Prince de Condé. He had bequeathed and assigned to her the château and extensive domain of St. Leu and de Boissy, with a sum of upwards of a million *francs*. Afterwards she desired that the forest of Enghien might be added to these very princely gifts, and her request was granted.

The scandal ensuing on her separation from her husband, who rejected with indignation all attempts to bribe him into silent complaisance, excluded the lady from court, where the occasional appearance of "the duke's daughter" had been tolerated for her father's and husband's sake. Her influence with the duke seems to have declined at this time, and violent scenes took place between them. The baroness, however, assumed the attitude of injured innocence, and sought to be again received in court circles through the influence of the Duchesse de Berry. A person in her confidence who was acquainted with some of the superior officers of Madame's household, referring one day to the Baronne de Feuchères, said: "She was overwhelmed with grief; she had been so severely and so wrongly judged. What a kind and just act it would be if she could be reinstated at court." Then, cautiously leading to the point, it was hinted that if Madame la Duchesse would deign to employ her good offices on *la baronne's* behalf, she both could and would give ample proof of her gratitude.

"The Duc de Bordeaux has the crown for an heritage," continued the injured lady's emissary, "and, of course, is thus amply provided for; but Mademoiselle is not. The House of Condé is immensely rich, the Duc de Bourbon is far advanced in years, and Madame de Feuchères's influence over him is greater than ever." The officer thus addressed declined to undertake the proposed negotiation, adding that he doubted not that any one doing so would be very ill received by Madame. When this was reported to the Duchesse de Berry that evening, she entirely approved the answer, adding that she certainly would not listen to any such proposals.

Failing in this quarter, Madame de Feuchères's agent addressed himself to the Duc d'Orléans, who received his overtures with eagerness. Then began those unflagging persuasions and entreaties, which resulted in Madame la Baronne's reception at court, and (the prince being worried, pressed on all sides) the securing of that valuable testament by which all the wealth of the House of Condé, save that portion bequeathed to Madame de Feuchères, passed to the Duc d'Aumale.

On hearing afterwards that Madame de Feuchères was received very flatteringly at the Palais Royal, the Duchesse de Berry inquired of her aunt, "Have you really received that woman?" The Duchesse d'Orléans replied: "I am a mother, and have a numerous family." *

The Duc de Bourbon-Condé had been anxiously awaiting news of Charles X.'s safe arrival in England. He then proposed to follow, feeling that his presence in France, though politically he exercised no influence, made him the accomplice of usurpation. He was to have left St. Leu on

* Nettement, "*Mémoires de Madame la Duchesse de Berry*."

the morning of the 31st for Chantilly *en route* for London. Two or three friends dined with him on the evening of the 30th. He played a rubber of whist with them, and bade them adieu, in good health and spirits, afterwards charging his valet to be punctual in the morning.

Louis Philippe's warmest partisans were much grieved to see him so materially served by the *apropos* of such a catastrophe. An inquiry was ordered at Pontoise; but every means were taken to hush up the matter and to throw a veil over it. If Louis Philippe had nobly repudiated an inheritance on which such tragic suspicions rested, he would have gratified his friends' hopes and have advanced greatly in the esteem of the nation. "But," as a French writer remarks, "he loved money too well — it was his ruling passion; and, as in other matters touching his pecuniary interests, he followed up the affair with unwearying earnestness." The Rohan princes, who were the duke's heirs, instituted a *procès en captation*. They lost it in the tribunals, but gained it in public opinion. Madame de Feuchères was believed to be capable of the crime; but it was not proved that she was guilty of it, though it clearly appeared that she was opposed to the duke's departure, believing that the testament he had so unwillingly signed would be annulled when he was no longer under her influence. The whole nation interested itself in the progress of this painful two years' struggle, whose result was so unsatisfactory and cast so dark a shadow over the commencement of Louis Philippe's reign.

The new king endeavoured to win over M. de Châteaubriand to his interests; and, from the liberal opinions he had frequently advocated, and his known pecuniary embarrassments, Louis Philippe probably thought that the offer of a prominent and lucrative post in the government would secure the support of the viscount's eloquent tongue and flowing pen. But the old royalist, though it has been said, with some apparent injustice, that he might be bought, was not to be tempted to swerve from his allegiance to the King of France by any offers that the King of the French could make him. He so thoroughly detested Louis Philippe that Madame Récamier is said to have found it difficult to dissuade him from allying himself with the republicans, who, from the day that a vote of the deputies placed the Duc d'Orléans on the throne, sought his downfall.

Another of Madame Récamier's friends, and once ardent lover, Benjamin Constant, was less firm in his purpose to hold aloof from the new *régime*. His passion for gambling had reduced him to as great straits as bad management of his income and general carelessness of his pecuniary interests had brought M. de Châteaubriand into. M. Constant, however, did cherish hopes of happy results from the July revolution when he accepted a seat in the council of the citizen king, with a salary of 30,000 *francs*. Yet in the short space of five months he had not only thoroughly awakened from his dream, but had undergone such excessive moral agony in the bitter reproaches of his conscience at having, to use his own words, "advocated the cause of the best of republics," that it produced a painful nervous affection, which terminated in death on the 8th of December, 1830. Sixty thousand citizens in deep mourning followed to his grave the brilliant orator whom they named the "first victim of the July monarchy."

The impeachment of Charles's ministers seemed likely to lead to another revolution, so frantic were the people when they learned that instead of death their sentence was perpetual imprisonment. Assembling in thousands, with muffled drums and black flags, and in their sanguinary rage gesticulating violently, and screeching, "*Aux armes! aux armes! Vive la république!*" they surrounded the Palais Royal, and demanded that the traitors snatched from the vengeance of the people should be given up to them. A similar demonstration was made at Vincennes, where it was supposed that Polignac and his colleagues were imprisoned. But they had been secretly conveyed to the fortress of Ham. This raised the fury of the people to the highest pitch, and matters looked exceedingly threatening, when this tumult was unexpectedly quelled in a singular manner.

About four thousand youths of the École Polytechnique, wearing their uniform, and the students of the schools of law and medicine, their students' tickets in their hats, accepted the rather hazardous mission of attempting to restore order in the streets, proposed to them by Général de La Fayette. They formed a column, marched along the principal thoroughfares, urging as they went all good citizens to respect law and order. The unexpected appearance of this improvised brigade of youthful police is said to have had an almost magical effect on the riotous assemblages they encountered. The novelty of this mode of inviting a disorderly crowd to be peaceable seems to have both surprised and captivated them. With characteristic mutability the cry of "*Aux armes!*" was at once exchanged for a no less vociferous one of "*Vivent les écoles!*" many of those who had been most clamorous joining in the march and the exhortation of the students, while others gradually dispersed.

The election of Louis Philippe's first Chamber took place under the still passionate idea that he recognised as the basis of his power the conditions laid down by the representatives of the people. The journalist M. Thiers now first appeared on the legislative benches. M. Laffitte had undertaken to make him eligible, and, in spite of the sentiments evinced in his "*Histoire de la Révolution Française,*" the ministry accepted him as a candidate.

The new king was desirous of freeing himself from the tutelage of Général de La Fayette, to whose popularity he owed so much, and who had been named commander-in-chief of the national guards of the kingdom. It was suggested in the Chamber by the Orléans family lawyer, Dupin the elder, that only to the king should such a command belong. Instantly the general sent his resignation, which Louis Philippe, though much delighted, feigned unwillingness to receive, and pressed him greatly to accept the honorary title of commandant-general of the citizen militia, with whom, being his creation, he was, in a measure, identified. The general firmly declined it.

Louis Philippe was well pleased that he should do so. Having divested him of the prestige which his command-in-chief gave him, and centred it in himself, he had greatly strengthened his throne. He also adopted the device, "*Chacun chez soi, chacun pour soi*," formulated by Dupin the elder, in the name of the *bourgeoisie* — the *bourgeoisie* personifying the royalty of Louis Philippe, and tending towards arbitrary monarchy.

He was now really king of both France and the French. Besides the *dotation* of the crown, a civil list of eighteen millions was voted him, free from all the charges that encumbered Charles's civil list. For his extraordinary expenses for the five months of 1830, the Chambers, in their great liberality, awarded a sum of twelve millions. But that he could not, with all his secret scheming and intriguing, secure for his son Nemours the throne of the compact little kingdom of Belgium, as well as other good things that fell to him, was very vexatious, and distressing, no doubt, to his anxious feelings as a parent.

Prince Talleyrand was growing old, perhaps really dozing in the council-chamber instead of, as formerly, only appearing to do so. At all events, he allowed himself, say the French, to be outwitted, dominated by Lord Palmerston; and an English prince — as Prince Leopold was called — took the crown that should have graced the brow of a French one. But, in mitigation of his chagrin, it enabled him to dispose satisfactorily of a daughter; and this to the happy man, whosoever he may be, who hath several of them in his quiverful of blessings, must be a real pleasure and cause for rejoicing.

CHAPTER XXIV.

Restoring the Tuileries. — The "Monarchy à *Bon Marché*." — "We Are Subjects of the Law." — Caught in Their Own Trap. — A Sacrilegious Carnival. — Sack of the Archbishop's Palace. — Fast Waning Popularity. — Paganini's First Concerts. — The Opera and Opera Stars. — Madame la Comtesse Merlin. — Grand Musical *Réunions*. — *Petits Soupers Fins*. — The Literary *Salons*. — Private Concerts at Neuilly. — The Garden of the Great Lenôtre. — Cits and Citizenesses.

THE interior of the Tuileries had been so extensively damaged, its furniture so recklessly destroyed, by the wanton destructiveness of the mob that invaded the palace on the 29th of July, that the new royal family could not for some considerable time take up their abode in this royal residence. Preparations for their reception might have proceeded more quickly, but that, the populace having become so thoroughly disorganised, large numbers of the working classes were unable calmly to resume at once their usual occupations. There was great distress among them; much crying for bread and demand for work, though so few were disposed to settle down to it. Their minds were constantly kept on the stretch in expectation of the "*Réveil du peuple*" — in other words, the breaking out of a fresh insurrection.

The Tuileries being thoroughly swept, the floors repolished or carpeted, and walls repapered, such of the furniture as could be used again was furbished up, gilding retouched, damask cleaned, and so forth. It was suggested that what was wanting might be supplied from the superfluous grandeur of St. Cloud, Compiègne, or even from the Palais Royal, for the Chambers were beginning to think the "monarchy *à bon marché*" a dear bargain, and to repent of their liberality in the amount of the civil list, voted in the first flush of their loyalty.

The various members of the government had discarded their embroidered coats for plain ones; the king, too, was always *en habit bourgeois*. "What need had he, then," they asked, "the chief of a popular monarchy, of so many country residences?" Such luxury was but a remnant of the false grandeur of feudal times, wholly incompatible with the new order of things.

To these ardent republicans, of whom M. Dupont (de l'Eure) was the head, the *intendant* of the civil list replied that "if luxury and splendour, which promoted the prosperity of a nation, were to be banished from the residence of the 'King of France,' they would soon disappear from the homes of his 'subjects.'"

The Chamber had echoed with many a burst of indignation, but probably with none more frantic, more prolonged, and again and again renewed, than that which responded to the word "subjects." Louis XVIII. had been told that there were citizens only in France, no subjects. But that such a word should be repeated in that Chamber after the "glorious July days" passed all tolerance.

"Retract! retract!" they vehemently cried. But the offender, the Duc de Montalivet, had the courage to decline to do so. A solemn protest was therefore drawn up and signed by 160 deputies against the use of such expressions as "King of France" and the "King's subjects." "We are subjects of the law," they said, "but not of the individual will of any man."

Some obscure individuals, in their rabid zeal for the republic, thought to turn this incident to account, expecting that with a call to arms they could rally all the restless spirits of the capital around them. Entering Notre-Dame they sounded the *tocsin*, which alarmed the city; then ascending the towers, after barricading themselves in, they began to light what they called beacon-fires. The *gendarmerie* were sent out, and the arrest of the delinquents was soon accomplished, the defences they had set up forming a trap of their own making from which they were unable to effect their escape. The assembled crowd made merry over this disaster; hooted, hissed, and jeered at the would-be insurgents, whom nobody knew; and since they had no leader or definite plan of their own, Paris laughed at, instead of rising *en masse* to follow, none could tell whither.

But although this little episode of a most unquiet period, having its ludicrous side, afforded more amusement than alarm, nevertheless, not only in Paris, but in all the chief towns of France, Lyons especially, a most feverish state of feeling prevailed.

A solemn service held by the clergy and legitimists at St. Germain l'Auxerrois on the 14th of February, to commemorate the assassination of the Duc de Berry, led to very serious consequences. A catafalque without insignia was placed in the centre of the church. A lithograph portrait of the duke was attached to it, and a bust of Henri V. placed above. The assistants arrived in carriages, and all were in deep mourning. But their manner, it was thought, was more defiant than devotional. The people of course assembled, if only to see the sight; but great offence was taken by them when a woman began to collect contributions for the benefit of the royal guards wounded on the 29th of July, 1830. Vows of devotedness to the deposed dynasty were audibly murmured, and at the close of the ceremony the church doors were shut and locked.

The people resented this. Excitement increased, and an attack was made on the presbyter's house, which was speedily destroyed and pillaged. Following, as is asserted, the impulse of some unseen agency, the furious mob broke into the church, tore down altars, broke statues, destroyed pictures, and, arraying themselves in the priests' vestments, held high carnival within the sacred edifice. "*À bas les Jésuites! À bas les Bourbons!*" they raved, as, with fiendish glee, they carried on the work of destruction, no attempt being made to check or put a stop to these infamous proceedings.

"You must do as with a fire, let it burn out," said Louis Philippe to the *préfet de police;* "but look well to the safety of the Palais Royal." The police were indeed so careful not to interfere with these carnival revels, that they complied with the request of the revellers to aid in striking down the cross, on which was a *fleur-de-lys*, from the summit of the church, they being unable, unassisted, to accomplish it. All crosses bearing the emblem of the *fleur-de-lys* were also destroyed in other churches, national guards assisting. Next day the archiepiscopal residence was completely sacked by the mob. The furniture and the valuable library were thrown into the Seine, and when the rioters had been allowed full time thoroughly to accomplish their work, a legion of national guards appeared, and the building at their request was immediately evacuated.

Among the crowd of masks on the boulevards to whom this memorable carnival scene appeared to afford much amusement, some of the ministers, and, it was asserted, Louis Philippe and M. Guizot, were recognised. As if to identify himself with these shameful orgies, the citizen king that same day renounced his family arms. The *fleur-de-lys* was effaced from all his carriages, and, to please the mob, the Archbishop of Paris was ordered to appear before the judges of the Cour Royale, to account for his conduct in authorising the performance of a ceremony so repugnant to the sentiments of the people.

But this neither restored order nor revived Louis Philippe's waning popularity. Calm and peace seemed banished from France. Even the *préfet de police*, M. Baude, — who, in obedience to superior orders, had looked only to preserve the Palais Royal from a riotous attack, — declared that "if the government persisted in the erroneous course it had pursued during the last six months, the country would soon be left entirely to the mercy of circumstances."

Plots, intrigues, and street riots more or less menacing and sanguinary, succeeded each other throughout the first half of Louis Philippe's reign. During the concluding eight years the struggle between the monarchy and the people continued, though it assumed a different character. But of those ministerial crises and political contests, no particulars, of course, will be looked for in these pages. In spite of them Paris contrived to be gay, and luxury and pleasure were even more in favour, it was thought, than in the distinguished aristocratic circles of Charles's court.

If in the new *salons* there was less distinction in manners, with fewer grand names and antique escutcheons, than in the old, there was on the other hand much artistic talent and great literary ability that had been waiting its hour for development. The Opera-house opened its season brilliantly with a galaxy of stars of the first magnitude, and at the Théâtre Français and other houses old favourites and promising *débutants* attracted large audiences. Some alterations were made in the interior arrangements of the Opera-house, to denote that the exclusiveness of the former state of society was abolished, and that the *régime* of *liberté*, if not *fraternité*, now prevailed throughout France under the auspices of the son of Philippe Égalité.

To suit the spirit of the times and the economical habits of the new *bourgeois* court and society, the prices of admission to the opera were lowered. But they were considerably increased when, on the 9th of March, 1831, the great violinist, Paganini, gave the first of his opera concerts. So pressing was the demand for places, so eager the desire to see that strangely weird being and to hear his marvellous performance, that a profitable traffic was carried on for some time in the purchase and sale of tickets.

If the reports are not exaggerated, really fabulous prices were paid for places by those who could not restrain their curiosity to hear the screechings and wailings of the tortured demon in Paganini's violin until the first *furore* was past. There was, it seems, a real fascination in his personal appearance, and in the ectasy, real or feigned, with which, drawing his bow with a triumphant air across his instrument, he compelled his imprisoned familiar spirit — as some were inclined to believe it — to give forth those sounds that enraptured his audience.

Rossini's "*Guillaume Tell*," which, in five acts, did not in 1829 meet with the favourable reception its merits deserved, was reproduced this season in three acts and achieved a triumph. Madame Cinti-Damoreau, with Nourrit, and Mdlle. Taglioni as *première danseuse*, also delighted crowded audiences in Meyerbeer's first successful opera, "*Robert le Diable*." Again, too, Auber's "*Muette de Portici*" — the subject, apart from the lively and inspiring airs of the opera, being so much in accordance with the sentiments then predominating in France — received another popular ovation. The music sung by Masaniello would have softened no rocks, probably, and bent no knotted oaks; but it had done more than that, it had stirred a people to rise up against oppression and to demand their rights. They had obtained them, too, with a king of the Belgians, as the *grande nation* believed they had secured theirs with a king of the French. Hence " *Vive Auber! Vive Masaniello!* "

Of musical *salons*, that of the Comtesse Merlin was the most distinguished in Paris. The countess herself was a highly talented amateur; she was young, elegant, and personally attractive; and, above all, she was rich. Generally, the Faubourg St. Germain did not frequent the *salons* of the new *régime*. The denizens of that aristocratic *quartier* had either entirely withdrawn from society, or received only a small intimate circle exclusively royalist. Others had retired to the solitude of their country châteaux, while a few had followed Charles and the Duchesse d'Angoulême into exile. Yet the certainty of meeting the stars of the musical world, both vocal and instrumental, assembled at the countess's grand musical receptions — for she had her *grands jours* and *petits jours* — often attracted to them two or three of the less rigid members of the old court. If they found less etiquette, perhaps greater geniality, without much, if any, loss of *distinction*, atoned for it.

Rossini generally presided at the piano. He also sang occasionally, and with great *verve*, generally some air from his " *Barbier de Séville.*" Mesdames Malibran, Persiani, Orfila, and the Comtesse de Sparre — formerly Mdlle. Naldi of the opera, but now *très grande dame* — were the songstresses usually present, professional engagements permitting. Even Rubini, who did not often vouchsafe to display his vocal powers at private receptions, added the charm of his magnificent voice to the Comtesse de Merlin's grand concerts. Lablache, too,— "so big, so good, and so gay," — was often there, and Geraldi, then known but as an amateur ; also a young Sardinian officer, the Marquis de Candia, whose voice had a peculiar charm, and who was destined, under the name of Mario, to fill a distinguished place on the operatic stage.

At these receptions, not only the *élite* of the musical world assisted, but other artistic celebrities and *littérateurs* of distinction. The countess, being desirous that her *réunions* should bear a certain impress of exclusiveness, strove to revive the *petits soupers fins* of the old *régime* after her concerts, and on those evenings spent in acting Alfred de Musset's proverbs, composed expressly for Madame de Merlin's intimate circle. Musset himself, with MM. Villemain, Dupin the younger, Berryer, Arnault, and other eloquent speakers and writers of that day, took part for a while in this amusement, and contributed largely to the gaiety and witty badinage of the lively *petits soupers*.

But the march of time had done as much as revolutions to bring about a change of manners, a change in the habits of life, to introduce new amusements and dispel the taste for old ones. The time and thoughts of the men who frequented the new *salons* were chiefly engrossed by the lamentable events and political questions of the day. They took an interest, and many of them took a part, in those oratorical skirmishes, those duels of the tribune, of which the journals vaunted the grandeur and the importance. The elegant triflers of the olden time were not disquieted by stormy debates in the Chamber, but had leisure to employ themselves *usefully* with embroidery or *parfilage*, while whispering pretty nothings to the patched and painted reigning *belles* of the old *salons*. To revive this graceful frivolity and the pastimes of the *salons* of the old *régime* in times so prosaic as those in which the Comtesse de Merlin attempted to do so, though but for two or three hours in the week, was to fail, as Charles X. had failed to restore its despotism and hypocritical piety. But if in that she failed, she none the less continued to bear the sceptre as undisputed queen of the musical society of Paris.

The passion for letters, and particularly for poetry, invaded all the *salons*, and those especially of the Comtesse Baraguay-d'Hilliers, Madame de Mirbel, Madame de Lacretelle, Madame Auger, wife of the perpetual secretary of the Academy, and the very blue *salon* of Madame Ancelot. The last-named was, indeed, considered almost as a branch of the Academy. There, not only short pieces of poetry were recited, but whole tragedies were read, and often portions of historical works.

Under the July monarchy the *opéra comique* regained its former vogue. Louis Philippe was an admirer of Grétry's music. His pieces were full of charming airs, but they were too weak in orchestral effects to suit the taste of the musicians of later date. Adolphe Adam brought them forward again, increasing the effects of orchestration; and Grétry's operatic works achieved once more the success they had always commanded, until the ever increasing demand for noise caused them to be laid for a few years on the shelf. Grétry himself disliked what he called the *musique tapageuse* that was coming into favour when his career was drawing to a close. "Mark my words, child," he said to a young lady who was with him at the first representation of Cherubini's "*Medea*," "you will some day hear the time beaten with cannon-balls."

Both Adam and Auber were in high favour with the new royal family, and often were invited to Neuilly to the private family concerts. The pupils of the Conservatoire played and sang there, while the queen and her daughters and Madame Adélaïde knitted and knotted or worked at their embroidery-frames. Louis Philippe was often employed at the same time at his writing-table, and the young princes and officers of the household, collected in groups, *sans façon,* and listened to the music or conversed.

The musical afternoons at Neuilly doubtless pleasantly varied the daily routine of the quiet life of the *bourgeois* royalty. They had, too, the further advantage of costing next to nothing. Paris, however, was neither amused nor quieted by them; and as the Tuileries were now decently, if not, as of old, superbly furnished, it was as well to migrate there and invite the citizens to a dance or two. All classes of the Parisians had indeed been very indignant of late at the digging of a deep trench, or ha-ha, across the Tuileries gardens, thus cutting off and enclosing a portion of it for the special use of the new royal family.

Artists exclaimed against this defacement of the garden of the great Lenôtre. The people saw in it an invasion of their rights. "Napoleon, Louis XVIII., and Charles X. had inhabited the Tuileries, and had never attempted to appropriate any part of the garden. Should, then, the Orléans family, a new royal dynasty that could not claim to be wholly a popular one, be allowed to deface, to mutilate, to restrict for its own use and pleasure, the plan of the great *artiste?*" The Théâtre des Variétés produced the vaudeville "*La Fosse des Tuileries,*" and crowded audiences applauded. But it was soon withdrawn; for, although the revised Charter of 1830 decreed "The censorship can never be reëstablished," "it soon reappeared," says Théodore Muret, "in the form of *le sabre et de la botte forte*, which placed the theatre in a state of siege."

Public excitement was beginning to calm down when Louis Philippe took possession of the Tuileries, and found it necessary to oppose some check to the wide spread of his reputation for extreme avarice. Some gay carnival balls were given, at which liberty, equality, and fraternity presided — the worsted epaulets of the national guards figuring side by side with the gold epaulets and gold lace of the army. The citizenesses of the Marais who appeared at these courtly *réunions* were far less plainly attired than the wealthy citizens, their spouses. Their fashionable *toilettes* of rich brocades, laces, and jewels threw quite into the shade the pretentiously simple dresses of the princesses, who are said to have been "rather good-looking but without much distinction or manners."

CHAPTER XXV.

A Grand Carnival Ball. — King, Queen, and Family. — A Dreaded Enemy Advancing. — An Affray with the Rag-pickers. — Ravages of the Cholera. — Disastrous Results of a Funeral. — An Ill-advised Adventure. — Madame and Her Aides-de-Camp. — Death of Napoleon II. — The Prisoner of Blaye. — A Visit to Exiled Royalty. — " Madame, Your Son Is My King. — The Sisters Elsler. — " *Le Roi s'Amuse.*" — Death of Général de La Fayette.

THE dancing which had served as a sort of *bourgeois* house-warming when the citizen king took possession of the Tuileries was followed on the 11th of January by a brilliant ball, surpassing even the famous Neapolitan *fête* in the splendour of the arrangements. The guests, too, were of distinguished rank, chiefly foreign, and in the variety of their costumes gave to this grand entertainment almost the appearance of a fancy-dress *fête*. The Emperor and Empress of Brazil were present with their daughter,— a girl of thirteen,— the fair, fat Donna Maria da Gloria, Queen of Portugal, whose throne that monster of cruelty, Dom Miguel, had then usurped. The very magnificent Hungarian costumes of the Austrian ambassador, Count Apponyi, and his sons, were especially remarkable for their elegance as well as for the great value of the jewels that adorned them. But in pearls of great price and the size of his diamonds, the envoy of the Dey of Tunis appears to have surpassed all other guests, no less than in the richness and picturesqueness of his gracefully draped Oriental costume.

Queen Amalie also was resplendent with jewels, her dignified bearing strikingly contrasting with the *bourgeois* demeanour of the king, who, meaning to be gracious, was only obsequious. Madame Adélaïde, who so much resembled him in her opinions and sentiments, was remarkably like him in manner; and naturally so, both being *chefs-d'œuvre* of Madame de Genlis, trained according to the system of Jean Jacques, as developed in "Émile." However, together with the young princes and princesses, the new royal family formed a by no means uninteresting group.

All was laughter, life, and gaiety in that fairy scene, with music's sweet strains and the perfume of flowers; but what was going on without? A band of conspirators was being arrested. That night had been chosen for the realisation of what they fancied was a well-planned scheme to seize the person of Louis Philippe and to proclaim Henri V. Money had been lavishly spent in buying adherents, one or more of whom sold the information thus obtained to the government, and thus the affair collapsed. The conspirators in council were arrested, the editors of several royalist journals imprisoned and fined, which gave great offence, as they were merely suspected, while others, whose aid had been promised and paid for, kept quietly out of sight, consoling themselves with having at all events put a little money in their purses.

But an enemy far more to be dreaded was then on the confines of France, slowly but surely advancing towards the capital; it was the fatal cholera. So great was the consternation its approach inspired that, as gradually it from day to day crept onward, many persons, in their terror of being attacked by the disease, died of fright. It was expected to fall chiefly on the poor, and preparations were made to alleviate their misery and to prevent the spread of infection. But Paris was a very hotbed for the propagation of disease; and sanitary measures, though ordered by the municipal authorities, none cared to adopt.

The attempt to enforce them was violently opposed by the *chiffonniers*, or rag-pickers, who, collecting in a body, for three days successfully repelled the efforts of the street-sweepers to cart off the collections of dirt and rubbish from the fronts of the houses until it had been thoroughly turned over by them in the exercise of their calling. They lived in dirt, and picked up their living — sometimes a very good one — out of dirt, and they saw no necessity for or benefit in cleanliness. The struggle, therefore, between pickers and sweepers caused the streets to be dirtier than ever, — the rag-picking community considering the maintenance of their rights and privileges to be of far greater importance than any arrangements for cleansing the city.

Nothing surely can be more terrible, more heartrending, than the accounts of this fearful visitation — the rage, the despair, the madness of some of the unhappy people; the wild orgies of others at the opera balls, where, with mad profanity, they defied death and the cholera, and after dancing through the night, often with the disease upon them, ended their revels in some instances in the streets before they could reach their homes to die. A malignant report was spread that the rich had plotted to destroy the poor by introducing poison into the water-carriers' barrels, the milkwomen's pails, the bakers' flour, and the casks of the wine-shop. Unbounded rage, a frantic desire for revenge, led to fearful scenes of strife and bloodshed, the cholera meanwhile carrying off its daily increasing number of victims.

All who could leave Paris did so. Louis Philippe and his family were at St. Cloud when the Chambers suddenly brought their session to a close. Several of their most eminent men had succumbed to the prevailing epidemic. Casimir Périer was one of the first; among men of science was Baron Cuvier, the naturalist. Général Lamarque, a distinguished general of the empire and one of the most brilliant orators of the Chamber, was its latest victim. His death was regarded as a public calamity. Ten thousand of the national guards in uniform attended his funeral, and the same number of civilians in mourning, carrying emblems and banners. Several detachments of troops were officially convened to attend. A vast crowd followed, very clamorously disposed, misery and wretchedness being so general and the people in so unsettled a state.

The funeral service ended, there was a struggle among the young men of the Polytechnique for the honour of carrying the coffin to the Panthéon. A collision took place on the way between the people and the military, who fired on the crowd. The fire was returned, there was a call to arms, the *rappel* was beaten, barricades arose. The people got possession of the bank, the post-office, and the Hôtel de Ville, and obstinately defended them. For two days this lasted, and only after cannon had made sad havoc among the insurgents, and on both sides a loss of between four and five hundred killed and wounded had occurred, was the revolt put down. Louis Philippe then returned to Paris to sign the dissolution of the École Polytechnique, the veterinary school of Alfort, the national guards' corps of artillery, and to order that Paris be put in a state of siege.

The cholera was still desolating Paris when, on the night of the 29th of April, the Duchesse de Berry, in pursuance of her purpose of returning to assert and proclaim her son's rights, landed on the western coast of Marseilles with Général Bourmont and a number of adherents to the cause of Henri V. The expedition, as at first planned, failed entirely. But the adventurous and courageous, though ill-advised, princess was not disposed to look on this repulse as a defeat. Her maid, who had remained on board the steamer (*Carlo Alberto*) that brought the party from Genoa, was arrested by the police under the idea that she was the duchess, who, in disguise, and accompanied by Général Bourmont, was then making her way across France to La Vendée. There, the zeal of some of her partisans, and the imperious enthusiasm which, inspired by her maternal ambition and the effervescence of wounded pride, she herself displayed, roused many of the younger men to respond to the old royalist cry of "*Ouvrez à la fortune de France,*" and to rally around her.

In some of the towns of La Vendée the people and the military came into collision. In le Bocage armed bands paraded the villages and placed the white banner on the church steeples. In the South rebellion seemed imminent; but it was rather from dissatisfaction with the general state of misery and poverty in France than from any sympathy with the cause of Henri V. The duchess by no means spared herself; no hardships or privations dismayed her that seemed to lead towards the success of her project. It has been called "romantic folly worthy of a heroine of the Fronde."*

But in the midst of her army, mounted on her Vendéen pony and arrayed in a semi-military costume, with her two aides-de-camp, Maréchal Bourmont and Général Clouet, to advise and assist her, Madame certainly inspired a temporary enthusiasm in her cause. Bands of armed peasantry enrolled themselves under the command of chiefs bearing the celebrated names of Larochejacquelein, Charette, Cathelineau, Cadoudal, etc., and Madame mistook the passing excitement for loyalty and attachment to the expulsed dynasty. There was much skirmishing and pillaging, and many incendiary fires; but this did not advance the cause.

Louis Philippe had lately been occupied with the final arrangements respecting the dowry of his daughter; he now returned from Compiègne and despatched an army to put down the civil war. This was soon accomplished; and, meanwhile, MM. de Châteaubriand, Berryer, Hyde de Neuville, and the Duc de Fitzjames were arrested in Paris, with the hope that they would be proved to be in complicity with Madame or the Vendéen

* Nettement.

chiefs. In this he was disappointed. But while the police were tracking the vanquished heroine from farm to farm, where, in the disguise of a Vendéenne peasant, she was concealed in barns and outhouses, a piece of great good fortune rejoiced the heart of the citizen king. He feared not Henri V. or his romantic, imprudent mother, whose capture he only awaited to ruin at one blow both her reputation and the legitimacy of her son. But he had at times feared that a Napoleon II. might yet reign over fickle France. How then must his mind have been set at ease when it was announced that the Duc de Reichstadt had died on the 22d of July of a long-standing malady called languor!

But the Duchesse de Berry is at last in the clutches of her "dear, kind uncle." None had been found to betray her but a German Jew, named Deutz, who had affected to be convinced of the "errors of his faith," as his pretended renunciation of Judaism was called, and whom the Pope, deceived by the new convert's supposed piety, had recommended as a person in whom she might place entire confidence. "*Trahissez, mon ami, et vous serez riche,*" M. Thiers is reported to have said to him,* and 20,000*l.* was the reward he received for betraying Marie Caroline into the power of Louis Philippe. She was concealed at Nantes, and was arrested there, and

---

* Marchal, " *Mémoires de la famille d'Orléans.*"

thence transferred to the fortress of Blaye. She had privately married the Comte Luchesi-Palli, in Italy, and was now obliged to publicly declare it — the *Moniteur* having announced that she was *enceinte*, and her partisans refusing to believe it.

This was sufficient to put an end to her pretensions as regent, and, without making it public, she should have been sent to her family, being henceforth a powerless enemy. But Louis Philippe preferred to make her drink the cup of humiliation to the very dregs; her aunt, Queen Amalie, gave no reply to her letters, and it does not appear that she interceded for her. Securely locked up, and closely watched, she was for seven months a prisoner in the fortress of Blaye, where, in the presence of her gaoler, Maréchal Bugeaud, and others, she gave birth to a daughter. In her distress of mind, she wrote to M. de Châteaubriand, who made himself her champion, and went to Prague with her letters to Charles X. and his son, and to Carlsbad to entreat the Duchesse d'Angoulême to take care of her children while she was retained in captivity.

The viscount was coldly received, and the only message of comfort he brought back to the prisoner of Blaye was: " I pity my sister-in-law greatly; tell her so." The children were not allowed to return to her. The deposed king deposed the regent; and thus Henri V., who, as M. de Châteaubriand remarked, was being deplorably educated, was brought up in ignorance of the world and in narrow-minded bigotry. During the three or four days he remained to recover from the fatigue of his journey, the viscount saw enough of the fallen royalties to be amazed at the *petitesse* of their lives. He was also astonished and a little vexed at the badness of their dinners, notwithstanding that the staff of the royal kitchen was still so numerous.

When Madame was released, M. de Châteaubriand went to Ferrara to meet her. She had recovered her spirits, her journey from Palermo having been almost a royal progress, so enthusiastically was she everywhere welcomed. At the inn where she alighted at Ferrara a guard of a hundred Austrian and as many papal troops awaited her. The balconies, the *salons*, the staircases, were garlanded with flowers, and all the officials, all the grandees, were waiting to be introduced. Luchesi-Palli, too, was there. When her carriage drove up, the soldiers presented arms, there was a flourish of trumpets, the drums beat, and the regimental bands struck up a national air. Scarcely could she alight, so eagerly did the people crowd around to welcome her.

"Ah!" she exclaimed, when she saw Châteaubriand, "my son is your king, is not he?" He had written in his pamphlet on her captivity, "Madame, your son is my king," and, from some misunderstanding respecting him which arose on this occasion, he was addressed as "your royal highness;" while Madame, to her great amusement, was complimented on her beautiful book on Christianity. Everybody was delighted with her, and she delighted with everybody. Thus ended Madame's adventures. Louis Philippe would have had her refused an asylum in the papal dominions; but the Pope declined to accede to his wishes. She subsequently lost a large part of her fortune, and was compelled to dispose of her pictures and valuable collection of *objets d'art*, owing to the unfortunate speculations of her husband, for whom she had become guarantee. However, her elastic spirits and great light-heartedness availed at least to soften the blow.

The cholera abated towards the close of the year, and the theatres were beginning to be more frequented. They had never been entirely closed, lest it should spread further alarm among the people; but the audiences were naturally of the thinnest, and the theatres redolent of camphor, as, indeed, for a considerable time they continued to be, all persons wearing camphor-bags in the *salons* and places of public resort. The principal singers and dancers had migrated to London, where the cholera was on the decline when at its height in Paris; and M. Véron, the director of the Opéra, succeeded there by flattering offers in inducing the sisters Fanny and Theresa Elsler to visit the French capital. Fanny was a popular favourite and a formidable rival to Mdlle. Taglioni. A sort of interest also attached to her from the report — which, however, seems to have had no real foundation — that the young Napoleon had been very deeply in love with her.

It was about this time that Victor Hugo's play of "*Le roi s'amuse*" was produced at the Théâtre Français. By ministerial order it was suspended on the day following its first representation (the 22d of November, 1832), and the next day was definitively prohibited because of its immorality. Its author protested, printed his play, brought an action against the director, and claimed 25,000 *francs* compensation. The matter was tried before the tribunal of commerce. The court was crowded to suffocation; there were cries of distress, many persons fainted, and the struggle of some to get out, and of others to open the windows, occasioned a scene of tumult and confusion that delayed for some time the opening of the proceedings. M. Hugo addressed the judges, and, as is generally known, — from the accounts of this play at its recent revival, — after an eloquent speech the poet-orator obtained a triumph, described as "bordering on frenzy."

Several plays were subsequently suppressed, but rather for political reasons than as offending morality. Press prosecutions were also frequent, Louis Philippe being disposed apparently to play the part of Charles X. But fortune seemed to favour his views by removing his most vigorous opponents out of his way when they were becoming too dangerous or troublesome. An instance of the kind occurred at this period in the death of Général de La Fayette. It was the extinguishing of "the torch of liberty" at a moment most favourable to his purposes. The general's funeral was a grand and imposing spectacle, conducted with the greatest order, the demeanour of the vast concourse of all classes attending it being calm and deeply reverent.

To divert the public mind from the trials of editors and journalists, Louis Philippe took his family to Fontainebleau, invited thither the *corps diplomatique*, and, reviving the long-suspended splendours of the imperial court, gave a series of brilliant *fêtes*. Balls, concerts, and plays, hunting in the forest, riding parties, *fêtes champêtres*, acting of charades, filled every hour of the day with gaiety and pleasure. Such unwonted mirth and extravagance in the royal household was indeed a novelty, and, as expected, greatly occupied public attention.

CHAPTER XXVI.

The Rule of Life in Paris. — Fieschi's Infernal Machine. — In Quest of a Wife. — "*Vive Napoléon III.!*" — The Marriage Bells Are Ringing. — Arrival of the Bride. — Wedding *Fêtes* and Presents. — A Great Theatrical Event. — *Les Débuts* of Mdlle. Rachel. — Success, Fortune, and Glory. — Rising with Her Circumstances. — Birth of the Comte de Paris. — Ste. Helena and Boulogne. — The Spanish Marriages. — Mr. Smith and His Passport. — M. Guizot "Disguizoted." — Death of M. de Chateaubriand. — Death of Madame Récamier.

WHILE Louis Philippe, with his family and court, was reposing from cares of state in a round of festivities at Fontainebleau, Paris resounded with cries of "*À bas Philippe! Plus de Bourbons!*" elicited by the audacious press prosecutions. There were rumours of secret plots and terrible vengeance in preparation; but they were unheeded — plotting and intriguing being now the rule of life in Paris and chief cities of France, and generally more menacing as the celebration of the "glorious July days" drew near.

In the course of his reign six attempts — three of them supposed to be mere ruses on the part of the government and the police — were made to assassinate Louis Philippe, from all of which he escaped unharmed. The most serious, in the injuries and loss of life it inflicted on others, was that of Fieschi with his infernal machine. The explosion took place after a review on the 20th of July. The horses ridden by the king and his sons were, it seems, slightly wounded, but its effects to his numerous staff were fatal. Maréchal Mortier was killed; two generals and twelve other officers, with twenty-one persons among the crowd nearest to them, were either frightfully wounded, or killed on the spot. The face and hands of the assassin himself were terribly injured, and blood was streaming from them when he was arrested.

The funeral of Maréchal Mortier and the general officers, together with the other victims of this crime, was, perhaps, the grandest that France, so famous for such pageants, had hitherto witnessed. Fieschi, with two accomplices, was executed in February of the following year, after a trial which, in the manner of conducting it and the strange liberties of speech and behaviour permitted to the assassin, probably never had its counterpart except in a recent trial in America. But this crime, so fatal to others, served well the views of the citizen king. Fate or fortune, or another powerful and occult influence, seemed always at hand to aid him, and to divert attention from his and his ministers' attempts — even more arbitrary than those of Charles X. and his advisers — to restrict the liberty of the press and to influence the elections.

But Louis Philippe is now anxious to marry his sons, and the heir-apparent and his brother Nemours are about to visit the German courts. Vienna being inquired of beforehand as to the reception they might expect at that court, Metternich replied to the Austrian ambassador, "We are at peace with France, and of course the Duc d'Orléans will be suitably received; but if a marriage *with us* is believed in as probable, there will be disappointment." The young princes, however, met with a splendid reception both at Vienna and Berlin. "It was a new Holy Alliance," says a contemporary writer, "into which the legitimate and absolute sovereigns did not fear to introduce the government of July, now absolved of its origin."

Alibaud's attempt to shoot the king recalled the princes to Paris. The assassin's pistol broke a pane of glass, but did no further harm. But scarcely had his execution taken place when a vast military conspiracy, which was to extend like a train of gunpowder to all the garrison towns, first broke out at Strasbourg, on the 30th of October, to the cry of " *Vive l'empereur! Vive Napoléon III!* " Louis Philippe is said to have displayed intense anxiety on this occasion. He was up all night, receiving frequent despatches and sending off messages; and when the prince and the officers concerned in the plot were arrested, his agitation still continued, until he knew that the bearer of the name so magical in its influence was on board the vessel that awaited him and on his way to America.

The acquittal, at Colmar, of all persons compromised by the Napoleonic conspiracy at Strasbourg greatly startled and annoyed the king and his Cabinet. It was the cause of some insubordination in several regiments. *Fêtes* in honour of the decree and of the judges who decreed the acquittal were celebrated in Alsace, and both the accused persons and their judges assisted at them. It seemed as if the throne of the King of the French were slightly shaken by this untoward event. But again it was steadied by the death of Charles X., at Goritz, on the 6th of November. All the European courts, with the exception of the court of the Tuileries, went into mourning. The Duc d'Angoulême, at the desire, or command, of the duchess, assumed the empty title of king; but they were unable to proclaim it to those courts who had — and few had not — acknowledged the King of the French.

But again, for a brief space, plots, assassinations, and the visits of the King of Terrors must yield place to festive throngs. The hymeneal torch is lighted, the marriage-bells are ringing, and Louis Philippe and family are assembled at Fontainebleau to receive the royal bride — the

Princesse Hélène of Mecklenburg-Schwerin. Her brother, it appears, was not very anxious for a union with the French royal family; he thought the country and the throne unsettled. However, his objections were overcome, and his sister became Duchesse d'Orléans. She was then twenty-three, her disposition said to be very amiable, the expression of her countenance charming, and, as all princesses are, or should be, she was highly educated and accomplished. The Chambers had been liberal towards the prince, though they refused to endow the rest of the sons and daughters, with the exception, very unwillingly, of a million *francs* to the Queen of the Belgians.

Louis Philippe had also opened wide his purse-strings. The Chamber had voted a million for the expenses; but that was not enough, it appears, as this royal marriage was to surpass in splendour all former ones. On the 29th of May, 1837, the princess, accompanied by the Grand Duchess Augusta Frederica, reached Fontainebleau. From the time she crossed the frontier, her journey had been a sort of triumphal march, and deputations from all classes and from all parts were waiting her arrival. The rolling of drums and a grand flourish of trumpets announced the entry of her carriage into the Grande Cour. At the foot of the grand staircase she was received by the Duc d'Orléans and his brother Nemours. When presented to the king, he embraced her as effusively as though she had been Général de La Fayette, and, assuming an air of dignity, led her first to the queen, then to the different members of his family.

On the 30th the civil marriage took place in the gallery Henri II., the religious ceremony afterwards in the chapel — first by the Bishop of Meaux, then, the bride being a Protestant, by the Lutheran pastor, Cuvier. Amongst the witnesses were Prince Talleyrand, "a spectre of evil omen," but who departed this life in the following year, and Louis XVIII.'s *cher enfant*, the Duc Decazes, now one of the adherents of the new dynasty.

The bride's dress of *point d'Alençon* is said to have cost 30,000 *francs* — 1,200*l.* It is described as a magnificent specimen of that lace, and would probably cost a larger sum now. The queen and princesses were also very richly dressed; but the fashions of the day were hideous. The *corbeille de mariage*, or wedding presents, filled three large *salons*, and formed a real exhibition of the highest class of French industrial manufactures. The entry into Paris on the 4th of June was a very grand affair. Never had Louis Philippe looked so radiant since he had worn his crown of thorns — for such it really was, though he pressed it so closely on his brow. Banquets, balls, illuminated gardens, and public festivities for the *canaille*, followed.

On the 11th a *fête* took place at Versailles "of a grandiose and national character, intended," says Lacroix, "to cast on this union and on the reign of the citizen king a reflex of the glory of the *Grand Monarque's* reign ; the vast galleries of Versailles, transformed into an historical museum, dedicated to all the glories of France, were then for the first time thrown open." The festivities in Paris continued until the end of the month. Several persons were killed and many injured by the pressure of the vast crowd assembled in the Champ de Mars to see the illuminations and fireworks. "Ah!" exclaimed the princess, "it is as when the marriage of Louis XVI. was celebrated. *Quel affreux présage !*"

The theatre had, of course, its part in the marriage festivities. A grand piece was arranged expressly for the occasion, in which the stars of the musical world, as well as poets and others, were included.

But one of the greatest theatrical events of this reign was the appearance of Mdlle. Rachel at the Théâtre Français on the 13th of June, 1838, when she made her *début* as Camille in "*Les Horaces.*" She was then but seventeen. Though a finished actress, her appearance was not at all attractive. Her complexion was swarthy, her stature short, and she was meagre rather than slight in figure — "poor *physique*, but much talent," said M. d'Henneville in 1836. "So short, too." "But she will grow," replied Mdlle. Mars. Cherubini thought her voice and style against her, but that she had "infinite intelligence."

These opinions were given when she declaimed before an *audition audience*, or official committee, arranged for her by M. Lasalle, the director of the Français. On his application to the Minister of the Interior, she was placed as a pupil of the Conservatoire, which she left the next year for an engagement at the Gymnase with a salary of 3,000 *francs*. She appeared in "*La Vendéenne.*" Her *début* passed unnoticed; but she was an indefatigable student, and M. Samson, teacher of declamation, who had had several distinguished pupils, was then her master. Yet when, in June, 1838, she appeared at the Théâtre Français, she at first excited little attention, except from two or three inveterate old playgoers, who predicted success. The weather was exceedingly warm; the classical drama, too, was not in favour, and some few cases of cholera had reappeared, which causing alarm, all who could leave Paris hastened out of it.

But towards the end of September the Parisians began to return; the *habitués* of the Français resumed their accustomed places, and ere a month had passed away Mdlle. Rachel had become famous. Reared in poverty, the poor, thin, faded girl, when prosperity came to her, revived and bloomed like a flower in the sunshine. Rachel grew too, as Mdlle. Mars predicted, and grew until after she was twenty. Though she was not tall, her dignified carriage, the graceful pose of her head, the easy fall of her arms, and the remarkable elegance with which she draped herself, gave her the appearance of height; while a peculiar movement of the shoulders that was noticed in her "marked, as it were, the rhythm of her steps."

Horace Vernet thought Rachel a perfect type of Oriental beauty. "If he could have had such a model," he said, "when painting his 'Rebecca at the Fountain,' he would willingly have paid her a thousand *francs* an hour." She was for a long time the favourite subject of the artists of the day, whether in lithography, painting, or sculpture. Portraits innumerable appeared of her; but rarely one that did full justice to her expressive countenance and the powerful glance of her deep, dark, searching eyes. Rachel brought both fortune and glory to the Théâtre Français, and drew them also on herself. Crowded houses nightly greeted her; the boxes were filled with the *élite* of the *beau monde*, who applauded with enthusiasm; recalled her again and again, to repeat this frenzied applause, and covered the stage with bouquets. "It was not the tragedy," says one of her biographers, "that was listened to, but Rachel herself."

The curtain rises; there, draped with the classic elegance of a statue from the antique, motionless, she stands. How calm she appears.

But when she speaks, that authoritative but perfectly modulated voice thrills the audience, and with the first word she utters she communicates to them the fire of her own feelings. Journals of all shades of opinion vied with each other in praising her and surrounding her with romantic interest, never wearying of recording how perseverance had triumphed over the poverty and suffering of a wandering life in infancy, and her great genius obtained its patent of nobility. So variously, indeed, has the story of her early years been related, that, further than that it was a period of misery and obscurity, little is accurately known.

Her triumph was as great in private society as on the stage. The most distinguished of the aristocracy were eager to receive her, and, rising with her circumstances, she dropped the tragic mask on leaving the stage and entered the *salon* a perfect *grande dame*. She was a great favourite at the Abbaye-aux-Bois, where Madame Récamier still received all that remained of the old royalist society and all the *élite* of the new *régime*. There, too, it appears, Mdlle. Rachel was accustomed to read her new parts; and there and everywhere "this spoiled child of fortune, of the *grand monde*, and the public, was welcomed by that society which a few years later was to exaggerate her weaknesses and mercilessly accuse her of unpardonable disorder, but who in the dawn of her celebrity would see in her nothing but virtue and purity of heart and mind, unsullied by any vicious sentiment, and ignorant of any of those passions which, as they were accustomed to say, she so thoroughly depicted yet without experiencing them."*

But other events have to be mentioned, and mentioned only, being too recent and too well known to need further notice here.

On the 24th of August, 1838, a son was born to the Duc d'Orléans, on whom Louis Philippe conferred the new title of Comte de Paris. It was an axiom of his that "to reign over Paris was to reign over France." In 1840 the Duc de Nemours married the beautiful Princess Victoria of Saxe-Coburg-Gotha, and the July dynasty was further strengthened by the birth of a second son to the Duc d'Orléans.

In 1840 an application was made to England for the transfer of Napoleon's remains from Ste. Helena to France. When proposed in the Chambers it was represented as "a solemn act of national gratitude," and the sum necessary for it was voted with enthusiasm. But instead, as was intended, of getting rid by these means of the phantom of Napoleon, it gave renewed force to the popular sentiment. While the Duc de Joinville was despatched to bring the body of the hero from his island tomb, Louis Napoleon,

* Véron's " *Mémoires d'un bourgeois de Paris.*"

who had returned from America in 1838, landed at Boulogne on the 6th of August, believing that the people of the Pas de Calais were ready to rise in his favour. He was arrested, and sentenced to perpetual imprisonment in the fortress of Ham, whence he escaped in 1846.

A great domestic affliction befell the king and his family on the 13th of July, 1842, in the death of the Duc d'Orléans, who was thrown from his carriage and killed on the spot. In the following year Queen Victoria and Prince Albert visited the King of the French at the Château d'Eu, and again in 1845, Louis Philippe having in the interval paid a return visit to England.

The marriage of the Comte de Chambord to the Princess Maria Theresa of Modena took place at Burg in October, 1846. The long-closed *salons* of the legitimists of the Faubourg St. Germain were then thrown open to *fête* their queen. To these unwonted festivities the citizen royalties replied by fêting with great *éclat* the arrival of the Duc de Montpensier's child-bride, sister of the young Queen Isabella; married also against her will, by the arts and intrigues of Louis Philippe and his minister Guizot, to the Duke of Cadiz — the possibility of a Spanish crown for the citizen king's youngest son looming deceitfully as a mirage in the distance.

The unexpected death of Madame Adélaïde, on the 31st of December, closed the calamitous year 1847. The persistent demand for electoral reform led to the overthrow of the July monarchy in February, 1848, and the flight of Louis Philippe and family to England. Thus ignominiously ended a reign of nearly eighteen years, which has been branded as one of "egoism and corruption."

The ex-king and queen landed at Newhaven on the 3d of March, and went to the Bridge Inn, where apartments had been taken for them. There were many offers of services from families in the neighbourhood, but they were of course declined. Louis Philippe was, however, much delighted when the rector, the Rev. Theyre-Smith, was announced. He hailed him as a namesake, gave him some particulars of his escape, and showed him his passport as Mr. Smith. He wore a blue pilot coat, and a pocket-handkerchief for a cravat. He had abandoned his lofty wig, and his beard was untrimmed.

On the 4th they left Newhaven for Claremont, travelling from the Croydon station in private carriages, having declined the offer of the queen's.

Some days after Louis Philippe's arrival in England, Madame Guizot received a letter from her son, giving the particulars of his royal master's hasty journey across Normandy disguised as a peasant and wearing a red cotton nightcap. Of course he gave her the details of his own escape and his disguise — a workman's blouse and cap. This letter Madame Guizot sent to Madame Récamier by a friend, who was to read it to her, she being then quite blind. The political *intrigante*, Princesse Lieven, with whom M. Guizot had been on terms of very intimate friendship, happened to be in the *salon* of the Abbaye-aux-Bois reading to Madame Récamier the newspaper accounts of the same events. The reader of the letter, it appears, stopped short when she came to M. Guizot's own adventures. "But Guizot?" said the princess, yet without lifting her eyes from the newspaper. "Madame," replied the lady addressed, making a sort of pun on the name, "he "disguizoted (or disguised) himself (*Il s'est déguizoté*) as a workman." "I recognise him there," said the princess. "There need be no anxiety about him. He is sure to bring himself safely out of the affair."

It was with difficulty that another person who was present was made to comprehend what had taken place. This was M. de Châteaubriand. When at last it dawned upon him that the man he once so thoroughly detested had ignominiously fled the country, he merely said he cared nothing about it. For the last two or three years he had been in a pitiable state of senile debility, yet with occasional very brief flashes of his former self. In March, 1848, he took a severe cold, and was carried no more to the Convent *salon*. But he lingered on for nearly four months, and the devoted Madame Récamier went daily to the Rue du Bac to sit an hour with him. He smiled, and gazed on her, and seemed to listen to what she said, but rarely spoke. Her grief was that she could not see him. Sometimes his old friend Béranger was there, and he and Madame Récamier were the only friends at his bedside when, on the morning of the 3d of July, he passed quietly away. He had nearly completed his eightieth year.

Madame Récamier was now aged, blind, and nervous; yet all whom death had spared of her once pleasant circle of old friends, as well as those of a more recent date, still regularly found their way to the Abbaye. Something of the old spell yet lingered there. For an hour or two every day some one of her friends read to her; others brought particulars of passing events, for it was still a most anxious time, and the evenings were enlivened by music and conversation. Thus the even tenor of her life might yet have flowed on for some years; but again, in April, 1849, that dreadful scourge, the cholera, reappeared in France.

All who remembered its ravages in 1832 were filled with terror. Madame Récamier, alarmed for the safety of her niece and family, though dreading death in so frightful a form herself, contrary to advice, left the Abbaye-aux-Bois to stay with Madame le Normant at the Bibliothèque

Nationale. Two days after, the fatal symptoms appeared, and the next morning she breathed her last. Thus, painfully, closed the life of this celebrated woman. She was seventy-two, and from the age of sixteen, upwards of half a century, may be said to have reigned as a queen of society; for the greater part of it as queen of beauty also, and she was by no means deficient in *esprit*. She has generally been represented as a very charming person, without much heart, which is doing her scant justice; for it may at least be said of her that her disposition was amiable and her nature kindly.

THE END.

INDEX.

Adélaïde, Madame, training of, II., 337, death of, 360.
Alexander I., admiration excited by, I., 14 et seq., visits Queen Hortense, 49, king of all Paris, 67, forces Louis's hand, 68, change in, 242, pleads for La Bédoyère, 251, comes to the rescue of France, 324; illness of, II., 167, death of, 168.
Algiers, taking of, II., 258.
Amalie, Queen, deportment of, II., 337.
Ambray, M. d', panegyric of, I., 114.
Ancelot, Madame, *salon* of, II., 332.
Angoulême, Duc d', effort for popularity of, I., 52, sketch of, 58, embarks for Spain, 177; returns victorious from Spain, II., 63, anger of, 284, opposes all concessions, 286, abdication of, 295.
Angoulême, Duchesse d', hatred of, I., 73, characterisation of, 95, her marriage, 96, her severity, 118, jewels of, 149, leaves Bordeaux, 178; receives pardons from the Pope, II., 99, supports the Jesuits, 214, received with hisses, 305.
Anne, Grand Duchess, proposed marriage of, I., 256.
Artois, Comte d' (see Charles X.).
Assembly of royalty, I., 174.
Auber, Daniel François Esprit, opera of, II., 329.
Bagatelle, La., life at, I., 97.
Bagration, Princess, beauty of, I., 311.
Bassanville, Comtesse de, anecdote told by, I., 218.
Béranger, songs of, I., 156.
Berry, Duc de, oratory of, I., 53, sketch of, 57, assassination of, 325, death of, 326, 327.
Berry, Duchesse de, proposed for royal marriage, I., 281, reception of, 297-304, marriage of, *ib.*, description of, 306, 307,

birth of daughter of, 321; birth of son of, II., 31, visit to Chambord, 221 et seq., costume ball of, 227, her patronage of *belles lettres* and the arts, 232, gains adherents for her son, 341, betrayed by Dutz, 343, imprisonment of, *ib.*, birth of daughter of, *ib.*, release of, 345.

Berry, Miss, her description of Madame Récamier, I., 236.
Berthier, Maréchal, speech of, I., 63; death of, II., 216.
Blacas, M., counsels Louis XVIII., 66, 67.
Blücher, Maréchal, narrow escape of, I., 212.
Bonaparte, Caroline, influences Joachim, I., 125, rewards Benjamin Constant, 129, leaves Naples, 207.
Bonaparte, Louis Napoleon, heads the revolt at Strasbourg, II., 351, escape from prison of Ham, 360.
Bonaparte, Napoleon, at Saint-Dizier, I., striking manœuvres of, 3, at Fromenteau, 4, blow falls upon, *ib.*, meditates a new campaign, *ib.*, at Fontainebleau, 29, deserted by marshals, *ib.*, signs abdication, 30, humiliated, 34, accepts Elba, 36, his suffering, 38, his adieu, 39, arrival at Elba, 41, family of, 56, reaction towards, 139, lands in France, 168, enters Lyons, 171, arrival at the Tuileries, 181, betrayed, 211, at Waterloo, 213, signs abdication, 214; death of, II., 46.
Bordeaux, Duc de, christening of, II., 43, 44, education of, 175 et seq., made Henry V., 303.
Bouilly, J. Nicholas, writings of, II., 177, interview with Duchesse de Berry, 178, 180, writes tales for the royal children, 181.
Bourbon-Condé, Duc de, murder of, II., 313.
Byron, Lord, characterisation of, I., 313.
Cambacères, Jean Jacques Regis de, death of, II., 213.
Campan, Madame, deportment of, I., 100.
Candia, Marquis de, voice of, II., 331.
Caroline, Queen (see Caroline Bonaparte).
Caulaincourt, M. de, his interview with Alexander, I., 32; death of, II., 213.
Chambord, description of, II., 219.
Champ de Mai, fête of, I., 200.
Charles X., speech of, I., 41, prudent act of, 47, repents past life, 50; at St. Cloud, II., 84, reception at the Tuileries, 88 et seq., abolishes restrictions of the press, 101, address to the Chambers, 102, coronation of, 132–140, disbands the Na-

tional Guard, 199, his reception at the theatre, 242, description of cabinet of, 246 et seq., hissed, 257, reëstablishes absolute ordinances, 261, orders seizure of printing-presses, 266, disturbing news brought to, 267, remains obstinate, 272, orders Marmont to resist, *ib.*, withdraws ordinances, 287, abdication of, 295, retires to Holyrood with royal family, 307, removes to Bohemia, 308, removes to Austria, 309, death of, 353.

Charter, reading of, I., 114, 115.

Châteaubriand, M. de, pamphlet of, I., 27, 28; at Verona, II., 54, turned out of office, 70, his opposition to Louis XVIII., 149, friendship for Madame Récamier, 150 et seq., aids in overthrowing the ministry, 209, made minister to Rome, 211, illness of, 237, eloquent address of, 292, arrest of, 342, death of, 363.

Cholera, ravages of, II., 338 et seq.

Cockades, the white, I., 13; the tricolor, II., 273 et seq.

Congress of Vienna, I., 112; of Verona, II., 52.

Constant, Benjamin, marriage of, I., 123, his love for Madame Récamier, 128, hostile philippic of, 187, interview with Napoleon, 194, appointed Councillor of State, *ib.*, faithful to Napoleon, 238; death of, II., 318.

Constant, Madame de, her marriages, I., 123.

Coronation of Louis XVIII., I., 123; of Charles X., II., 132 et seq.

Corpus Christi, pageant of, I., 133.

Court of the Tuileries, I., 82 et seq.

Cuvier, Baron, death of, II., 340.

Decazes, M., made Prefect of Police, I., 220, tact of, 262; made duke and peer of France, II., 4, death of, 354.

Dey, Hussein, French consul struck by, II., 212.

Donizetti, il Signor Gaetano, talent of, I., 312, sad end of, 313.

Dreux-Brézé, Marquis de, death of, II., 252.

Duchesnoy, Mlle., plainness of, I., 270.

Elsler, Fanny, popularity of, II., 346.

Eugène, Prince, offends the king, I., 109, withdraws from public affairs, 110.

Fay, Général, death of, II., 146 et seq.

Ferdinand VII., aided by the French, II., 61.

Feuchères, Madame de, accused of murder, II., 313.
Fieschi, infernal machine of, II., 350, execution of, *ib.*
Fontan, M., imprisonment of, II., 234.
Fouché, Joseph, generosity of, I., 249, his marriage, 250, resigns his office, 259.
Francis I., visits France, II., 251 et seq.
Francis II. enters Paris, I., 53.
Hélène, Princess of Mecklenburg-Schwerin, marriage of, II., 353 et seq., sketch of, *ib.*
Hortense, Queen, made Duchesse Saint-Leu, I., 109, her reunions, 145.
Hugo, Victor, prohibition of play of, II., 347.
Indemnity, law of, II., 102, 103.
Joséphine de Beauharnais, visits Louis XVIII., I., 108, death of, 109.
Jouy, M. de, turns his coat, I., 185.
Junot, Général, his style of living, I., 102, death of, 103.
Junot, Madame, description of, I., 101, her dislike to Blücher, *ib.*, her *salons*, 102, refuses to leave Paris, 104, favoured by Louis, 105, her extravagance, 106.
Krudener, Madame de, her prophecy, I., 140, her belief, 142, influence over Alexander of, 244, her receptions, 246; death of, II., 169.
La Bédoyère, Général de, his loyalty, I., 250, death of, 251.
La Fayette, Général de, tour through the provinces of, II., 239, citizens under the lead of, 276, organises a new commune, 293, death of, 348.
Lafitte, M., advances large sums of money, II., 268; proposes Duc d'Orléans as lieutenant-general of the kingdom, 288.
Lamarque, Général, funeral of, II., 340.
La Valette, Général de, escape of, I., 287 et seq.
La Valette, Madame de, loses her reason, I., 288 et seq.
Law of "justice and love," II., 187.
Letort, Général, anecdote of, I., 11.
Louis XVI., obsequies over ashes of, I., 159.
Louis XVIII., recalled to the throne, I., 27, overjoyed, 43, restoration of, 59, 60, at Compiègne, 61, 63, offends Alexander, 66, motto of, 67, signs manifesto, 69, enters Paris, 70, 81, at the Tuileries, 82, at the Opera, 94, speech of, 113, house-

hold of, 135, his debts, 137, his receptions, 143, invokes legislative chamber, 169, leaves Paris, 179, at Ghent, 191, return to the Tuileries, 228; his regard for etiquette, II., 24, 25, his decline, 42, final speech of, 67, condition previous to death, 73, 74, death of, 77, lying in state of, 85, his *cortège*, 86, 87.

Louvel, M., murders the Duc de Berry, I., 325; execution of, II., 18.

Maria Theresa (Princess of Modena), marriage of, II., 360.

Marie Antoinette, finding of remains of, I., 162.

Marie Christine, marriage of, II., 252.

Marie Louise, deserts Napoleon, I., 27, visited by Alexander at Rambouillet, 55, at Schönbrun, 172.

Marmont, Maréchal, treachery of, I., 8, denounced, 271; ordered to quell the people, II., 267, message of, 271, reported dead, 274, defeated, 282, arrested, 284.

Mars, Mdlle., partisanship of, I., 157, 158.

Marsan, Pavillon, etiquette of, I., 116, 117.

Martignac, M. de, made president of the Council, II., 208.

Merlin, Comtesse, *salon* of, II., 330 et seq.

Metternich, Prince, enters Paris, I., 54, negotiations of, 204; his self-esteem, II., 96, visit to Paris, 111 et seq., estimate of the Revolution, 294.

Mirabeau, Comte de, message of, II., 27.

Molière, his "*Tartufe*," II., 158.

Moncey, Maréchal, pleads for Ney, I., 253.

Montalivet, Duc de, gives offence to the Chamber, II., 324.

Montlosier, Comte de, his crusade against the Jesuits, II., 185.

Montmorency, Duc Mathieu de, resigns his office, II., 55, made governor of Duc de Bordeaux, 165, death of, 166.

Mortier, Maréchal, killed, II., 350, funeral of, *ib.*

Murat, King Joachim, desertion of, I., 125, his repentance, *ib.*, declares for Napoleon, 205, lands in France, 208, death of, 256.

Napoleon II. (King of Rome), afflicted with melancholy, II., 48, weak condition of, 288, death of, 343.

Navarino, victory of, II., 205.

Ney, Maréchal, urges regency, I., 35, feasts Alexander, 99, joins the emperor, 175, death of, 255.

Orléans, Duc d', death of, II., 360.
Orléans, Louis Philippe de, returns to Paris, I., 230; made the wealthiest man in the kingdom, II., 107, grand *fête* of, 255, proposed arrest of, 260, suspicion falls upon, 316, declares he will never be king, 290, proclaimed lieutenant-general of the kingdom, 293, opens the legislative session, 294, called to the throne, 296, made king, 297, at the Tuileries, 335, at Fontainebleau, 348, attempts to assassinate, 350, his visit to England, 360, flight of, 361.
Paginini, Nicolo, first concert of, II., 328.
Palastron, Marquis de, death of, I., 49.
Paris, Comte de, birth of, II., 359.
Paris, capitulation of, I., 4, 5, rioting in, 19, welcome of, 23, filled with foreign guests, 82 et seq., left to govern itself, 180, capitulation of, 220, occupied by soldiers, 226, spoliation of, 238, 241; garrison ordered out, II., 207, in a state of revolt, 268 et seq., defences raised in the streets of, 273, excitement prevailing in, 327, gaiety of, 328 et seq., Louvre and Tuileries sacked by mob of, 282, disturbance among the people of, 340.
Paul, St. Vincent de, remains borne through the streets of Paris, II., 244.
Peace of Paris, I., 61.
Périer, Casimir M., oration of, II., 147, death of, 339.
Peyronnet, M. de, introduces law of "justice and love," II., 187, demonstration against, 198, encourages Charles X., 275, imprisonment of, 318.
Pius VII. refuses to recognise Louis XVIII., I., 132.
Polignac, Duc Jules de, visit to Paris of, II., 213, organises a new ministry, 234.
Rachel, Mdlle., debut of, II., 355, description of, 357 et seq.
Ragusa, Madame la Duchesse de, *salon* of, I., 100.
Rapp, Général Comte, grief of, I., 46, 47.
Raucourt, Mdlle., her burial, I., 164.
Récamier, Madame, lovers of, I., 124, received by the Queen of Naples, *ib.*, influence with Benjamin Constant, 127, coldness to Wellington, 235; characterisation of, II., 56, returns to Paris, 150, death of, 364.
Rémusat, Madame de, treachery of, I., 13.

Romarowsky, Col., warns Charles X. of his danger, II., 276.
Rossini, masterpiece of, II., 329.
Rubini, vocal powers of, II., 331.
Sacrilege, law of, II., 115 et seq.
Saint-Cloud, description of, I., 265, 269.
Staël, Madame de, returns to Paris, I., 119, interview with Louis XVIII., 120, 122, receives two millions, *ib.*, hostility of, 123, leaves Paris, 176.
Taglioni, Mdlle., popularity of, II., 329.
Talleyrand, de Périgord, Charles Maurice, missive of, I., 1, at the head of the government, 27, expostulates, 31, instigates insult of Napoleon, 39, his account of Waterloo, 213, exposed, 214, resigns his office, 260; death of, II., 254.
Treaty of Paris, I., 111.
Vernet, Horace, opinion of Rachel of, II., 357.
Vicenza, Duc de, death of, II., 213.
Victoria (Princess of Saxe-Coburg-Gotha), marriage of, II., 359.
Vigée-Lebrun, Madame, description of, II., 156.
Wellington, Duke of, at the opera, I., 93, ball given by, 223.

www.ingramcontent.com/pod-product-compliance
Lightning Source LLC
Chambersburg PA
CBHW022046160426
43198CB00008B/140